Successful Dog Breeding

Successful Dog Breeding

The Complete Handbook of Canine Midwifery

2ND EDITION

Chris Walkowicz
and
Bonnie Wilcox, D.V.M.

Illustrations by Mary Jung

New York

Maxwell Macmillan Canada
Toronto

Maxwell Macmillan International
New York   Oxford   Singapore   Sydney

Howell Book House
Macmillan Publishing Company
866 Third Avenue
New York, NY 10022

Maxwell Macmillan Canada, Inc.
1200 Eglinton Avenue East
Suite 200
Don Mills, Ontario M3C 3N1

Macmillan Publishing Company is part of the Maxwell Communication Group of Companies.

Library of Congress Cataloging-in-Publication Data
Walkowicz, Chris.
    Successful dog breeding : the complete handbook of canine
midwifery / Chris Walkowicz and Bonnie Wilcox.
        p.   cm.
    Includes index.
    ISBN 0-87605-740-7
    1. Dogs—Breeding.   2. Dogs—Reproduction.   3. Veterinary
obstetrics.   I. Wilcox, Bonnie.   II. Title.   III. Title: Complete
handbook of canine midwifery.   IV. Title: Canine midwifery.
SF427.2.W35   1994   93-13560   CIP
636.7'0824—dc20

Macmillan books are available at special discounts for bulk purchases for sales promotions, premiums, fund-raising, or educational use. For details, contact:

Special Sales Director
Macmillan Publishing Company
866 Third Avenue
New York, NY 10022

10 9 8 7 6 5 4 3 2 1

Printed in the United States of America

This book is dedicated to our husbands,
Ed Walkowicz and Tom Wilcox,
who first interested us in mating and reproduction.

Contents

Acknowledgments

APPLAUSE, applause to our illustrator, Mary Jung, who so perfectly pictures our words.

Our appreciation also to Carol Walsh Peterson for the two medical illustrations on pages 111 and 123.

We are grateful to those who supplied us with photographs, especially International Canine Genetics and Dr. Patricia Olson, University of Minnesota.

Special thanks to the hundreds of breeders who answered our survey and supplied us with the experience of a thousand years.

Our gratitude to Marcy Zingler, our oh-so-patient editor, and to Howell Book House for welcoming us to their house and for supplying the Fancy with priceless information through their books.

Forward!

Foreword

WHEN WE WROTE the first edition of *Successful Dog Breeding,* we had no idea how much progress would be made during the ensuing decade. When it comes to dog breeding, things appear to be rather simplistic. After all, there are only so many ways Tab A can fit into Slot B.

Researchers have made great strides, however, during the last few years: DNA, paternity and progesterone tests have burst upon the scene. We are fortunate to have access to ever-improving veterinary knowledge that can lessen the chance of learning the hard way—through heartbreaking experience.

In a way, breeders should be considered artists, with the ability to create beauty and bring pleasure to others. But, unlike those who spawn discordant notes of music or a garish painting, we work with living, breathing creatures. When we make a mess of things, they pay. So do their future owners, the breed and, eventually, our reputations.

With all this responsibility, breeding is hard work. It can be a scary proposition for the newcomer and even more frightening to someone who has suffered a bad experience. The sage advice of veteran midwives is invaluable in assisting us to make the best choices. The knowledge that, no matter what happens, someone else has walked this path before us is comforting.

Through our surveys, we've shared the tears and laughter of breeders. We've found most enthusiasts have a good sense of humor. Despite puddles, tooth-scarred furniture and midnight whelpings, we hang on with the tenacity of a Bulldog.

In Bonnie's nearly thirty years as a veterinarian and exhibitor, and my equivalent time as a breeder/exhibitor, we've learned a lot, but perhaps one of the most important lessons is that we will never know it all. So we breeders take

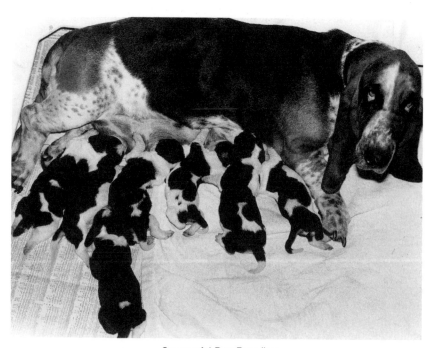

Successful Dog Breeding

advantage of every opportunity to indulge in our favorite topic: dogs. Whether it's imparting knowledge to others or drinking from the fount of wisdom, the path must be well lit, or we will stumble.

As the years pass, events tend to blur together, and we are unlikely to remember just how tiny our smallest surviving puppy was—and how big that puppy grew to be. When planning your next litter, keep this handbook nearby. Add a dog, a friend, a veterinarian, a thermometer and your record books, and you've got Successful Dog Breeding.

Taking the first step.

1

Taking the First Step

SHOULD I OR SHOULDN'T I?

A decision concerning living creatures should never be taken lightly. All factors must be carefully considered. Let's face it. The life of a breeder is demanding. Sure, it's fun to cuddle adorable puppies. But more time is spent dealing with the mundane. Midnight whelpings, weighing squirmy pups, mixing goopy cereal, wiping puddles, scooping poop and clipping countless nails are all part of a breeder's life. And it doesn't stop there. Selling puppies isn't posting a sign in your yard or running a newspaper ad. It begins with the decision to breed and doesn't end until the last puppy dies of old age—because *we are responsible for every animal we bring into this world*.

It seems easy when Mom's taking care of the crew. When she says, ''I quit!,'' our work multiplies by the number of puppies.

A Breeder's Day

A typical breeder's day starts with the first puppy yodel (usually at sunrise). The yowling continues until those tummies are full. So, bleary-eyed, before shower and coffee, you mix cereal or puppy food with nutritional goodies aimed at making the crew forget Mom's Home Cookin'. While the pups are tasting, gobbling or scrambling through the food, you clean the pen and replenish the water. Then you mop goop off the puppies. Between four and eight weeks (your

I QUIT!

half of the parental duties), this must be done four times a day—every day—including holidays, when your in-laws are visiting and when you have the flu.

The all-important socialization process comes during the time you spend loving and stroking. It also is implemented during bathing, lead breaking and grooming. Periodically, you weigh, cut nails, change ID tags, make trips to the vet, collect stool samples and record all this information for future reference. In between, pedigrees must be typed, feeding and grooming instructions gathered and papers sorted for each puppy.

You pray you'll have not only buyers but also the right home for every pup. *Veteran breeders never plan a litter without advance deposits.* But these don't come without work either. Designing attractive ads, taking pictures or videos, answering phone and written inquiries (many of which are only window shopping), screening buyers, temperament testing and matching the right pup with the perfect home all take a lot more time than you would imagine. A conscientious breeder logs more than 200 hours per litter from breeding to sale. If complications arise—such as illness, a Caesarean section or a mother that won't tend to the puppies—double the hours.

Sometimes, especially if you have not established a reputation in your breed, you must be prepared to keep the little darlings until they become sharp-fanged little devils or even gawky, not-so-little adolescents. You must be able to present them as the sweet pups you know in your heart of hearts they still are.

Professionalism and Responsibility

The person who is the breeder of an occasional litter does not have to be synonymous with a poor one. On the contrary, the quantity of litters has nothing to do with the quality of the puppies produced—unless the quantity outweighs the care.

Breeders should act professionally even though they do not breed dogs as a business. In fact, commercial breeding practices—puppy mills—are contrary to professionalism.

Whether breeding is a life's dedication or only a hobby, professionalism means that breeders intend to produce happy, healthy, attractive dogs. They refuse to mix breeds or to pair dogs indiscriminately because of proximity, convenience or financial appeal. There is no reason to perpetuate mediocrity— or worse. If a dog has a genetic problem, why pass it to its pups and their owners? Professionals research the conditions existing in their breed, and particularly in their own dogs. Sellers should discuss a breed's drawbacks, as well as its appeal, with buyers. Honest representation of the breed and the individuals is a must. Breeders are sure of the soundness of their breeding animals. They have proved their dogs' worth in at least one area of competition: breed, obedience or performance.

Even the most successful exhibitor receives more calls for companions than for show puppies, and nearly every litter contains pet-quality puppies, even those from top-notch parents. Despite this abundance of pet homes, each breeder's goal should be to strive to improve. While a show prospect still makes a good companion, *a pet-quality pup rarely makes a show dog of breeding quality.* Sweetness, loyalty and cuteness are not enough reason to breed a dog. Sweet, loyal, cute but unwanted dogs die every day.

With five million plus dogs euthanized annually because of a lack of homes, we feel no one should breed who is not willing to sign the following pledge:

I pledge that all animals that I breed are sound, both mentally and physically, and that they are outstanding examples of their breed.

I pledge to sell all pets on spay/neuter contracts and to enforce my contracts.

I pledge to stand behind my sales with health guarantees for those problems that may result from my breedings.

I pledge to assist in providing a loving home during its lifetime, to the best of my abilities, for every animal I breed.

Each year, millions of ex-pets, once-upon-a-time cute puppies, die or live out their lives in cells. They die in pounds; they die under cars; they die of starvation or disease. Often they die in agony. *Remember that anyone who creates a life is responsible for that life . . . for a lifetime.*

Another consideration for those who wish to breed is a toughie. Reproduction is not only the miracle of birth. Sometimes it brings the tragedy of death. Breeders must be able to face the terrifying possibility of losing a puppy or the entire litter—or, even worse, losing the bitch to one of several whelping complications.

NEUTERING

If you decide not to breed your dog, have your female spayed or your male castrated. Neutering eliminates pesky seasons, unwanted pregnancies, straying and lovelorn males. Desexing focuses the dog's attention on you, the owner, rather than on dogs of the opposite sex. This, in turn, aids training.

Dogs don't miss what they never had. Sexual frustration intensifies after they have been bred. In other words, breeding a dog once makes sexual behavior more likely.

A recommended age for neutering is when the dog is between six and twelve months old, nearing puberty or sexual maturity. A clue to approaching puberty is the first season, or when leg-lifting commences. The hormones released at this stage cause the development of sexual characteristics, so a male will still look like a male and a female will still appear feminine after surgery.

More than fifty[1] animal shelters have been using **juvenile spay/neuter** procedures (eight to twelve weeks of age) and are achieving great success. Proponents state that pigs and calves are castrated at five to ten days of age without problems. Veterinarians have found that the younger pups are less stressed and handle the anesthesia better than the pubescent or mature animal. Puppyish behavior—joy of life and trust in all humans—continues without the pubescent personality quirks.

Juvenile neutering prevents the animal from littering future pounds. Euthanasia statistics are decreasing in the areas where shelters practice this procedure. This certainly outweighs any possibility of minor side effects. Unfortunately, some adoptive families do not carry out the mandatory spay/neuter requirement of shelters.

Juvenile neutering is not yet common among the average pet owner or breeder, but it is a boon for shelters seeking to decrease euthanasia statistics. It also ensures that an animal with an obvious Standard fault visible at eight weeks (e.g., color, coat) cannot ever be bred.

Spaying is a relatively simple and inexpensive operation, certainly cheaper than an unwanted litter (or even a much-desired litter). It is also easier than caring for puppies during a minimum of eight weeks.

Those old wives who are blamed for all unsubstantiated beliefs state that altered dogs become fat. Nothing makes them fat except too much food and lack of exercise. Watch food intake. As dogs mature, their bodies, just like ours, do not require as many calories, and owners may need to increase exercise, cut down on portions or switch to a ''light'' food.

Those same old wives advise not spaying a bitch until she has had a litter. Doing this accomplishes nothing, especially since a dog does not have the human urge for maternity. Dogs do not have parental yearnings or a drive to have their line perpetuated. They don't mope when their kids forget to call on Mother's

---

[1]Diane Calkins, ''An Early Start,'' *Dog Fancy* (July 1991): 21–23.

Nothing makes them fat except too much food and lack of exercise.

Day or when they can't dandle grandpups on their knees. In fact, having a litter may cause myriad complications for the bitch and her owner.

Castration is the removal of the testicles from the scrotum. Spaying, or ovariohysterectomy, is the removal of the uterus and ovaries. Although pregnancy may be avoided by a vasectomy or excision of the uterus only, these procedures do not eliminate the sexual urge or prevent the heat cycle. Since the reason for birth control in dogs is to eliminate not only puppies but also the cause of them (i.e., SEX), part of the difficulty with having an intact dog remains.

Spaying stops recurrent false pregnancies and prevents uterine infections and ovarian or uterine cancer. It also decreases the likelihood of breast cancer. Current research indicates that 40 percent of females (particularly those above ten years of age) develop mammary tumors, half of which are malignant.

Mammary neoplasia represents 82 percent of reproductive tumors in females, according to Shirley D. Johnston, D.V.M., Ph.D.[2] Intact bitches have a three to seven times greater risk than spayed ones. Spaying before the first estrus lessens the chances to 0.5 percent. After the first season, this increases to an 8 percent chance, and after the second season, the risk factor rises to 26 percent. In other words, spaying after the first season has little effect on breast tumor occurrence, although spaying once neoplasia has been diagnosed may prevent progression.

In lifetime studies conducted by Johnston, approximately 50 percent of four- to eight-year-old bitches had **uterine abnormalities** that could have impaired reproductive function. Two-thirds of bitches had lesions by nine to seven-

---

[2]Shirley D. Johnston, "Health Benefits of Spay-Neuter," *JAVMA* (April 1, 1991).

teen years of age. Thus, *spaying at any age can give health benefits* in preventing reproductive organ disease.

Testicular tumors are the second most common malignancy in males and represent 4 to 7 percent of all those in canines (and 97 percent of male reproductive tumors). Testicular growths can occur as young as two years, with the average ten to eleven years. Undescended testicles (cryptorchidism) increase the cancer risk, with seven to eight years a common occurrence.

Testicular torsion is potentially life-threatening and is more frequent in abdominal testes, especially if they are enlarged with a tumor. Infection, trauma, wounds and frostbite can also give pain and stress to the intact male.

Benign prostatic hypertrophy occurs in more than 60 percent of intact male dogs above five years of age. This leads to infection and/or cyst formation of the prostate. Treatment of prostatic cysts is very unrewarding, with serious postoperative complications. Castration is both a prevention and the recommended treatment.

Neutering often helps calm an overactive dog, although maturity sometimes has the same effect. Castration helps curb the wanderlust and indoor urination. In addition to preventing prostate enlargement and infection, it often checks aggression, particularly if performed at or before puberty. Some owners also find another positive effect: female dogs shed less when spayed. Instead of blowing coat with every heat, they often shed only during Nature's heat, the summer.

The Surgery

When you make an appointment for surgery, withhold food and water from dogs for twelve hours; otherwise, they might become ill and vomit during anesthesia, thereby causing asphyxiation.

Recovery from neutering is swift, particularly if the dog is young and in good health. Pups in one juvenile neuter study were up and playing within three hours! Restrict exercise and feed lightly for the first day. Your dog may feel so good that these might become your most difficult tasks.

Take your dog's temperature after any surgery. Normal rectal temperature is 101.5 degrees F. (38.6 degrees C.), or within a range of 100 to 102 degrees F. (37.8 to 38.9 degrees C.). A fever is often the first sign of infection or other problems. Examine the incision for heat, discharge or redness. Contact your vet if any of these symptoms appear.

A Surgical Alternative

At the time of writing, canine chemosterilants are being tested. In males, the testicles are injected directly with the vaccine. No viable sperm are found within forty-eight hours. Over the next two months, the testes shrink. Experimental research is also being conducted on a vaccine which would prevent the egg from being fertilized, thereby sterilizing females.

The advantages of using this are enormous. The expense for owners would be much smaller, thereby encouraging more to neuter their pets. Adoptees could be sterilized easily at shelters without the expense of a surgeon, operating room or the time consumed performing the surgeries. The animal would not have to undergo the risks always involved with anesthesia and surgery. This is particularly important for dogs that are sensitive to anesthesia, brachycephalic breeds or sighthounds, or those at high risk, elderly or ill dogs. Owners should be aware, though, that these procedures are only for hormone and birth control and will not afford other health advantages.

The Pill and Other Options

A few factors might influence your decision to delay neutering. For instance, an altered animal cannot show in the breed ring, although it can compete in Obedience and other Performance Events. (The American Kennel Club does permit neutered dogs and bitches to compete in Veteran classes, as a boon to the health of these canine seniors. They may not, however, compete for any higher award than Best of Breed.)

Heat cycles do exactly what Mother Nature intended them to do: attract males. In addition, the blood flow can be messy, particularly with long-coated breeds, and seasons often result in the bitch shedding her coat. Whatever the reason, you might want to prevent a pregnancy until the appropriate time. Several alternatives exist.

Disguising agents for heats, such as chlorophyll pills, Vicks VapoRub[R] or commercial sprays, mask the odor and help control the attraction. These products do not, however, curtail the breeding advances of the persistent female or male. They are an aid at shows or classes during the first and last days of season. Intrauterine devices, likewise, have not met with much success or acceptance.

Oral birth control, the ''pill'' for canines, is available only through veterinary prescription. Owners' and pets' birth control prescriptions are not interchangeable—although your bitch's pill would certainly prevent you from having puppies.

The pill's active ingredient is megestrol, a progesterone-type hormone normally produced during pregnancy. Under the brand name Ovaban[R], or a generic, it is given orally daily for eight days, starting at the third day of heat, according to the weight of the bitch. Doing this extinguishes the season until the next cycle. Exhibitors occasionally wish to postpone an estrus. To do this, a much lower dosage of megestrol may be given at least one week prior to heat onset and continued for thirty-two days.

Breeders should follow directions explicitly and be aware of possible side effects of the hormone. Reproductive experts warn that the pill should never be used on the first heat or for more than two consecutive cycles. Irregular heats, transient weight gain and decreased activity level sometimes occur. Used on more than two consecutive heats, the pill may increase the risk of endometrial disease and pyometra. Oral products should not be used on bitches with active mammary or uterine disease.

The "get-rich-quick" scheme.

Of course, besides neutering, the next-best way to avoid pregnancies is to restrict the dating privileges of the female as well as the male. Do not assume from averages that any time is safe. Your bitch may be far from average. Conception has occurred on every day of the season.

Males have been known to perform Olympian feats to obtain the lady of their dreams. Do not depend on a screen or a fence to separate the lustful twosome. To avoid a surprise birthday, the only safe precaution is to keep both dogs in security kennels or in crates, separated by solidly closed doors.

THE GET-RICH-QUICK SCHEME

Breeding dogs is a *costly* business if done right. It is even more costly—to your reputation—if done poorly.

Few people make money from litters, and none become rich. Most breeders are content to break even. Those who do have a "profit" use it to help defray expenses.

A typical dream fades as follows: Your bitch whelps a normal healthy litter of five, and you see the dollar signs toddling about.

- You sell the first pup, and the sale pays for the pre-breeding veterinary fees and the lovely whelping box you built.
- The next sale goes for advertising and for the pups' exam, first shots and worming.
- The sale of the third pup covers the food bill, the second inoculation, registration of the litter and the pedigree forms.

By this time, the others need their next shot (six for each pup in the first four months) and more food (boy, do they eat a lot!). The local market is saturated, so you continue advertising in desperation for the last two prospective owners, wherever they may be. Finally, one more sells, which means you can reimburse your brother for the stud fee he lent you. You cut the price to sell the last one (which is all knees and elbows by this point) and pocket the "profit." That is, unless you have tail docking, dewclaw removal, ear cropping or shipping expenses. Wait a minute . . . did you forget to deduct the expense of purchasing the dam and several forays into the showing arena? There go the profits.

Ah, but there's next time. The last enlightening experience taught you a few lessons. Eliminate shipping and breed to a local stud.

So the pups come. Or rather pup, because it's a litter of one. That one goes as the pick pup to the stud owner, because you worked out a clever deal. But you must still pay the vet, the food bill, registration. . . .

Well, this can't happen twice in a row, can it? You breed the bitch on the next season since she only had one pup. So you pay the fee, paint the box, buy food and count the people who said they'd like one. This time there are ten pups, but all the interested buyers have an excuse for why this is a bad time, and the pups hang around for six months.

You buy a ton of food, give sixty shots, buy a large exercise pen and dream up ads and more ads. Then you buy two kennel runs, because the girls are starting to come into season. Heaven forbid any of them are bred! Someone from your first litter calls and needs to return his pup because he's being transferred overseas. You welcome her back, stacking crates like egg cartons.

Finally, the last two pups are given away. Never again, you think! But a year later, you've had six calls for puppies, and pain diminishes in memory. So you take a deep breath, collect deposits and decide to try again. After all, your bitch has three champions in her lines! She whelps eight pups. Six are reserved at 300 dollars apiece. At last, you relax. But they contract a virus when they're six weeks old, and all but three are lost. Of course, you've already sunk a fortune into food, shots and the other necessary accouterments.

The remaining pups must be kept for another month until they're back on their feet and no longer contagious, and it's cost you ninety dollars per pup for hospitalization and intravenous fluids to keep them alive. The six people cancel their reservations because (1) they don't want a pup that's been sick, (2) the pups aren't as cute at three months as they were at two, and (3) they've already found another one.

That's it, you say, and you tell people you can't afford it anymore. You've

Sexual maturity is not a green light for breeding.

never received anything from all your work. Three years and nothing to show for it but bills.

Too bad.

If you'd counted the genuine affection from the pups, the loyal love of your bitch, new friends along the way, the delight in watching puppies bounce after one another, maybe the end of this story would be different. Experience and knowledge may not put dollars in your pockets, but they do add up to a certain amount of wealth and can be shared with others at no expense.

AGE

The breeder can be any age. The brood bitch and stud dog, however, should be in the prime of life. Sexual maturity is not a green light for breeding.

Although capable of breeding and conceiving at the first heat, the bitch is no more physically or mentally able to care for babies than the pubescent human teenager. Neither is the adolescent male wise in the mating procedure, no matter how eager he may appear.

The American Kennel Club's registration rules state that sires must be at least seven months and under twelve years. Likewise, dams must be more than than eight months and no older than twelve years. Any litter conceived and whelped outside those age limitations must be attested to with reasonable proof and affidavit. Although legitimate, these extremes are far younger and older than we recommend.

This does not mean these age limits are suggested—just physically possible. Most veteran breeders recommend waiting until the second or third heat, around two years, depending on the breed and individual. The bitch should be bred for the first time by three years of age, preferably. As a female ages, there is less flexibility of the bony pelvis and other tissue; this makes it unwise to wait until the bitch is middle-aged or ready for Social Security before her maiden attempt at motherhood.

Top age for breeding depends on the health, condition and breed, but most breeders retire a bitch between six and eight years of age (sooner if there is a problem). Certain breeds—Miniature Schnauzers, for instance—maintain fertility into advanced age. They often produce well with no ill effects at seven or eight years.

Litter size seems to increase until three or four years of age, after which advancing age causes a reduction in the number of eggs released. It is sad, and not uncommon, for an elderly bitch to go through a belated pregnancy only to produce a sole survivor.

Young males can be introduced to the joys of prospective fatherhood, depending on the breed and inclination, between ten and fourteen months. Regular use of the stud is not recommended until two years. The majority of genetic problems manifest themselves by the age of two. Many studs continue to service bitches until the age of nine or ten (or older) with proper care and good health.

Smaller breeds reach sexual maturity earlier than large breeds. Therefore, a Pomeranian often stands at stud at a younger age than a Saint Bernard.

The optimum age for breeding is young adulthood—two to five years. A commonly held but mistaken belief is that the best puppies are produced at the age of three.

The reason for the prime time may be lusty youth but is more likely the stud's being at the peak of his popularity. Good bitches are sent to him, and he hasn't yet been challenged by the young bucks.

A FIRM FOUNDATION—SOUNDNESS

A dog cannot function well in any arena—work, show or pet—without being physically and mentally healthy. Soundness is the ultimate prerequisite for a breeding animal. Any dog that is not totally sound should not be bred. There are no buts.

An observer should be able to tell a breed by its silhouette.

Dogs with a severe physical defect, such as hip or elbow dysplasia, von Willebrand's disease, esophageal or heart defects or retinal atrophy, pass such hereditary ailments to their progeny. X-rays are the only positive method of diagnosing bone deformities like dysplasia, and a veterinary ophthalmologist is the only expert qualified to detect eye disease. Unless deterioration is severe, afflicted dogs may live fairly normal (though celibate) lives.

Mental soundness is also hereditary, and only dogs with stable temperaments are good breeding prospects. A shy, aggressive or hyperactive personality should not be projected into the next generation. If something about your dog bugs you, it'll irritate someone else as well. And if you knowingly breed a dog with a problem, the blame you'll receive from buyers is justifiable.

TYPE

Ranking high with soundness is type. An observer should be able to tell a breed by its silhouette. Of course, many non-Fanciers do not know what a Lhasa Apso looks like, nor are they even able to pronounce it. But a knowledgeable person should be able to identify a Bichon Frisé or an English Setter at a glance. Fanciers should be able to discern a Boxer from a Mastiff and an Akita from a Malamute. Even the uninitiated should be able to tell that a Poodle is a Poodle and that an Afghan Hound is an Afghan. What is a Dalmatian without spots or an Old English Sheepdog without the shaggy-dog appeal?

The Standard . . . defines the ideal.

This means that whatever gives the breed individual characteristics, or "peg," should be apparent in a breeding prospect. A Belgian Sheepdog's ears should stand erect. A Great Pyrenees should be large. A Sheltie should be small—at least in proportion to a Collie. And a Bearded Collie should be hairy—and have a beard!

PLAY BY THE RULES—THE STANDARDS

The Standard of each breed was formulated to define the ideal. This super-dog should be able to perform the task for which it was developed and be breathtaking in stance and movement—in other words, it should make onlookers gasp. The purpose of the breed could be the ability to trot for long periods under a coach, to swim in icy water, to save a drowning person or simply to be a loving companion.

While you might not care about showing, you should not remain ignorant of the breed Standard. Everything was put into the Standard for a reason. If there is a size maximum, it is possible that the breed forefathers discovered that bone disease increased with size or that larger specimens were too clumsy to do the work for which they were intended. If the Standard calls for a scissors bite, perhaps it was found that teeth wear down with a level bite or that a bitch with an underbite could not sever the umbilical cord.

The mere fact that *your* dog is not used for sledding, herding or coursing does not mean that the dog no longer needs to be able to function. Therefore, first-time breeders, as well as those with more experience, should study their Standards again and again, breeding only dogs that comply. The ideal dog has not yet been achieved. When it is, the rest of us can quit.

The Standard, of course, is open to each individual's interpretation, and that's what keeps us going. Often there appear to be three or four or more "types" within a breed. "Types" is a misnomer, however, since this word describes any dog that typifies the breed; the more correct word would be "style." After all, a thirty-inch brindle Greyhound is as typical of Greyhounds as a twenty-seven-inch fawn one.

A copy of a breed Standard may be obtained from the appropriate national breed club. Addresses are available through the American Kennel Club or from dog magazines.

MATE SELECTION

If you've decided your female is good enough to breed, would you settle for anything less than the best for her? Once it is determined that the bitch is in good health and condition, the search for a mate begins.

In some human societies, the girl's parents select her mate. The males may dance attendance on her, and now and then the girl herself may run off without her parents' permission. But good parents want the best for their daughter and are selective—even persnickety—in their choice.

Today, most breeders probably spend more time choosing their dog's mate than we do our daughters'. This may be because dogs don't complain when we make the choice.

Because it is the dam's owners who pay the stud fee and who whelp the litter, raise the pups and place them in good homes, it is the dam's owners who pick the contest winner.

Sire owners may offer their dogs at stud but seldom have the variety of choice that bitch owners do, other than the obligation to turn down a poor-quality or unsound female. In fact, in a less common breed, there may be *no* takers. If a male is handsome, record-setting and highly advertised, his owners might be able to persuade a bitch's owner to breed to their male. But if he has all of those qualities going for him, he doesn't have to ask. The girls will be waiting in line.

Some newcomers make the mistake of starting with a male and then attempting to buy a bitch to match. Even if your male is exceptional, he will not be the right mate for every female in your kennel. The bitch's owners may take their choice of nearly any male in the country or hemisphere. In fact, with frozen semen, a breeder has the advantage of upgrading through a world of males. Your

Puppies that hide behind furniture . . . and sport airplane wings for ears.

selection for your bitch should be at least as good as she is. What is the sense of downgrading for proximity or a few dollars? A bargain is seldom a financial success—or any other kind.

Good health and temperament on both sides are paramount. The dog should be a good example of the breed. You want Pointer puppies that look like Pointers, not like Whippets. If you need help in choosing a stud, ask experienced professionals, such as judges or trainers. Vets know whether a local stud has sired hearty, happy puppies or progeny suffering major medical or temperament problems, but they may not know if the pups adhere to the breed Standard.

If you're pleased with your bitch, ask her breeders. You thought enough of their opinion to buy her; now ask their advice.

Club members, long-time breeders and handlers can give suggestions, although they may have personal reasons for recommending or not recommending a stud. Still, input from several sources should give you enough information to weigh and balance. Usually, people are happy to show off their knowledge of such matters.

A potential breeder should study prospects. Breed books and magazines can help you evaluate what is appropriate for your breed. Watch the stud's get. Do you like what you see? Do not settle on a stud because the dog is convenient, is cheap or belongs to a friend. If you wind up with a bunch of puppies that are knock-kneed, hide behind the furniture, are crippled by the age of six months and sport airplane wings for ears, the friendship may not remain beautiful either.

Titles should not be the only consideration. Sometimes, because of luck or finances, unworthy dogs finish championships and good ones don't. Pick a male for the dog himself, for his ancestry and progeny. Worth is not in titles alone, but in the flesh.

If you are attempting to breed show-quality pups, your study of the breed must be even more intensive. Faults of the bitch must be compensated for, and her attributes allowed to dominate. Remember that what you see may not be what you get (see Chapter 2). And some of the stud's attributes might be good for other bitches, but not right for yours.

Kennel owners must eliminate animals that yield hereditary defects or poor quality from their breeding programs. Be honest in your evaluation of dams, sires and their progeny.

PEDIGREES

What's black and white and red all over? Answer: the ideal pedigree. Because titles are often typed or highlighted in red, we can increase our knowledge about litters or prospective studs through studying a pedigree. By looking at the actual dog, we can see whether or not it is a good specimen. By researching its pedigree, we can make an educated guess at how it will produce.

Breed experts can read between the lines and speculate on whether an anticipated litter will produce good coats or fright wigs, noble heads or weak chins, substance or scarecrows, mediocrity or WOW! Even newcomers can decipher symbols to determine valuable lines. The blood of two or three champions can be watered down to a drip if the rest of the family tree is flushable. The same holds true for Obedience titles or health certifications. A couple of Companion Dogs (CDs) could still produce a Simple Simon, and two Orthopedic Foundation for Animals (OFA) parents might have a Quasimodo behind them, but a pedigree rich with titles shows depth of quality. This increases the percentages of building our own foundation with soundness.

Look for championships from the United States and other countries to show superior type, movement and presence. Obedience titles (CD, CDX, UD, TD, TDX, OTCh.) demonstrate the ability to learn and the will to please. Dogs with conformation and Obedience titles are usually sound in body and mind, but the breed student can be certain of those ancestors with health certifications, such as OFA, CERF clear or vWD-free.[3] When notations such as sable, merle or liver

---

[3]OFA (Orthopedic Foundation for Animals)—certification of disease-free hips and/or elbows; CERF (Canine Eye Registration Foundation) clear, free of eye disease; vWD (von Willebrand's disease)-free, free of bleeding disorder.

. . . whether an anticipated litter will produce good coats or fright wigs.

are included, we may be able to predict colors likely to be produced by various pairings.

A breeder combines not only the genes of the sire and dam but also every ancestor of the two.

GOLDEN RULES OF BREEDING

Although courtesy is not a requirement of dog breeding, ethical, caring breeders become more successful as that reputation spreads. These are some suggestions for owners:

- *Call on the first day of season to make an appointment.*
- *Inform the stud owner of any idiosyncrasies of your bitch's cycle or personality.*
- *Exchange pedigrees.*
- *When shipping, call on departure and arrival.*
- *Use only healthy, clean dogs with no parasites.*
- *Pay the stud fee promptly.*

- *Notify the stud owner when your bitch is in whelp or misses.*
- *Do the same when she whelps, giving statistics on the litter.*
- *Don't blame each other's dogs.*
- *Refuse any bitch that is unsound or of poor quality.*
- *Provide good food, attention, security and necessary medical treatment to the bitch.*
- *Charge a smaller fee for an unproven male.*
- *Do two breedings forty-eight hours apart.*
- *Provide for a return in case of a miss.*
- *With an outside or extremely short tie, do another breeding within two days.*
- *Discuss alternative artificial inseminations (AIs) and substitute studs.*
- *Make sure no other male can sample her wares.*
- *Provide for return breeding for no fee or a reduced fee with a small or nonsurviving litter.*
- *Remember that a stud can produce more puppies per week than a dam in her lifetime. The responsibility for these puppies belongs to the stud owner also.*

ETHICS

Dogs have always played a part in the media. We've enjoyed the Little Rascals' Petey, Lassie, Rin Tin Tin, the Shaggy Dog, 101 Dalmatians and 1,001 others. In the last few years, however, we have seen a darker side of the canine world portrayed on the front page and our television screens: puppy mills, the Pit Bull anathema, millions of unwanted animals and resulting euthanasia statistics. The world has revolved, and once again "Dog Bites Man" is news.

Because of these horrors, humane society officials, animal control officers and animal rights activists have pressured lawmakers to pass legislation concerning dog ownership. Lease restrictions, breeding bans, breed-specific bans, pet number limitations, puppy lemon laws and compulsory spay/neuter programs all have some merit to their cause. It is up to the Fancy to monitor these proposals and assist in modifying them to do the most good and the least harm to the world of purebred dogs as we know it.

If breeders do not maintain squeaky-clean reputations and put pressure on their peers to do the same, hobby breeding may become a part of history, with no present or future. For instance, the breeding ban proposals, which erupted around the country in 1991, following the lead of California's San Mateo County, initially required all pets to be neutered. Shocked breeders realized the ramifications, rallied together and proposed a compromise that would not eliminate breeding by the Fancy but would discourage indiscriminate or careless littering.

To help eliminate the image of throwaway pets, make sure buyers understand that their pup is never to become a statistic, that you can find her another home if the need arises. Obviously, all pets should be sold on spay/neuter contracts. But that is not enough. We must follow up on sales to make sure the neutering agreement is adhered to.

We should assist in rescue programs—even though these pound pups are not ''our fault.'' We can help educate other owners, through training, with helpful suggestions and by example. All exhibitors and breeders should participate not only in clubs but also in regional and statewide federations whose goals are to protect us and our animals. We all must budget some time and funds to help in these efforts.

We must diminish the painful picture portrayed by dying pets. If we do not, someone else, possibly a court or a legislature, will do it for us.

Then breeders may become an endangered species. Worse—so might dogs.

A mixed bag.

2

A Mixed Bag

IF YOU'VE EVER PLANNED a litter, you've used the principles of genetics—whether or not you realized it and even if you didn't achieve the desired results. All reproduction involves genetics—from the fleas that plague the dogs to the dogs themselves. So the more you can learn about practical genetics, the more predictable (or at least *explicable*) your breeding results will be. This knowledge can even help you understand your human family!

Genetics comes from *genes*, the units of heredity we all carry inside our body cells. At the moment of conception, each dog acquires the genes that determine not only what it will look like and much of how it will behave, but also what it will be capable of producing in *its* offspring. This means, literally, one breeding is responsible for the future of the entire line—the good, the bad and the ugly.

It's hard to understand why a dog may look one way but produce pups that are different from each other and might not appear anything like the parent. To comprehend this and use it to your advantage, you have to learn how genes work.

GENES / CHROMOSOMES

Genes are submicroscopic particles, but imagine they are objects you can see and hold. In the body, hundreds of genes are attached in a long string called a *chromosome*. Visualize genes as beads of different sizes strung together. Like any other string of beads, some are valuable; others are faux.

Even though scientists don't know yet where all genes on the chromosomes

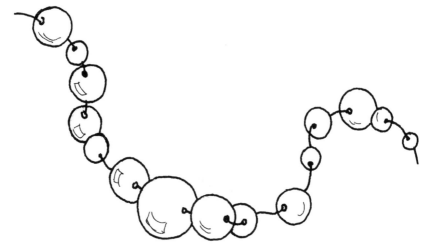

Visualize genes as beads of different sizes strung together.

fit, we do know that the order (site) is always the same and predictable. Pretend that on this imaginary chromosome, gene (1) controls eye color, genes (2), (3) and (4) have to do with shape and structure of head, (5) and (6) affect tail shape and placement, (7) determines coat color, (8) is for coat texture, and (9), (10), (11) and (12) control temperament. To act, genes must occur in pairs, so picture a second string of beads to go with the first.

Thus chromosomes, as well as genes, always occur in pairs. For instance, in gene pair (8), which controls coat texture, the larger bead causes wirehairs, and the smaller bead is for smooth coats.

DOMINANT / RECESSIVE

Unlike football, where the fastest or the smartest sometimes wins, here the larger, more **dominant** bead always wins. The small bead loses out in *this* generation. But it stays hidden and is carried as a **recessive** gene for the future, sometimes resulting in a surprising sneak play. Therefore, if we use our above example of coat texture, wire coats are dominant and smooths are recessive to wire.

Let a large bead (*O*) represent a dominant gene and a small bead (*o*) a recessive gene. A Dachshund that inherits the gene pair (8) *OO* (double dominant), of course, will be a wirehair. A Dachshund that acquires the pair (8) *Oo* will also be one because the wire gene (large bead) dominates, or wins over, the smooth gene (small bead). Only if our example, Moxie the Dachsie, inherits the gene pair (8) *oo* (double recessive from both parents) will he have a smooth coat.

Substitute a capital letter for a large bead and a small letter for a small bead, and you can talk like a geneticist! If the gene pair at *locus* (site) number

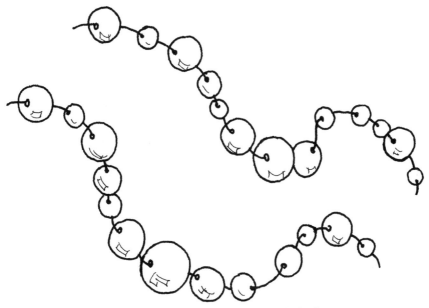

Picture a second string of beads to go with the first.

(8) is for wire versus smooth coat, use *W* for the large bead and *w* for the small bead. Again, the pairs *WW* and *Ww* would both produce wire coats, and *ww* would produce smooth.

Try to predict the following gene combinations:

* Black *B* is dominant over liver *b*. If a Flat-Coated Retriever inherits the genes *bb*, what color is this dog? Answer: liver.
* Self-color (solid color) *S* is dominant over spotted *s*. If a German Shorthaired Pointer inherits *Ss*, what is the dog's color pattern? Answer: solid color. *But* this animal carries the gene for spotting and could produce spotted offspring.

HOMOZYGOUS / HETEROZYGOUS

When both genes in a pair are the same, either dominant or recessive, we say the dog is **homozygous** (pure) for that trait or character and *must* pass this characteristic to any progeny. If the genes in a pair are different, the dog is **heterozygous** (carries a dominant and a recessive) for that trait and could pass either the recessive or the dominant gene to offspring.

Simple genes consist of one pair controlling one trait. Other simple genes on our imaginary chromosome would be at loci (1) and (7).

Eye color is produced by (1). Moxie is heterozygous for dark eyes (*Ee*); that is, he has one dominant and one recessive. If dark eyes are dominant over light eyes, our Dachsie would have the preferred dark eyes.

Coat color locus (7) would be the sable or red (dominant) vs. black-and-tan (recessive). Because Moxie has two small beads (homozygous recessive), he is black-and-tan.

ADDITIVE GENES

Complex traits, such as gait, hip structure, shoulder angulation and hunting ability, are controlled by several gene *pairs* that act together to produce the visible result. These are additive genes. If good shoulder assembly is dominant over poor structure, and there are seven pairs of genes that control the shoulder formation, fourteen dominants would be a perfect shoulder—and fourteen recessives would be the pits.

Most dogs fall somewhere in between. The more dominants they inherit, the better shoulder they exhibit. In most additive gene groups, dominants yield Mother Nature's desired result.

This lesson started with beads and had a chromosome pair that looked like this:

Locus	1	2	3	4	5	6	7	8	9	10	11	12
	O	o	O	O	O	o	o	O	O	O	o	o
	o	O	O	O	o	O	o	o	o	o	O	o

If we substitute letters, we end up with this configuration:

E	h	H	H	T	t	a	W	P	P	p	p
e	H	H	H	t	T	a	w	p	p	P	p

If we look again at Moxie and the six possible genes for head shape, his five dominants would create a classy head. With only two out of four dominants for tail set, he would be average on that end.

Five of the eight temperament genes are recessives, which means he takes no guff from other dogs. Perhaps you would like a more mellow dog. In this case, temperament could be improved by breeding him selectively.

Once we know that *Ee* stands for eye color, *HHHHHh* is for the head, *TTtt* is for the tail, *aa* is for black-and-tan color, *Ww* is for wire coat, and *PPPppppp* is for personality, you can figure out what Moxie looks like and why he behaves in the manner he does. Moxie the Dachsie has dark eyes, a lovely head, a low-set tail, black-and-tan color, a wire coat and a bossy temperament.

Knowing this helps you as a breeder in two ways. First, you're now equipped to learn more about genetics, especially in your breed. You're armed with the knowledge and the language of genetics. Second, you can analyze the reverse of the above (which is the way dog owners have to do it): start with the dog and try to sketch out the genetic configuration.

By studying sources, you can distinguish the single (simple) gene patterns in your breed. The multiple (additive) genes will be mostly guesswork, but you can keep in mind that the harder a trait is to modify from one generation to the

Moxie the Dachsie.

next, the more genes are involved. For example, length, color and texture of coat are relatively easy to change, and they all involve single or few genes.

On the other hand, traits like head type, herding ability and rear angulation don't change much from generation to generation and involve many genes. They are harder to improve upon than simple gene traits.

MODE OF INHERITANCE

While our imaginary chromosome duo had twelve pairs of genes, in reality there are many hundreds of genes on each chromosome. Dogs have seventy-eight chromosomes (thirty-nine pairs). People have forty-six. Cattle have sixty, and mice forty. Birds are varied, which is why you don't see mixed-breed birds or bird-dogs! Donkeys have sixty-two, and horses sixty-four. Their offspring, the mule, has sixty-three, which leaves one chromosome with no pair. Mules are sterile, which is Mother Nature's way of getting back at us when we mess around with her laws and cross-breed closely related species.

Again, each species has a different number of chromosome pairs. This is why you cannot cross-breed very dissimilar species, such as tigers and pythons or dogs and cats, even in a laboratory. When the chromosomes line up, there is no match, so they can't make the connection to produce offspring.

When the body prepares for reproduction, the chromosome pairs split up; only one chromosome, containing half of each gene pair, ends up in each egg or sperm. (Isn't that a miracle?)

Bird-dog.

In our example, half of Moxie's sperm cells would contain E-h-H-H-T-t-a-W-P-P-p-p (sperm b), and half would have the chromosome e-H-H-H-t-T-a-w-p-p-P-p (sperm B).

But because *there are thirty-nine pairs in real dogs*, the probabilities become innumerable—which is why we can end up with so many variations in repeat breedings, or even within the same litter. Try another analogy: imagine chromosomes as blocks of different shapes. Our imaginary animal has six pairs of chromosomes—two stars, two triangles, two squares, two circles, two rectangles and two half-moons. One of each pair is white, and one is black.

Put all these blocks in a bag. Reach in without looking, and pluck out one of each shape. You will end up with a combination of the six shapes, and a variant combination will be left in the bag (see illustrations at right). In fact, mathematically, there are 128 different combinations that could occur by chance with only these six genes, which is why we sometimes wind up holding the bag!

This same chance combination of the chromosome pairs arises in the production of sperm and eggs. This explains why repeat breedings of superstars can be disappointing.

With thirty-nine pairs in the bag, several million combinations are possible. So it becomes evident why it's hard to produce a carbon copy.

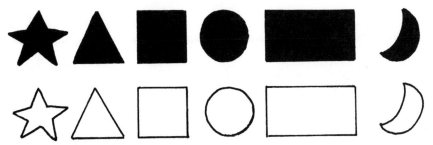

Imagine chromosomes as blocks of different shapes. Put all these blocks in a bag. Reach in without looking, and pluck out one of each shape.

The first time you may end up with

and

left in the bag.

The next try may result in

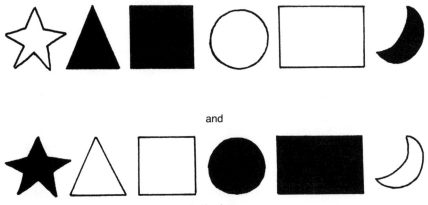

and

in the bag.

Roxie the Dachsie.

BREEDING ROXIE THE DACHSIE

Go back to Moxie, and examine the possibilities with just one chromosome pair. Half of his sperm contain the chromosome *E-h-H-H-T-t-a-W-P-P-p-p*, and the other half *e-H-H-H-t-T-a-w-p-p-P-p*. Suppose Moxie finished his championship and was much admired for his typey head. If you had a sable wire Dachsie female, Roxie, with *sweet* temperament and good tail set, but you wanted to improve her head quality and eye color, you might choose this male.

Roxie's chromosome pair can be presumed from her appearance:

e-H-h-h-T-T-A-W-p-P-P-P

e-h-H-h-T-t-A-w-P-P-P-p

Her *ee* results in light eyes; only two *H*'s give her a poor head type; three *T*'s make an above-average tail set; *AA* makes her sable; *Ww* gives her a wire coat; the six *P*'s generate her friendly, outgoing temperament.

Half her egg cells, when the pairs split, would contain the chromosome *e-H-h-h-T-T-A-W-p-P-P-P* (egg *a*), and the other half would carry *e-h-H-h-T-t-A-w-P-P-P-p* (egg *A*).

FERTILIZATION

Breeding is accomplished—that was easy—and fertilization transpires. When the sperm containing the thirty-nine single chromosomes unites with the egg, also containing thirty-nine single chromosomes, each chromosome lines up with its corresponding mate. Voila! We now have seventy-eight again. These newly paired chromosomes with their thousands of genes tell each new cell how to develop.

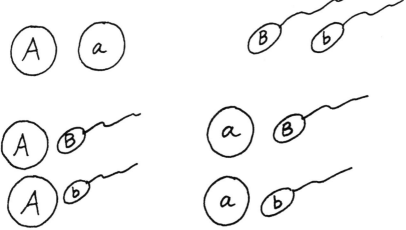

Four possible pairings exist.

Moxie and Roxie have two genetically distinct classes of eggs and two kinds of sperm between them. How many combinations could you see in the pups?

Four possible pairings exist: sperm *b* with egg *a*, sperm *b* with egg *A*, sperm *B* with egg *a*, and sperm *B* with egg *A*. The law of averages says that 25 percent of the pups would have sperm *b*/egg *a*, 25 percent sperm *b*/egg *A*, 25 percent sperm *B*/egg *a* and 25 percent sperm *B*/egg *A*.

Probabilities are accurate only with large numbers—in the hundreds. In a litter of six or seven, it's possible all sperm *b* could be Olympic swimmers and reach their goals first, fertilizing the *A* and *a* eggs. But for an overall view, assume one of each combination appears in every four pups. So a litter of four might include:

Pup 1   *E-h-H-H-T-t-a-W-P-P-p-p* (from sperm *b*)

   e-H-h-h-T-T-A-W-p-P-P-P (from egg *a*)

Mopsy the Dachsie had dark eyes, average head, good tail set, sable color, a wire coat and a good temperament.

Pup 2   *E-h-H-H-T-t-a-W-P-P-p-p* (sperm *b*)

   e-h-H-h-T-t-A-w-P-P-P-p (egg *A*)

Foxy the Dachsie had dark eyes, an average head, an average tail set, sable color, a wire coat and a good temperament.

Pup 3   *e-H-H-H-t-T-a-w-p-p-P-p* (sperm *B*)

   e-H-h-h-T-T-A-W-p-P-P-P (egg *a*)

Mopsy the Dachsie.

Flopsie the Dachsie had light eyes, a good head, a good tail set, sable color, a wire coat and an average temperament.

Pup 4 e-H-H-H-t-T-a-w-p-p-P-p (sperm B)

e-h-H-h-T-t-A-w-P-P-P-p (egg A)

Joe the Dachsie had light eyes, a good head, an average tail set, sable color, a smooth coat and average temperament.

Now, be honest—did you improve on your female? Did you eliminate Moxie's faults?

Foxy the Dachsie

Flopsie the Dachsie.

PHENOTYPE/GENOTYPE

Moxie's dark eyes didn't dominate. Why? Because he is **heterozygous** for this trait *(one dominant and one recessive)*. The *phenotype* is the characteristic Moxie shows on the outside, the dark eyes. This is contrasted with the ***genotype***, the configuration of *genes* for this trait, which is not visible (one dominant, dark-eyed gene and one recessive, light-eyed gene).

Breeders often say, "Rambo carries the light-eyed recessive," or "He is a carrier of light eyes." Or they say the reverse, "Igor is free of light eyes."

Joe the Dachsie.

If he had been a homozygous dominant for dark eyes, *EE*, he would have looked the same (dark eyes); thus, the phenotype would have been the same. But his genotype would have been different, double dominant, and all his pups would have been dark-eyed, even from our *ee* female.

What about heads, which you really wanted to improve? All four pups had a better head than Mom, but no one's was as nice as Dad's. Remember that the more genes involved in the trait, the harder it is to improve. Taking one of the pups with a good head from this litter and breeding it to another mate with a superior head would improve head type even more. This time, the litter would contain two pups with good heads that could compete in the show ring.

Tail sets were average to good. All of our sample pups had average to above-average temperaments, so they would fit happily into their new homes.

You know the color genotype of our male, because black-and-tan is recessive *aa*. After seeing that all the pups are sable out of our sable female, we can be fairly certain of her genotype, a homozygous dominant for sable, *AA*. The result is all sable pups, carrying the black-and-tan recessive, *Aa*.

Notice you produced one smooth pup out of four from two wire parents. You know both parents must carry the smooth recessive. It takes two recessives *ww* to produce the smooth, and *one gene from our pups' pair comes from each parent. Each parent has to have at least one* W *to be wire-coated*, so you can figure that both parents have the genotype *Ww*.

TEST BREEDING

Because so many of the medically dangerous traits that crop up from time to time are recessive, it is probably wise to reemphasize them. Traits such as generalized PRA, hemolytic anemia, cleft palate and dwarfism are all known recessives. The same is true of show faults, such as "fluffies" in Pembroke Welsh Corgis, smooth coats in German Wirehaired Pointers and parti-color in Boston Terriers.

If your Alaskan Malamute stud produces forty (or 140) pups without a dwarf *and* the bitches he is bred to don't carry the recessive, you'll never see one. But if the twelfth litter contains a dwarf, we know *he* has carried the recessive for dwarfism all along. We also know that 50 percent of all the other pups he has produced up until now are carriers of dwarfism. (Whoops!) You can't blame the dam of that twelfth litter alone, although she is also a carrier. *A known recessive has to come from both.* In order to avoid such surprises, do your homework and be aware of recessives, especially those with health aspects, carried in your breed. (See Appendix I.)

You have no way of knowing about a recessive trait except by test breeding. "Proving" your dog carries (or is free of) a recessive is accomplished by breeding your dog to one that is homozygous for that characteristic. Another accepted alternative in making the claim is breeding to three *known* carriers without producing it. An educated guess of whether the dog carries the recessive, however, can be made by studying the ancestors and their progeny.

If a sire's twelfth litter contains a dwarf . . .

In Beardies, for example, a male would not be a carrier of the dilute colors, blue and fawn, if he were bred to three blues (or fawns) and did not produce dilutes. German Shepherd Dog stud owners often advertise "free of the long-coat factor" after they've been bred to three bitches that have previously produced long coats.

SEX-LINKED

One chromosome pair is distinct from the others. The two in the female's pair are alike and are called the *XX* pair. But in the male, one chromosome of this twosome is shorter than the other, as if half of the beads were removed from one string. His is called the *XY* pair. When the female's chromosomes split apart, all of her eggs contain an *X* chromosome—since that's all she has. Each sperm, however, contains either an *X* or a stubby *Y* chromosome. At conception, the *X* egg can unite with an *X* sperm to produce a female pup (*XX*) or with a *Y* sperm to produce a male (*XY*). So *it's the male who determines gender*, and the chances are fifty-fifty.

The genes on this pair include those that produce sex organs and hormones, secondary sex characteristics, maternal and mating behavior—all the things that make boys different from girls. Many other genes are also on this chromosome pair, and these can produce traits known as *sex-linked*.

Generalized myopathy and hemophilia A are two examples of sex-linked recessives that occur in dogs. Others can be found in Appendix II.

We know a single recessive never expresses itself on the other chromosomes, since it is overpowered by its paired dominant. But on the male's *XY* chromosomes, the genes on the long end of the *X* have no opposing pair on the shortened *Y*. Single recessives that occur here express themselves without a matching pair. Thus, a

33

recessive *sex-linked* trait (that is, one that occurs on the X chromosome) can express itself in the male offspring even though only one parent passed it on. (This is how male pattern baldness is inherited in humans.) Recessives on all other chromosomes must come from both parents in order to be expressed.

Hemophilia is represented by *h*, and a normal, nonbleeding condition by *H*. A female theoretically could be *HH* (normal/noncarrier), *Hh* (normal/carrier) or *hh* (bleeder). With no pair in the male, there is no carrier state. An *HH* female can produce only normal males (*H*) since she is the only one giving X chromosomes to her sons. Even if she were bred to a bleeder male (*h*), her male pups would be normal (*H*), and all her females would be normal carriers (*Hh*). An *Hh* (carrier) female bred to an *H* (normal) male could produce *HH* (normal) and *Hh* (normal/carrier) females, as well as *H* (normal) and *h* (bleeder) males. Only in a laboratory, where a carrier female (*Hh*) might be bred to a bleeder male (*h*), would you expect both male (*h*) and female (*hh*) hemophiliacs, as well as carrier females (*Hh*) and normal males (*H*).

Therefore, the *sex-linked traits are carried by the female and expressed mainly in the males*. Don't forget there are thirty-eight *other* pairs at work at the same time. Before you despair, read on about breeding programs.

NATURAL EVOLUTION

If you're using genetics the way you should, trying to produce better specimens that will be prepotent superdogs, you are attempting to change the genetic pattern of the breed. Did you ever wonder why, even in a puppy mill, where the breeding is indiscriminate, without even the pretense of genetic selection, the products still look like dogs, still have their eyes, ears and legs in the right number and places? Even a poor example of a Basenji looks more like a Basenji than a Bloodhound or a Borzoi.

A million years of natural selection by survival of the fittest, as well as hundreds of years of prudent artificial selection by breeders, rest behind your dog's genetic makeup. Selection created the majority of gene pairs as homozygous. Evolution provided the correct gene pairs for teeth, eyes, four well-muscled legs and adequate coat protection, as well as other physical and mental traits vital for survival.

A few recessives still lurked in the gene pool. In the wild, defective whelps die; they don't thrive. Even if the recessive matched with another to produce an undesirable feature (e.g., a short coat in an arctic climate), the resulting offspring would succumb. Even a neutral trait such as color variation wouldn't breed true, because it is a recessive.

It is clear why the majority of desirable traits are dominant. In addition. Mother Nature also provides a small percentage of heterozygous genes, allowing for adaptation and evolution. An example of this would be the adaptation of a population of smooth-coated dogs living in a warm climate that slowly becomes colder over the centuries. Eventually, the smooth-coated dogs would perish. A few long-coated specimens could be produced, however, through recessive genes. Because they would be more vigorous and more able to thrive in the frigid climate, the long-coated ones would be the pack leaders and would multiply.

SELECTIVE EVOLUTION

By actively selecting breeding partners, we accomplish the same effects as nature but manage in less time. People began by opting for superior attributes, then went on breeding to fix the new characteristics. Without realizing it, early breeders were tinkering with the small percentage of heterozygous traits present and making them homozygous, artificially prodding evolution.

Most prehistoric dogs, upon scenting prey, immediately leaped, seized and killed it. Notably, a few dogs crouched, hesitating briefly before springing at prey. While of unknown value in the wild, this trait was an immense help in allowing hunters (long before the days of gunpowder) time to throw their nets and capture several birds.

The breeding of dogs with this quality developed "setting" breeds, which freeze into the classic point upon scent or sight of game and hold the pose for long periods. This trait is now essentially fixed and homozygous, whereas it once was an oddity.

Breeders achieved homozygous traits over the years, with preferred color patterns, coat qualities, distinctive head and body types, and temperaments, as well as other working qualities. Modern geneticists are finding that vigor, longevity, reproductive quality and freedom from many organic diseases are also genetically based.

GREAT EXPECTATIONS

Before you select a male, make a list of your bitch's good traits and those you'd like to see improved. Study books and photos, watch dog shows, evaluate litters and ask questions. Seek advice from several people whose dog knowledge you respect. Forestall an attack of a disease peculiar to dog breeders. When this disease, kennel blindness, strikes, all dogs with a certain kennel name on them appear more beautiful and less faulty than dogs of other bloodlines.

If your female is *linebred* and has a couple of areas that need improvement, you might choose an *outcross* mating. This means there will be no common ancestor in the preceding three or four generations.

In selecting a male for your outcross, you should designate one that is particularly strong in the areas that your bitch lacks. If you need topline and rear angulation, find a male strong in those aspects. But ascertain whether he is prepotent in producing these traits. If you discover most of the pups he has produced have no better topline and rear angles than your bitch, the male probably has a better phenotype than its genotype. You'd better keep looking.

It matters very little that your girl's pedigree is full of Champions if she is faulty herself.

Don't let big wins and advertising hype sway you. All the ribbons and trophies in the world can't guarantee or alter genotype.

With a bit more experience and a female who doesn't have too many faults, you might want to try to establish a strain. This is a line that breeds true and is consistently stamped with the traits and characteristics you find desirable.

This will, of course, take many generations and can be accomplished only through *linebreeding* and/or *inbreeding*. These established breeding tools differ only in degree of intensity. Select a mate that has ancestors in common with your female; how many times and how close names appear in the pedigree determine whether the term used is "linebreeding" or "inbreeding."

Close breeding of similar animals is used to cement traits—that is, we try to make the offspring homozygous for the desirable characteristics and thus accelerate evolution. Naturally, homozygous animals tend to be prepotent and produce animals that look like themselves. Genetically, their genotypes and phenotypes are close to being the same.

It matters very little that your girl's pedigree is full of champions if she is faulty herself. The Dachshund family mentioned earlier in this chapter proved that two nice dogs may not produce superstars. Pedigrees are only as good as the dogs that represent them, just as royal families have skeletons rattling.

When the long-awaited litter arrives, select the female pup that carries the strongest attributes you want. She will be the foundation for your next generation.

A good breeding program takes patience, planning, fortitude, hard work and a bit of luck. That all-champion litter surely won't come the first time, and maybe not the tenth, but intelligent use of these genetic principles should bring you closer to your goal each time.

OUTCROSSING

Uninformed people assume that outcrossing is the safest method of breeding. This is not necessarily true. The method is not what makes a pairing good or bad, but rather the individuals involved. For instance, the most extreme examples of outcrossing are what dogs produce on their own: mixed breeds.

Because it is difficult to obtain two dogs that do not have any common ancestor (six generations contain 126 names), most breeders consider outcrossing to be two dogs having no common ancestor in three or four generations. The first three generations have the greatest effect, since the great-great-grandparents' influence is well diluted.

The main reason for outcrossing from familiar lines is to introduce a much-needed characteristic. If you have been consistently producing good health, conformation and temperament, but have been losing pigment, a prepotent but unrelated dog with an ancestry of good pigment should be found. It is important that the dog have a good background of the desired attribute. He should not be a fluke. Of course, to maintain the qualities already secure in your lines, the selected sire should have adequate producing ability in other areas as well.

Outcrossing prospers best when you choose partners that have been line-bred themselves, although they are not related to each other. In this instance, there can be some expectation of results. The representatives should be first-rate if the efforts of past breedings are not to be diminished.

Another method of reaching the same goal is to use dogs from different lines, although with similar traits. In other words, two completely unrelated lines can produce plush, gorgeous coats. One side might be dominant in producing excellent attitude but needs better backs. The other side could carry iron backs but have a ho-hum attitude. Outcrossing can restore energy and vigor.

Don't expect a uniform litter; size and type are likely to be a potpourri. Choose the pup that most displays the attribute you are seeking. Then breed back into your own line to blend the best of both.

LINEBREEDING

Linebreeding is the method most commonly used by novice and veteran breeders alike. This is a safe method if the novice concentrates on the bloodlines of a quality dog that produces quality. The technique is valuable to the professional when used to enhance an attribute for a kennel. Linebreeding should be done on a superior animal. It does no good for anyone, especially for the breed, to double on a mediocre dog.

In selecting a male for linebreeding, it is especially important to look at the dog himself *and* at his production record, not just the fact that he appears in the pedigree. The value in linebreeding is the dog chosen, not in the method itself. If, for example, you want to breed back to your bitch's paternal grandfather, Ch. Famous Fred, you'd better make certain that the bitch's tendency for long loin and light eyes didn't come from him. If it did, you'd be fixing those poor qualities in the line permanently, rather than the gorgeous coat and good movement you wanted.

It might be better to go to the maternal grandsire, Good Ol' Guy, even though he's not a champion, especially if you've seen that he produces dark eyes and shorter bodies. Or perhaps there is a son of Ch. Famous Fred that produces the qualities you need and desire.

Linebreeding on a good dog with a superior upper arm and shoulder layback can build a sound foundation for shoulders. But breeders must not become so engrossed in producing superb shoulders—or rears or heads—that they lose sight of the total dog.

No matter what manner of breeding is used, the whole dog must be considered. If the line producing breathtaking movement also carries a gene for missing premolars, the fault will be set in as firmly as the desired attribute.

The procedure of linebreeding may not reach a goal as quickly as inbreeding but is less liable to produce undesirable traits.

ALL IN THE FAMILY

Whenever the uninformed see a dog with problems, they are inclined to blame it on inbreeding. This method, in breeder terminology, is mating to a close relative, for example, mother to son, daughter to father, half sister to half brother, or the closest: sister to brother. Inbreeding has been instrumental in establishing new breeds and creating famous prepotent strains within breeds.

The problem lies not with inbreeding itself, but with the individual dogs used. Naturally, when breeding closely, all defects are intensified, as are the assets. If you elect to inbreed, you must verify that the partners offer no severe faults and possess major attributes and only few minor flaws. In other words, they should be paragons of virtue.

In addition, you must expect whatever defects lie hidden in the line to surface and be prepared to deal with them in whatever manner you have chosen. A kennel that elects to use inbreeding should be familiar with the entire pedigree and the negative characteristics associated with the dogs in those lines. Inbreeding is *not* for the novice but is a valuable tool when used to establish sterling quality. It is also the fastest way to bring recessives to the forefront and eliminate undesirable characteristics *or* reinforce them.

Inbreeding does not create defects but uncovers them through homozygous progeny. Therefore, nutsy dogs are not more likely to be produced via inbreeding—unless two nutsy relatives are bred. A wiser choice, by far, would be two near-perfect individuals.

... one or two animals on each extreme end of the evaluation teeter-totter.

Inbred dogs are prepotent in producing their own type—even if absolutely awful. Inbred litters *must* be carefully evaluated; the breeder should retain the best and neuter the others.

The majority of puppies from an inbred litter are similar to those produced by the other methods. More probability exists, however, for one or two animals on each extreme end of the evaluation to teeter-totter. By selecting from the top, you are more likely to make genetic progress.

Selectors of this mode should be aware that continued inbreeding may decrease size, fertility and viability of pups. Good-sized, robust pups are the best choices for incorporation into an inbreeding program. Close breeding for several generations may also cement faults in your line and make them difficult to eradicate. The wise breeders study their dogs and take the appropriate route. A blending of all three methods—linebreeding, inbreeding and outcrossing—when needed is the program practiced by successful kennels.

One form of inbreeding is ***backcrossing***, which means finding an outstanding male, breeding that male to his best daughter (or his dam, if his dam is superb), taking the best female in that litter and breeding back to said male, and so on. Backcrossing can also be done with a female as the ancestor of merit.

Naturally, any system should be discontinued or changed once serious or multiple flaws crop up or threaten the advantages gained. We hope you have noted a consistency in the three types of breeding. That is, **the dogs chosen, whatever the method, should be healthy, sound, quality examples of the**

breed. To succeed, breeders must also make choices according to the goals of their program, rather than by sentiment because one pup looks more like the dam or the granddam. The aim is forward, not backward, no matter how much you loved your first dogs.

The world doesn't need more dogs. If you are going to breed dogs, consider it an art form. Use your knowledge of the gene pool to produce superior specimens. You know if you breed a Bedlington to a Bedlington, you'll get Bedlingtons. But this is not sufficient to satisfy the true dog connoisseur. The challenge must be to produce dogs a little sounder, a little more beautiful, a little . . . better.

3

Building a Solid Foundation

$\mathbf{A}$ WISE breeder keeps an eye on the future at all times, and this means the prospective parents. All dogs, just like their owners, have some faults. And if we're really, really honest (and we only have ourselves to fool at this point), probably even our world-beating, superstar wonder dog does too— at least an itty-bitty one.

Tests to determine the presence of hereditary breed defects in the prospective partners should be scheduled well in advance. An eye clinic can rule out eye disease, the University of Michigan can provide a thyroid panel, and X-rays can show elbow, hip or other bone deformities. Depending on your breed (see Appendix I, Breed Specifics and Predispositions), various other diseases can be ruled out with specific blood tests, biopsies or examinations.

Some of these diseases do not show up until the age of two or older. This is yet another reason to wait until your dog is mature and fully cleared from undesirable genetic traits before making it part of your breeding program.

THE FUTURE: DNA TESTS

Current research into DNA testing will prove to be a boon for breeders. Three mighty canine organizations, the American Kennel Club, Morris Animal Foundation and the Orthopedic Foundation for Animals, have joined together to fund the study. Geneticists at Michigan State University's College of Veterinary

Building a solid foundation.

Medicine are working hand in hand with University of Michigan geneticists who are delving into human mysteries.

Dog lovers believe canines come closer than humans to perfection, but we all have some defective genes. Scientists have discovered that some human and canine disorders appear similarly on chromosomes. **The average number of genetic defects for each breed is fourteen.**[1] Some faults are minor and do not prevent the puppies from competition or from living full, productive lives as companions. Others are lethal, causing stillborns or puppies that die as infants. Breeders necessarily cull major birth defects, such as cleft palates or spina bifida.

Although these problems are sad and frustrating, they are not as heart-breaking as those that appear in adulthood. This is especially true when they are crippling, like patellar luxation; cause major life-style changes, as severe epilepsy does; or are potentially fatal, as in subaortic stenosis. And it's even worse if you've bred the dog and passed these on to vulnerable puppies and their unsuspecting owners.

[1]George A. Padgett, *The Kennel Doctor* (June 1988). Dr. Padgett, D.V.M., is a professor of pathology at Michigan State University's College of Veterinary Medicine.

Some dogs' sterling qualities may outweigh a minor fault. These assets can be used to advantage by careful crossing into a line genetically free of the same disorder. The DNA testing will allow breeders to know if a dog is a carrier or not.

If all of this seems like modern-day wizardry, it isn't. It's better. A scientific test, simply by taking a small blood sample, will eventually pinpoint hundreds of diseases! The power of identifying and zapping disorders from our individual lines and breeds will lie in our hands.

Our dogs will move even closer to perfection while we, mere humans, will continue to make our genetic matches with our hearts rather than the microscope.

PRELIMINARY DECISIONS

Serious consideration should be given to who will best complement your bitch—accentuate her good points and offset the negative ones. What do you want to accomplish in this breeding? You can't build the Taj Mahal with one stone or make a silk purse from a piggy ear either. Bearing your nice, but slightly less than ideal, bitch in mind, what would you most like to improve? Movement? If I breed Dixie to Yankee and keep a puppy with her topline and his movement, I could breed her back to my Lincoln. . . . Hmmm, now we're cooking.

STUD OWNER RESPONSIBILITIES

It might seem as though the male's owner would not have to preplan, but important breeding decisions are better thought out ahead. Determine which health tests all incoming females must have. What if the bitch is flown in and she's not as represented in pictures or via the telephone wires? Who pays for an AI if needed? How many breedings will there be?

The wise stud owner wants the bitch to conceive on the first visit. A return on a miss is overtime work with no compensation. The only one that is happy is the stud. Most stud owners give at least one return for empty nests, and many offer a return for a small litter (another decision—how many constitute a litter) or a tragic loss of pups.

How much is your dog's service worth? The fee for an unproven stud is less and may be postponed until the time that pregnancy is apparent or even until the litter is whelped. As a rule, titled dogs' fees are higher than untitled; those with winning progeny are also worth more.

If you pick a puppy, which pick? At what age? What if there's only one pup?

A stud owner's life is not all gravy. The male's fasting, constant whining, pacing and territorial marking of furniture are no fun. Boarding a bitch who whimpers her homesickness all night, refuses to cooperate and goes on a starvation diet makes it seem more like cold, lumpy potatoes than gravy.

The stud receives (at least) 50 percent of the blame when things go awry, so it's not only advisable but smart to turn down a knock-kneed, cross-eyed, crotchety bride. In addition, *Daddy is accountable for each little life he eagerly brings into the world.* In the dog world, this means the stud owners. So if you feel the bitch's owner is not going to have the same sense of responsibility you do, don't allow the breeding.

Ask bitch owners:

- Why do they want to breed?
- Do they have reservations with deposits for puppies?
- How will they raise your grandpups?
- Will they, or someone who is qualified, evaluate the puppies?
- Have they tested for major heritable defects in the breed?
- Do they guarantee and offer lifetime security?
- Will they place the pets on spay/neuter contracts?

Unlike bygone eras when the male simply planted the seed and left everything else up to the female, fathers are becoming involved with their seedlings and accepting responsibility—whether scrawny weed or mighty oak. Stud owners cannot wash their hands when the bitch leaves their premises and the check has cleared, feeling they've done their job.

Another consideration is whether you expect the bitch's owner to live up to your standards. Stud owners should write into their contracts that puppies cannot be sold to pet shops or in litter lots or to people who sell to pet shops, that sales must be at a certain price or higher, and that pets must be sold with spay/neuter contracts.

GOOD HEALTH

Studs and brood bitches should be kept in peak condition. If the bitch is extremely thin or overweight, infested with worms or recovering from surgery or a serious illness, give her time to regain her health and condition.

The same is true of a male. During times of physical stress, reproduction is the first function to fall by the wayside, because the body labors just to maintain the necessity of life before adding the luxury of conception. The mating urge is dormant, and if a breeding is achieved, the number and vitality of ova and sperm are usually adversely affected. The stress of breeding can ravage a dog already suffering poor health.

Extra! Extra!

Feeding and maintaining a healthy brood matron or stud dog does not mean stuffing it with the fad of the moment. Prenuptial banquets mean feeding a premium dog food, providing a balanced diet and keeping dogs muscular and in ideal weight. Overweight bitches might develop problems during pregnancy or have difficulty whelping—or not conceive at all. They should be lean, if not a perfect "ten."

Overfeeding and too many goodies cause a dog to become sluggish. Breeding efficiency diminishes. No love handles for the canine couple!

Inoculations

Keep in touch with your vet about the latest vaccines to ascertain that your bitch has all the protection available for herself and her brood. Mom passes her immunity to her babies through the colostrum, which is the first milk. If the dam is not up-to-date on her inoculations, the pups are susceptible to disease. Nothing from nothing equals nothing.

Before she is due in season, take the dam to the veterinarian for a premarital exam, including current immunizations. It is not advisable to inoculate bitches in whelp, and it is preferable to do so *before* the season. Any little thing can make a cycle go off line, just as you and the stud are eagerly waiting.

Although rabies is not a disease that young pups are liable to come in contact with, airborne and other highly infectious viruses are extremely debilitating or fatal if pups catch them. It is most important that all dogs, particularly dams and puppies, be inoculated against parvovirus and distemper. Parainfluenza, hepatitis, leptospirosis, parvovirus and corona virus vaccines are usually incorporated into the distemper immunization.

A honeymoon with intruders.

Parasites

Would you dream of spending a honeymoon with intruders? It sure puts a damper on the fun. To avoid having uninvited guests crash the affair, the bitch should be flea-free and have her stool checked for evidence of parasites before she is bred.

If the fecal test is positive, worming can be done *prior to* breeding. Vermifuges can be toxic and are not advisable during pregnancy.

Nevertheless, many puppies are born with roundworm infestation. This happens because the larvae lie dormant in the dam, reactivate during pregnancy and then migrate directly into the fetuses. Parasites may also be transmitted while the mother is nursing, which proves that all is not pure, even mother's milk.

If the mother is infested, her condition is not A-one. Pregnancy and lactation will weaken her further. The pups will not be as robust as they would with a healthy mother, and these weakened pups will soon become infested themselves.

Of course, keeping a stud dog currently inoculated and parasite-free is important as well. His good health is advantageous to himself and his owner, to ensure the dog's producing ability.

At one time a problem only in the South or near water, the danger of heartworm is now widespread. In most areas, veterinarians advise an annual blood test, followed by administration of the preventive during the mosquito season.

Not only are fleas and ticks irritating pests themselves, but they carry other diseases as well. Be sure Mom is not bugged before breeding, as most insecticides cannot be used during gestation and nursing or on puppies under six weeks of age.

Routine Tests

Every stud dog and brood bitch should be examined for overall sparkling good health. A prebreeding veterinary appointment starts with a brucellosis test and a complete physical with emphasis on the genitals. An internal examination of the bitch shows whether a fibrous stricture or narrow pelvis is present. If a juvenile vagina is detected, AI might be substituted for a natural mating. In many of these cases, whelping follows normally, and a subsequent litter is bred via the time-honored method.

If reproductive history shows misses, stillborns, infections, weak pups, irregular cycles or other abnormalities, a culture to diagnose vaginal or uterine infections is suggested. Although some bacteria are normally found in the vaginal tract, an active infection might need to be treated.

The male's exam can detect paraphimosis or persistent frenulum, as well as the size and consistency of the testicles. Ideally, stud owners run a sperm count on an unproven male or one who has not sired a litter for some time. A semen evaluation shows motility (activity—we like to see them doing an Olympic kick) and morphology (normal shape—no two-headed, bent-tailed, freaky sperm).

Sperm Test

It is easier to obtain a specimen by using a teaser bitch, one exuding an alluring Eau de Season scent. The semen is examined for color, amount, any debris or foreign matter, and number and motility of sperm, as well as whether or not there are live or deformed sperm. The average stud dog has around 200 million sperm per ejaculate. It's hard to believe misses ever occur!

Stricture

The premarital checkup should include a thorough internal examination for a vaginal stricture. This is a tough ring at the end of the vaginal canal that an aggressive stud can sometimes tear. Occasionally, a natural oddity occurs and there are two strictures, one deeper than the other. The ring might have to be stretched by a veterinarian. Veteran breeders may be able to obtain the same results, using sterile gloves and petroleum jelly. Sometimes it is necessary to surgically sever the band. By whatever method, it is painful to the bitch and can make her a less than eager partner for a few days. Nevertheless, breeding should take place shortly after surgery so that scar adhesions do not prevent a later mating.

AI can be performed, if necessary, on a bitch with a stricture. Once pregnancy is accomplished, the ring does not interfere with delivery. A vaginal stricture can be a reason for an outside tie (see Chapter 5).

Heat Cycle

In terms of the average—which dogs never are, any more than their owners—small breeds first come into season at about six months of age, and larger breeds usually between ten and fourteen months. Bitches cycle about every six months. Some, however, come in as often as four times annually or as seldom as once a year. (See Appendix I, Breed Specifics and Predispositions.)

You can set your watch by a few females. Most, unfortunately, are not that timely and vary widely. As long as they are consistent, there is no need for concern. Make notes of cycles. The second or third heat establishes a pattern, and this pattern will facilitate your breeding plans.

The average heat runs twenty-one days. Some bitches show a bloody flow throughout the season, and others fade to pale pink after ten days.

Certain bitches have to be followed with a mop; others must be tested by flashlight and tissue to ascertain whether they are actually in season. Some bitches keep themselves scrupulously clean; others rise and leave a pool of blood. The safest method of detection is to tissue the vulva, particularly if there are males on the premises or a breeding is planned. Watch for licking, increased urination

Males often hoist a warning flag.

and/or enlargement of the vulva, which may precede flow. Males often hoist a warning flag by playing caboose, walking with their nose attached to the bitch's rear a day or two before the season starts.

Puberty varies widely. Small breeds tend to mature sexually earlier than large ones do. Nature has a way of equalizing everything. Toys reproduce younger and live longer than giants, but they also have smaller litters.

Parts of the Cycle

The estrous cycle contains four parts: anestrus, proestrus, estrus and metestrus. **Anestrus** is the R & R time between heats, lasting three to five months or longer.

Proestrus is the onset of the heat and discharge. The follicles containing the eggs mature over approximately nine days. Most females refuse mating at this time, by whatever method. Although flirtatious, they discourage males when it comes to actual mating by growling, baring teeth, snapping, running in the other direction and sitting on the target. Some eager matrons, however, cooperate at any time. Fertilization cannot occur during proestrus.

During **estrus**, the female accepts, in fact invites, coitus with a male. The bleeding often decreases and becomes pale in color. This receptive period of four days to a week is when ovulation takes place. Some females become quite shameless and obvious in drawing attention to themselves. They rub against fences separating them from the males, encouraging their advances. Green-light bitches eagerly flag (move) their tails to the side or curl them completely over their backs.

Timeliness can be checked by rubbing the bitch just above the root of her tail. If she flags, she is approaching ovulation—or is a hussy who doesn't care who, when or where. Toward the end of the season, the discharge becomes brownish.

Metestrus (or *diestrus*) is the stage that readies the uterus for pregnancy. If fertilization doesn't occur, this stage soon reverts to anestrus. A prolonged metestrus (called a false pregnancy) is common. If pregnancy exists, metestrus continues until delivery.

Disruptions in the heat cycle can happen through external influences. Cycles often change as bitches age. Illness or injury can interrupt the cycle, as might extended daylight or long periods of hard work (e.g., field trial or sled racing). Bitches living under the midnight sun often cycle more frequently, and unseasonable warmth brings early heats. Anestrus may be extended postpartum.

Indications of proestrus may include restlessness, frequent urination or indigestion. Bitches often lavish affection upon their owners. Personality changes often accompany this period—timidity, moodiness, flightiness and irritation with other dogs.

The rampage of hormones within the body sometimes causes physical changes as well. At least one bitch we know, a Miniature Pinscher, lifts her leg during her seasons. It's not unusual for a bitch to mount a male or even another female during this time.

The estrus "perfume" is inspiring to males, which can catch a whiff up to three miles from the source. Scent clinging to clothes makes the owners attractive to males as well, creating the embarrassment of dogs sniffing and mounting.

One female tends to bring another into estrus. This common chain is a frustration to breeders; with several bitches cycling at once, it's impossible to space out litters.

If you wish to investigate an individual's pattern for future breeding, run smears and/or progesterone tests throughout the season, starting on the fourth day. Record her behavior throughout the cycle. (See Smears in Chapter 4.) Then you—and she—will be prepared when you plan Mother's Day.

TRAINING THE STUD DOG—MR. MACHO

Sexual play is often observed in young pups, even among babes still in the whelping box! Behavior, such as mounting, is sometimes demonstrated by females as well as males and can represent dominance ploys aimed at becoming Top Dog as much as or more than the result of infantile hormones. Let them work out pecking order in the litter unless play becomes nasty. Even then, a slight "Uh, uh" should suffice since you're still Top Dog when you are present. Too much interference can upset the natural selection of leaders and followers.

An owner should not ignore the humps and thrusts of youngsters either, as the owner of a four-and-a-half-month-old sire discovered. A precocious young

Mr. Macho.

male should not be discouraged from mounting bitches but instead should be distracted when the act is inappropriate.

At sexual maturity, a male becomes more selective about mounting. Until that time, he is playing and experimenting. He is not discriminating; any bitch—or male dog, person or sofa pillow—will do. Once experienced, a stud becomes discerning and mounts only bitches in season. In fact, the ideal stud refuses to breed a bitch until the time is exactly right.

Training a stud dog should begin when he is a youngster. Accustom the male to having his genitals handled. Should the time come when he needs your help—and it will—touching him will not disturb him.

Males often have a creamy discharge from the sheath. This needs vet attention only if it appears abnormal in color or amount.

Break in a novice stud on a mellow matron so that his first service is pleasant rather than upsetting. A bitch that snaps or screams is intimidating to a stud, as well as to the handlers.

Use a phrase to coax that will later be his code word, such as "Up" or "Get the girl." Suddenly, a look of surprise enters his eyes, and he'll never be the same young innocent again.

Some new studs think this is their first and last chance and become over-eager. Fervor is good unless it leads to premature ejaculation or exhaustion. If he hasn't touched base with four or five thrusts, push him gently off, saying "Off" or "Enough," holding him still until he calms a bit. Then let him try again.

This routine should keep him from becoming overexcited. Should he show signs of tiring, put the girl in a crate for a bit so he can grab a few gulps of water and relieve himself. Take an hour break if necessary. Often a little break is all it takes. He returns with gusto, seeming to communicate, "Hey, I'd better get this right, or I'll lose out!"

Too harsh a correction or even the bitch's squealing can turn an untried male off, with a look of guilt as if he did something wrong. A young male is extremely impressionable, as demonstrated by the Keeshond that lifted his leg for the first time on a thornbush and didn't attempt that action again for three months. So be gentle and keep up the encouragement.

If a male misses on two consecutive bitches, particularly proven dams, have a sperm sample checked. The stud owner should keep records of all litters produced, including any defective pups.

It has only just begun.

HEAT CYCLES

Bitches can come into heat the first time as early as five months of age. This might not be a fertile heat, but since a puppy should not be a mother, care must be taken that she is not "caught." Although it is unlikely at that tender age, a precocious bitch may be receptive to males. The first heat may be "silent" or "dry." (See Silent Heat in this chapter.)

Delayed Heat

Those that wait . . . wait . . . and wait. Part of Murphy's Law of Dogdom is that if you are waiting to breed a bitch, her season will be delayed. If you want to keep her coat and show her, your bitch will be one of those that cycle three times a year.

If her season is unusually delayed as compared with what is normal for your breed, a cycle can be induced by following a course of hormonal treatment. The pet owner will probably be overjoyed at the reprieve. Breeders who have plans for a bitch in their breeding program prefer to know whether the coy lass will ever cycle normally and should discuss the treatment with their veterinarian. First, try crating or kenneling her near a bitch in estrus and a lusty mature male. The effects of their pheromones might start her own juices flowing.

If not, your vet can try hormonal treatment (IM injections usually), which may kick off routine cycling. Treatment with hormones should never be taken lightly, but these are fairly safe.

Sometimes all that is necessary is biding your time. If the family line shows late sexual maturity, don't despair. Remember a Saluki owner who waited patiently for three years for normal cycling to begin.

Silent Heat

Cases of dry or silent heat are occasionally reported. These heats are silent because no one tells the owner unless a stud conducting a private investigation sounds an alert. People who note vulvar swelling and proestrus behavior can resort to a progesterone test to determine whether it's the real thing. In one instance, an American Staffordshire Terrier bitch showed no external signs. Only the stud dog knew for sure.

A Samoyed breeder wrote of a bitch that cycled with a normal season in the fall and a silent season in the spring. Both were fertile. Owners should be aware that a common cause of silent heats is *hypothyroidism*.

Split Heat

Once in a while, a bitch appears to come into a normal season but ceases discharging after just a few days. Stress or trauma can cause such an anomaly. Similar cases have been noted during weather changes or extremes and in bitches who are shipped to the stud.

Although the delay is frustrating, these bitches often come back into season again in a few days. If there is a lapse of a day or two, it is safest to count from day one of the "first" season. If there is a span of several days to weeks, however, ovulation occurs normally during the delayed heat.

Extended Heat

An extremely long season could indicate cystic ovaries and subsequent hormonal imbalance. The use of birth control pills, such as megestrol, to skip a season often helps return the bitch to synch next time.

The bitch should be examined for other irregularities. One of those "you think *you've* got troubles" stories concerned a Black-and-Tan Coonhound bitch that remained constantly in season. During laparotomy, cystic follicles were discovered and ruptured. The bitch proceeded to cycle normally. She was bred six months later and whelped a normal litter.

INFERTILITY / MISSING[2]

Infertility is poor reproductive function, exhibited by irregular seasons, misses, abortions or delivery of puppies that are weak or die. In the male, infertility is displayed as low sperm counts, lack of interest or constant misses.

Lack of nutrition and poor condition are the major causes of infertility. Age, obesity or administration of many medications may interfere with reproduc-

---

[2]Cornell University's College of Veterinary Medicine has a Small Animal Reproduction Clinic, specializing in infertility. Call 607-253-3740 for further information.

Males can go into a batting slump, hitting and missing.

tion, as can overuse in breeding. Difficulties could also stem from a hormonal imbalance, congenital abnormalities or various diseases.

Don't always assume it's the bitch, even with a proven sire. Summer heat can decrease a stud's potency. Males can go into a batting slump, hitting and missing.

It is always important to establish a specific diagnosis because some causes are reversible and others are not. Whether breeding is worth the extensive examinations and treatments must be considered since some are hereditary. Sterility is the extreme of infertility.

Before alarm begins, however, the simplest approach to the frustration of an unproductive bitch is to find a highly fertile stud with cooperative owners. Run daily smears and progesterone testing from day four. Attempt breedings early. Continue breeding every other day until one or the other quits.

In one case, it was the owners who finally called a halt after four breed-

53

ings—their bitch conceived despite three previous misses. Nevertheless, this bitch never conceived again.

Unless the cause of chronic infertility is age, obesity, medication, scar tissue or some other nonhereditary cause, a breeder should consider whether quality outweighs perpetuating the problem. Infertility tends to be self-limiting, and the problem, along with the line, disappears.

Progesterone testing has helped in many situations where poor timing is the cause of misses. (See Chapter 4.) In two separate instances of Bearded Collies that had been bred on days indicated by smears and lusty studs, it was found that everyone was rushing Mother Nature. The progesterone tests showed ovulation to be occurring much later than owners and studs thought.

This can be explained by the possibility that the increasing level of estrogen, which brings on the come-hither scent, actually occurs earlier in these bitches. Usually, the estrogen rise coincides with the luteinizing hormone (LH) surge that causes ovulation. Once the tests indicated later ovulation, both Beardies conceived and delivered normal, good-sized litters.

Infertility and low libido do not necessarily go together. Therefore, a stud or bitch that is not interested might conceive through AI or forced breeding. Perversely, avid breeding partners may not reproduce after an orgy of mating.

A story is often told of a bitch bred to several carefully selected studs to no avail. But when she chose her own beau, often a kennel mate, the breeding resulted in a litter. Unfortunately, the choice may be not only wrong for her but the wrong breed as well.

Some causes of infertility are:

Female:
1. Stricture(s).
2. Vaginal hyperplasia in certain breeds, Boxers and Mastiffs, for instance, due to increased estrogen. (A big pink wad extends from the vagina. These bitches can be bred by AI. It does not interfere with delivery.)
3. Abnormal vulvar angle (such as inverted).

Male:
1. Persistent frenulum—a band under the penis that must be clipped.
2. Paraphimosis—too small a sheath opening for erect penis to retract into.
3. Prostate infection.

THYROID

An underactive thyroid gland is a common cause of infertility. Thyroid disease can be hereditary and must be a consideration when deciding whether to breed. Many breeds have a high incidence of hypothyroidism.

Symptoms are lethargy, weight gain, poor coat, loss of hair, darkened skin coloring (especially on the groin and abdomen) and thickened skin. Reproductive symptoms, which can appear without other signs, include loss of libido and abnormal heat cycle. The first indication might be lack of conception. The veterinarian will run a thyroid panel with Total T3, Total T4, unbound T3, unbound T4, and T3 and T4 autoantibodies to determine if there is a problem.

The disease is easily treated with oral hormones, but treatment must be maintained for life. A Golden Retriever showed irregular cycling, with two and a half years between seasons. An English Toy Spaniel, which had several misses, became pregnant on the first breeding after starting thyroid therapy. But serious thinking should be done about the possibility of perpetuating this condition.

VAGINITIS / BALANOPOSTHITIS

An infection of the vaginal tract (vaginitis) is apt to surface at any time but is more common during a heat or following a breeding. The same is true for an infection of the sheath (balanoposthitis) following breeding. A creamy discharge appears, which owners might mistake for a heat or pyometra.

The infection is spermicidal and thus is a common cause of misses. Breeding can transfer the problem. If the bitch receives the infection as a bonus from the male during mating, the vaginitis does not necessarily preclude conception, but antibiotics can also be lethal to sperm.

Treatment for breeding animals should include a culture/sensitivity to identify the cause and pinpoint correct treatment. Specific cultures for mycoplasmosis can be done in suspected cases. The veterinarian should be forewarned that the bitch may be in whelp when seeking care.

CANINE BRUCELLOSIS

A bitch should be tested for brucellosis before each breeding, and a stud tested once or twice a year, depending on the frequency of use. Smart owners require a clear test result.

Brucellosis is detected through a blood test. It is convenient to conduct it when blood is drawn for the annual heartworm exam. Results are obtained quickly in the vet's office. In-office tests occasionally show a false positive. Don't panic yet, but follow up with a specific test run by a state university or private lab.

If the initial diagnosis is positive, the dog should be isolated and not mated while suspect. Known by the term "canine VD" because the disease is transmitted mainly through sexual contact, brucellosis became widespread around 1962. The disease is highly infectious.

In active cases, the bacteria is present in vaginal discharge, urine and fetal fluids. Because of habitual licking and sniffing, the disease is disseminated throughout a kennel and can sterilize all inhabitants. An outbreak of brucellosis in a breeding kennel is tragic, because the only way to overcome it is to eliminate all positive dogs and isolate others until a safe period is past, then preferably to move to new premises. A shame when it is so easily avoided!

An infected bitch suffers spontaneous abortion around the seventh week of pregnancy. In some instances, pups are carried to term but either are stillborn or succumb shortly. Bitches usually have a discharge, and males suffer painful swelling of the testicles. Eventually, testicles can atrophy. Glands and joints may also swell and ache.

Although the disease is not fatal to adults, treatment has limited success, and most adults become sterile. Spaying/neutering is best after the active infection is controlled. The best prevention is to demand proof of health from the owners.

Don't take this disease lightly. Shelters report as high as 35 percent incidence, so breeders who are involved with rescue situations should include a brucellosis test along with others conducted on any dogs taken under their kennel roof.

OTHER REPRODUCTIVE DISORDERS

Any disease that lowers overall health can cause lowered rate of fertility. Some causes of lowered fertility are:

- **Orchitis** (testicle inflammation) caused by injury or infection. The testicles become hard, enlarged and painful. Autoimmune orchitis, causing permanent sterility in adult dogs, has been documented.
- **Hormonal imbalances**, which can cause testicles to atrophy. These include diseases of the adrenal glands, kidneys and/or pituitary gland, as well as the testicles and/or thyroid gland.
- A **sperm-duct blockage**, congenital or otherwise (such as epididymitis), which can be determined by a biopsy and perhaps corrected with surgery.
- **Hypoestrinism**, induced by low production of estrogen. It is exhibited by low libido or short, abnormal heats. Low production of testosterone will likely cause low libido in the male.
- **Cystic** disease of the **ovaries**, which can also cause irregular cycles and infertility.
- **Hermaphrodites**, intersex dogs that are a genetic accident and contain both testes and ovaries.

Timing and patience solve many puzzles. Run the advised tests to discover the solution.

4

Going by the Book

A FEW GEMS seem to have read the manual and follow averages like instructions. But many perfectly normal dogs and bitches seem to prefer to tease and surprise us.

TIMING

After the decision is resolved and the choice of the groom made, the date is the next determination. Timing is a prime aspect. Owners who have chosen a local dog or are boarding their bitch at the home of the stud are not under the same time constraint as those who must ship the bitch or travel to her liaison.

Bitches can be good indicators of correct timing, arching their backs and "flagging" their tails. Others flag during their whole season, and some old gals move their tail cooperatively whenever you rub their backs, even when not in heat.

The vulva "winks," tipping up, inviting a breeding. As prime time nears, the vulva becomes pouty and more and more swollen. One owner has described this softening as comparing the firmness of your nose with the pliancy of your lips.

The male, too, is a good timekeeper. An experienced swain will not be eager until the aroma signals that the time is now!

A bitch that flirts and invites the male to play by crouching and wagging her tail, bounces from place to place and refuses to stand still is signaling that it is too early. As the season subsides, however, bitches tend to lift a lip at the male's attentions.

Going by the book.

The average, true-to-the-book bitch is fertile between days nine through sixteen, with twelve and fourteen being the classic time for ovulation. Our survey, however, showed bitches that conceived anywhere from day minus four (four days before discharge) to day twenty-four! Reasons other than early or late ovulation may exist. For example, the heat could be dry or silent for the first two weeks, or stress or trauma might set back the cycle.

Nothing is certain. Ask the owners of the ten-month-old German Shepherd Dog male that bred a bitch four days before she showed any signs of season, with other kennelmates showing no interest. This stud broke all the rules—he was a novice stud, younger than average, and bred in the middle of household activity, with no visible season. Nah, Tom and Marylou said, it'll never take. "Never" resulted in five pups.

Breeders concur that the best way to mate a maiden bitch is to use a stud with cooperative owners. *The first priority should not be money or distance.* However, a quality stud that is not too far away is advantageous for first-timers. Good choices may be a young but experienced male or an older male that is not quite the man-of-the-moment. Stud and owners should have time to be patient with a bashful virgin.

A maiden should be tried daily from the tenth day until she willingly submits, then bred every other day until she refuses or the male becomes uninterested. If the breeding does not result in a litter, next time try even earlier.

Since the chosen male is not always able to be booked for a long run, and stud owners have other lives besides dancing attendance on a bitch, the breeder does well to study the bitch's signals. It is unnecessary to breed more frequently than every other day, for sperm remain viable for several days and ova for forty-eight hours. *Canine sperm live from seven to ten days in the female's reproductive tract.* Nevertheless, what matters is not the lifespan but rather the *fertility span*, and this is not yet known.

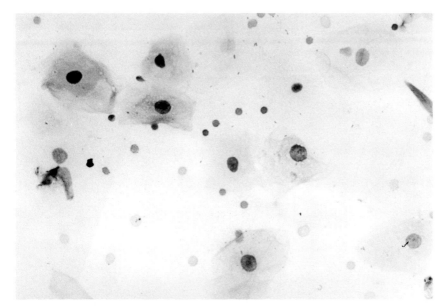

Proestrus—vaginal smear from a bitch in proestrus. Vaginal epithelial cells are of a mixed type, with large intermediate (superficial intermediate) and superficial cells present. Numerous erythrocytes (red blood cells) are also present in the background. (Magnification 400X.) Courtesy of Dr. Patricia Olson, University of Minnesota.

As a bitch ages, ovulation dates may change. She should be bred according to her actions or physiological tests rather than by the calendar.

Smears

Smears are helpful, although veterinarians agree that smears must be taken for several days to ascertain progress. The slightest incident can disturb ovulation.

Progressive examination of vaginal smears can identify the progress and ovulation time during the bitch's heat cycle. While smears need not be routine for the experienced brood matron, they are helpful when the bitch is a maiden, has missed before or must be shipped.

In breeds without tails (no flagging), the smear helps in planning an itinerary. When an AI is to be done, vaginal smears must be run in conjunction with the procedure.

Your vet will collect a smear from the upper vaginal tract with a sterile swab, dry and stain it, then examine it under a microscope. After researching the procedure with their vets, some veteran breeders take on this task themselves. A practiced eye is necessary to determine the changes that occur in the physical makeup of the cells during the course of their heat period.

As the season progresses, the cells from the vaginal wall change from the usual "fried egg" shape, slowly losing the nuclei (the eyes) and becoming

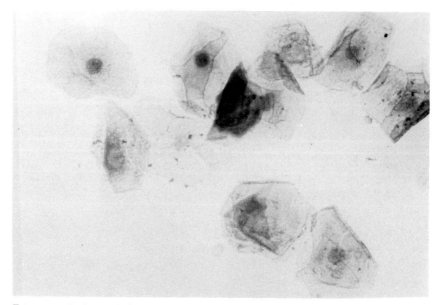

Estrus—vaginal smar from a bitch in estrus. Vaginal epithelial cells are of a superficial type (also referred to as cornified cells). (Magnification 400X.) Courtesy of Dr. Patricia Olson, University of Minnesota.

wrinkled and folded. Your vet will say they have become cornified (remember corners).

They also change from being attached in sheets to occurring individually. Red blood cells are present in the smear, along with white blood cells, mucus, and other debris that disappear as ovulation approaches. *On the day of ovulation, only cornified vaginal cells will be on the slide.*

Just after ovulation, white blood cells that are called neutrophils reappear in the smear. *Examination of one slide can't predict how fast the next stages will ensue.* But comparing smears over several days can show when D-day is close.

Metestrus

To identify the first day of metestrus, continue to take smears after breeding. *Recent veterinary findings indicate that due date is always fifty-seven days from the first day of metestrus.* This could prove helpful if a Caesarean section is planned, if your breed is prone to uterine inertia—or simply if you wish to plan around the date.

Depending on where the smear is collected from the vagina, smears can be inaccurate for several days in either direction. Other factors, such as changing from your veterinarian to the stud's midstream, can cause a variance in the technique and readings.

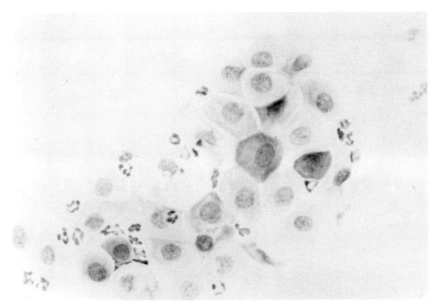

Metestrus—vaginal smear from a bitch in metestrus. Vaginal epithelial cells are of a noncornified type, with parabasal and intermediate cells present. Neutrophils (white blood cells) are also present but may also be absent from smears obtained from metestrous bitches. (Magnification 400X.) Courtesy of Dr. Patricia Olson, University of Minnesota.

PROGESTERONE TESTING

The highest conception rate resulting in the largest litter possible for each particular bitch occurs two days following ovulation.

Problem: How do we pinpoint ovulation other than by using the stud that may be eager enough to breed a knothole, the bitch that might stand throughout her season for anyone who scratches her back (or, conversely, snaps at anyone who comes near her) or the already admittedly less-than-perfect smears?

International Canine Genetics (ICG), which specializes in research concerning canine reproduction, has developed a progesterone test that accurately detects time of ovulation. This and other similar tests are performed through a blood sample drawn by a veterinarian. Run within the first five days of season, the test shows three dots in a baseline color, robin's egg blue, indicating low progesterone. When smears show 50 to 60 percent cornification, run the test every two days until the color changes to pale blue, indicating the initial rise (day zero). For most bitches, the lower dot disappears the day following the peak (day one). *Ovulation occurs two days following the color paling, with eggs maturing in another two to three days. Optimum fertility is on days four through seven.* For problem bitches, continue running tests every other day from the time of the baseline assay.

A stud that may be eager enough to breed a knothole.

The reproductive cycle is controlled by an amazingly complex waxing and waning of various **hormones** from the **ovary** and the **pituitary gland** in the brain. As the eggs ripen during proestrus, the **Graafian follicle** (in the ovary, containing the egg) begins pumping out **estrogen**. This hormone creates estrus. It causes vulvar swelling and changes in the lining cells of the vagina to prepare for breeding. It also creates her special stud-intoxicating perfume and flirtatious behavior that invites breeding: flagging and standing firmly for mounting.

Ovulation has to occur for true estrus to begin. In late proestrus, estrogen levels start to fall as the production of progesterone first begins. This change in the ratio of hormones triggers a one-day surge of the **pituitary luteinizing hormone (LH)** from the brain. LH causes the ripe egg to rupture (ovulation). Once the egg has left the ovary, the tissue that had fostered the egg (corpus luteum) will continue to produce progesterone (the nurturing hormone) to maintain pregnancy.

Once we understand this, we can see how the tests work. Vaginal smears and the stud dog's interest are based on estrogen-induced changes; however, because the estrogenic stage is long and variable, poor timing can still be a factor. But the LH surge is short and always occurs forty-eight hours before ovulation, just as the progesterone levels start up. The ICG test targets this first rise of progesterone, which tells us exactly when ovulation will ensue.

ICG suggests natural breedings on days two, four and six following the surge (indicated by the paling of color); chilled semen inseminations are best done on days four and six.

The progesterone level must stay elevated to maintain a pregnancy. Running the test two to three weeks following a mating, especially in problem bitches, can warn us of impending abortion. If the progesterone level has dropped, as shown by return to a darker blue color, hormonal treatment may be given to sustain pregnancy.

For owners who need to time Caesarean sections, progesterone testing two to three days prior to the due date determines the progesterone drop that occurs approximately twenty-four hours prior to delivery. The Status-Pro™ test takes away the guessing part of the mating game, saving wear and tear on everyone's nerves.[1]

BREEDINGS

Advance preparation facilitates the action. *Trim* long hair surrounding the genitals—just the bikini area for show dogs—and uncover the target by using a rubber band to gather profuse rear feathering on the bitch. Exercise both dogs. The mating act can stimulate more than the libido.

No candlelight dinners should be given before canine romance. A full meal can make the male sluggish or even nauseated during the excitement of the chase. If the erotic damsel is residing on the premises, however, most males tend to fast of their own accord.

Although some breeders recommend washing the genitals with a disinfectant soap both before and after breeding, it is generally not necessary for healthy animals. In fact, since soap can be spermicidal, it can be counterproductive.

If prenuptial *bathing* is necessary, plan it a few days *in advance*. The masking scent of shampoo might be a turnoff. Although it is more pleasant for owners to handle dogs that are clean and odorless, the dogs couldn't care less. Their mate might smell like a lump of very old Limburger cheese, and they'd be happy.

The Human Factor

The actual mating requires two dogs and, preferably, two people. One person holds the bitch still and keeps her calm, giving the bitch physical assistance in supporting the male's weight. The other handler aids the stud, guiding him, cheering him on and assisting him to turn or dismount. This helper can also move the bitch's tail to one side if she does not flag. With nervous or inexperienced dogs or large breeds, three people are even better.

When a certain English Setter stud was bred, assistance was not simply a luxury but an absolute requirement—for the dog would take his fun only on the

---

[1] For information, contact International Canine Genetics, 271 Great Valley Parkway, Malvern, PA 19355, 1-800-248-8099.

run. His intended had to be trotted ahead of him, with the stud tearing after her. The same dog that turned his head with boredom at a vamp soliciting on a stance bred with gusto when she took flight. Perhaps he thought he'd miss his chance!

A small bitch can be restrained with a hand under her belly. Larger breeds are supported with the loin resting on a handler's knee. The knee helps elevate the female, if necessary. Toy dogs are often bred on tables, which is easier on the helpers' legs and backs. One breeder holds her MinPins in her lap during the tie. Many owners leave collars on the dogs, giving themselves something to grab—besides the dog—if necessary.

Even the most placid maidens might object with a love bite, so have a muzzle handy. If the bitch is violently opposed to the seduction, she might have to be bred by AI (see Chapter 5). At the opposite extreme, one German Shepherd Dog brood bitch was so relaxed she'd fall asleep as soon as the tie was achieved.

Whether or not breeders intend to avail themselves of every helpful invention or test, they should still acclimate the stud to natural breeding with the assistance of a handler. If the stud is new at the game, encourage him to sniff and mount by patting the bitch's rump. When he makes an attempt, praise him— even if it's in the wrong vicinity. Scoot the bitch around to position, and he'll soon find that the right place is more fun.

Some dogs are coy and flirty, and they should be allowed time for courtship. Don't rush matters.

If the male becomes overexcited and is tiring himself to no avail, take him away and allow him to urinate. The idea that he might lose out if he doesn't do things right can spur him on to the goal.

Once the tie is accomplished, two people are able to keep the dogs from making sudden movements, help them stay content and keep each other company. It gets to be old and boring to watch two dogs carry on. Having two people present means that one person can call for help if there is trouble. If nothing else, you might speculate on the future litter while waiting.

We recommend that no breeding be unsupervised. If the stud has not been trained to accept handling or is too much of a mama's boy to perform in front of company, privacy might do the trick, but it is risky. Even the most congenial and cooperative dogs may move at the wrong time and injure one or both. A top producing German Shepherd Dog stud hemorrhaged when the bitch pulled away despite careful supervision. Flying solo should be attempted only under controlled conditions and with frequent checks by the handler.

Os Penis

The canine penis, unlike most other mammals', contains a bone, the os penis. This means that an injury could cause a fracture.

Fractures are painful, and this particular bone cannot be set in a cast or a sling. Care should always be taken during breeding.

The loving room.

On Location

Experienced stud owners recommend conducting breedings in the same location. Most males perform better when everything is familiar and they are alert to expectations.

Breedings are customarily conducted at the home of the stud. The reason for this chauvinistic approach is simple. The male is more dominant on his home turf, and the bitch will submit more readily when she is away from her territory. If the male were shipped or delivered to the bitch's residence every time he was bred, some popular studs would spend more time traveling than airline pilots.

The footing must be nonskid—a carpet or matting, for example. If feet slide at the wrong time, the results would be painful or awkward at the least. The rug should cover enough area to save the breeders' knees from hard floors as well.

Keep the room quiet and free of distractions—other dogs, kids, puppies, TV sets, extra people—particularly for the novice stud. A Don Juan may achieve a mating in the middle of a parking lot, as breeders have reported, but you should certainly not attempt to break in a youngster in a circus atmosphere.

Handler comfort should be considered also. A couple of low footstools or similar items are appreciated during the ties.

Two more pieces of advice for the comfort of dogs and handlers: do not plan matings during the heat of high noon; and find a place free of flies.

The Stud's Kit

One would think the stud wears all the equipment he needs, but owners soon learn to have a kit of helpful items nearby. Even if it is not needed, it's comforting to know that it is handy and that you will not have to search for it when you and the dogs are "tied up."

Helpful items include:

- lubricant cream, such as K-Y Jelly^R (not Vaseline^R Petroleum Jelly or other lubricants, which can be spermicidal)
- sterile latex gloves
- a leash
- a muzzle (pantyhose can be used)
- an AI kit
- a watch

Besides the kit, you'll need a dog crate and cleanup equipment in case of accidents. A pan of cool water should be accessible. Occasionally, after an AI or an outside tie, the male's penis does not retract into the sheath immediately. The cool water soothes and eases the swelling, and soon the male has forgotten the discomfort and is eager to start all over again.

Aiding

The stages of breeding are courtship, mating and tie. Some males get right down to the nitty-gritty without messing around. They consummate the sexual act without any of the amenities, and that's fine—it's normal.

Other males spend several minutes licking, sniffing, pawing and blowing in ears. They believe in taking it slow and easy, and this is normal too.

Most develop a routine. One stud might dance around, asking permission before he gets down to business. Another mounts, dismounts, whispers in her ear, resumes his position and Bingo! A third knows what's happening as he approaches his mating grounds. He struts into the room and possesses the bitch before she is even aware of his presence. The male mounts and thrusts until he hits the target. He then picks up momentum, and his legs seem to tread water for a minute. He has achieved his purpose, and ejaculation takes place.

The ejaculate has three parts. *The first is clear* and acts as a lubrication, rinsing the urinary tract. It is about this time that the tie is accomplished by the swelling of the bulb on the penis. *The milky second part contains the sperm*, and *the third portion (clear again) gives the sperm the oomph it needs to reach the waiting ova.*

If you have trained your male correctly, he will not object to your touching the bitch or him even in the throes of passion. The bitch's head should be held still, and her rear held in position. A little K-Y Jelly^R helps in a tight spot.

It is a mistake to allow a male to do as he wishes and take the bitch without handling. This is not only poor training; it's also unsafe. The time will come when he'll need help.

If the coupling must be handled by one person, the bitch can be restrained by a hitching-post method. This can be done by tying the bitch to a post by means of a short lead. When the handler's knee is placed under her groin, she will not be able to pull away. The stud should be well trained, and the handler confident that both dogs will remain calm.

One owner grew tired of wrestling with reluctant females and overeager males. Her husband and a design engineer developed a metallic assistant that they call a Bitch-Hitch™.[2] The equipment is made from welded steel with comfy chest and saddle pads and Velcro™ straps. The Bitch Hitch can be raised and lowered to the male's convenience. Not only is the device a safe aid to natural breedings and AIs, but it also saves the owners' backs and knees and is particularly a boon for those who handle matings alone. Users say that bitches react to the Bitch Hitch as though they were in a crate, calm and secure.

In the event that there is no tie, rest the dog for a half-hour and try again. Many times the second effort is successful. If not, the attempt may be twenty-four to forty-eight hours early (see Outside Tie in Chapter 5).

The Tie That Binds

On one occasion a client rushed into the veterinarian's office exclaiming that his dogs were stuck together—and how embarrassed he was when he found out why. This tie is normal, although peculiar to dogs. Once the act is accomplished, no amount of yelling or dousing with water will end it. You'll just have two sopping-wet dogs.

The tie is caused by the glans penis's swelling. At the same time, the vaginal muscles constrict, thereby resulting in the "stuck" dogs. Ties last from a fraction of a moment to forty-five minutes—or longer (see Extended Tie in Chapter 5). The average is ten to twenty minutes. Records of a Miniature Schnauzer breeder show variations of successful breedings ranging from no tie to ninety minutes, with five minutes the most common.

During this time, the male may choose to turn, and the handlers should aid him. Hold the bitch still, and help the male lift his leg over her back to turn so that they stand butt to butt. Holding the tails of small dogs together when turned

[2]For information, contact Bitch-Hitch, P.O. Box 1162, Studio City, CA 91614, 1-800-441-2258.

The serenade.

helps keep them still. This is the preferred position for wild canines because they can still protect themselves if attacked in this vulnerable position. They can also stand side by side. Lift the male down from the bitch's back, and help them assume a posture that is comfortable for them and for those assisting.

The dogs should be kept still, since sudden movement can be painful. If the bitch pulls away, there could be hemorrhage or tissue damage to both. Avoid this by exercising sufficient control over the dogs during breedings. Talk quietly and praise them, holding firmly. Before the separation, many studs lick themselves, anticipating the end of the tie.

Ties are normally boring even to the dogs—so much so that one Irish Terrier takes it lying down. A certain Beardie has become so blasé that he inches over to his dinner dish, taking the bitch along with him. Exceptions do occur now and then. The first time her Affenpinscher stud fainted during a tie, the owner was alarmed. Now she accepts it with humor. As she said, "He goes out with such a look of delight on his face!"

A tie is not necessary for conception but does increase the percentages. Once the tie is released, remove the bitch and crate her for at least half an hour. Do not allow her to urinate. A bitch may have a small amount of fresh bleeding, which is of no concern.

Examine the male to see whether the penis has retracted normally. Let him relieve himself; then give the dad-to-be water to drink and a treat to thank him for being so cooperative. Nobody ever mentions giving the bitch a treat, but why not? After all, it takes two!

Poor aim.

The Serenade

The male sings a love song only his mate appreciates, but once he has bred, he's strong and silent. The bitch, however, may tell the whole world what this lusty male is doing to her. Some females, even brood matrons, cry and voice their displeasure during the entire process. This can discourage an inexperienced stud, or even the owner.

A maiden often cries during the first penetration, particularly if the breeding is attempted early and she is not sufficiently dilated. Noise does not always indicate pain, for a sophisticated wench sometimes moans and utters little squeaks of pleasure. Unfortunately, this usually occurs about the time the poor old dear is ready to be retired from the mating game.

Poor Aim

Expect a youngster to try mating the ear, the third rib or a spot two inches too high or low. If a male has been conditioned to having his genitals handled from puppyhood, he should not be shy about a helping hand.

Scoot the bitch to the proper position, rather than shoving the male and distracting him. Encourage him to sniff her genitals. Suddenly he wakes up and aims in the general area. If the bitch is sufficiently swollen, a little boost or guidance should put him on the right track.

Let him try by himself for a time, but if he's just off the bull's-eye, don't let him become tired or discouraged. Aim the vulva a little higher or lower, as the case may demand, and guide the penis. Once the connection is made, Eureka!

Backup stud.

Frequency

A healthy stud (and there should be no other kind) can be used on an average of two or three times a week, or every other day. Occasionally, he can be used more frequently but not to the point of exhaustion. Excessive use can lower fertility, and the increased usage becomes futile.

Two breedings forty-eight hours apart should be enough to ensure conception unless the bitch has a history of infertility. Provided that owners and the dogs have no objection, breeding three times over a span of five days allows better coverage. Toy owners warn, however, that too much time in between breedings can mean teeny-tiny afterthoughts that will be whelped at the same time as their "older" siblings. Birth weight is a critical issue in Toys, where an ounce or two can make the difference in survival. The owners of some celebrity studs allow only a single breeding, and for these, a proven bitch and proper timing are imperative.

Backup Stud

Naturally, the bitch's owner should be informed if the preferred stud is unavailable. His owners will ask whether they should bring in the second-stringer or skip the breeding. If the backup is also a good dog, and particularly if he is related to the favorite, most bitch owners will agree rather than miss the breeding. A good choice for a substitute is a less famous brother, the sire, or a young son. The stud fee, of course, would be appropriate for the male used.

CHILLED AND FROZEN SEMEN

Chilled semen can be collected and shipped by the stud's veterinarian. Ask whether the vet has everything necessary: American Kennel Club (AKC) documentation, a vial of extender, frozen gel or ice bags, packing material, a styrofoam container and a shipping carton, in addition to the collection equipment. The semen is mixed with the extender, cooled for an hour and then packed so that it will remain chilled but not frozen.

The package must be sent express (twenty-four-hour delivery) to the bitch's vet, where she should be expectantly awaiting its arrival. After the semen is checked for viability, insemination can take place. Because the viability of the sperm is decreased during chilling, and the stud isn't present to signal his alert, zeroing in on the bitch's fertile days is even more important than with a natural breeding. Yet another reason for determining prime time is that this procedure is nearly as costly as shipping the bitch.

An old saw says you're only appreciated when it's too late. Owners can be sure it's never too late by storing their stud's frozen sperm at approved laboratories or cryobanks, which are advertised in canine publications. Use only labs approved for AKC registration. Freezing and thawing methods can be tricky and can kill the whole attempt, along with a future breeding program. Stud owners pay an annual storage fee. Optimum freezing success is aided by collection from a stud who is in his prime and in good health. Don't wait until the dog is debilitated by illness or old age.

Not only are shipping costs and danger of animal loss avoided, but timing errors are also minimized by having the same vet reading smears throughout the season. You also eliminate the frustration of the bitch's going out of heat because of the stress of traveling.

Paperwork is more complicated, and there is a lower conception rate, but these methods are a boon to the owner who lives in an isolated or quarantined area. Sperm-by-mail also gives wider selection to those who would like a broader choice of studs but cannot or will not travel or ship. One ejaculate can cover four or five breedings.

BACK-TO-BACK BREEDINGS

Successive breedings for a bitch should be very rare. At least a season's rest is needed between litters. Following back-to-back litters—for example, if the first litter produced only one pup—the bitch should be allowed to rest at least a year before her next breeding.

You might elect to breed a bitch twice in a row if you wish to have her whelp at a more convenient time of year, if she has had infertility problems or if she has whelped an extremely small litter. The bitch should be in tip-top condition. When she is bred on consecutive seasons, litters tend to decrease in numbers, and the size and vigor of the pups tend to diminish, so nothing is gained.

The exception may be the bitch who cycles only once a year. It is permissible to breed her on successive seasons since Nature has spaced her cycle for a year's sabbatical.

5

Dogs Don't Read
the Book

AFTER ENDEAVORING to mate an uncooperative bitch to a dud stud, we wonder how mixed breeds manage to procreate with such enthusiasm and success. Yet despite the best-laid plans with two superdogs, the path to success seems strewn with stumbling blocks like an Olympic steeplechase.

Overeager males sometimes work themselves up to the point of no return and suffer the dismay of premature ejaculation. Bitches with immature genitals can present a seemingly insurmountable obstacle. We can run interference for our males to achieve our goal.

A Scottie breeder has had success in dilating bitches with tight vaginal canals. This is when you'll use the sterile gloves and lubricating jelly in the stud kit.

Sometimes the male's spirit is willing, but his body isn't. A fold of skin might block the preputial (sheath) opening and keep the penis from extruding. This can be corrected surgically. Another problem that frustrates young dogs—and those trying to breed them—is a flexible penis, which bends like Silly Putty when it contacts an immovable object.

One German Shorthaired Pointer possessed two vaginal tracts. Although you'd think her admirer would be in ecstasy, it was the opposite for him, because each one was too small for penetration. One tract was surgically removed, and the breeding accomplished by AI. She whelped normally.

Dogs don't read the book.

OUTSIDE TIE

When you're anxious, it is natural to promote a romance a day or two early. If a breeding is accomplished, it might result in an outside tie, because the hormones aren't yet radioing "constrict" to the vaginal muscles. While these nonties are annoying, pregnancy *can* result. An outside tie decreases the percentages—possibly because swelling indicates poor timing or because the handlers do not hold the dogs together long enough. (This possibility is made apparent when, the first time you do a semen collection, you realize the second part of the ejaculate, which contains the sperm, appears after pelvic thrusting stops and can take several minutes to collect.) However, the third part of the ejaculate and the accompanying waves of vaginal contractions propel the sperm into the uterus.

To determine if there is a tie, the male's handler should run a hand along the penile shaft to see if the swollen bulb is on the outside or the inside of the vulva. If the swelling is external, you can simulate the tie by holding the dogs together for ten minutes after ejaculation is completed. This artificial tie stops the semen from leaking out. If outside ties are recurrent with a bitch, she should once again be examined for a stricture deeper in the vaginal tract.

Some breeds are lethargic, and an outside tie is more often the norm than not. But many who raise active breeds do not consider an outside tie a breeding. They back it up with another breeding and/or AI or wait payment until proof of pregnancy. For very small (e.g., Maltese), very large (Saints), short-legged (Dachshunds), or heavy-bodied breeds (Bassets), an outside tie is as common as

I've got a headache.

an inner one. In rare cases, older bitches develop scarring because of difficult delivery or prior infection, making a normal internal tie difficult or impossible.

If the bitch consistently experiences outside ties without complete penetration, surgery might aid the situation, or breedings can be completed with AIs. Many an outside tie turns into a normal breeding one to two days later.

LACK OF FEMALE INTEREST—I'VE GOT A HEADACHE

The bitch that prefers to ''sit on it'' most commonly has anxious parents who are trying to push her into marriage too soon. If owners are patient, often a day or two changes the little gal's mind, heart, and position. If she persists in being uncooperative, however, particularly after prior litters, it may be a sign of an abnormal season. It's also possible she could be a spoiled mama's or daddy's girl.

In the first instance, the season might have to be bypassed and tests run to determine the cause. Hormonal treatment sometimes helps. In the second case, the stud owner would be advised to remove the nervous in-law. The bitch often

Tantalize an inexperienced male.

calms down when her attention is focused on the male rather than on her hovering owner. Besides, the stud owner can take firm steps to make her stand, using physical restraint, without her owner protesting that his or her baby is being assaulted.

Sometimes it's best left to the stud. An aggressive stud often takes the situation in hand and shakes the bitch by the nape of the neck, intimating, "Hey! I'm here to do a job. Shape up!"

If the bitch continues to complain and tests show ovulation has occurred, the breeding can be accomplished with AI. The Bitch-Hitch (see Chapter 4) could work wonders in this situation.

LACK OF MALE INTEREST—NOT TONIGHT, DEAR

Trust your dog. An experienced stud almost always invites, dances and croons when the time is right.

Tantalize an inexperienced male. Kenneling him next to a bitch in season is similar to plopping a pubescent boy on a topless beach on the Riviera. Tease him by bringing in another male to demonstrate. The presence and scent of another male near "his" bitch is often enough to whet the youngster's (or jaded veteran's) libido. All dogs should be kept on leash if this is attempted, to avoid an accidental breeding by the wrong stud or a fight between the two competing males.

If this arouses no interest, let him grow up. He may just be too young, since all dogs mature at different times. A few precocious pups, mostly small breeds, are ready at six or seven months. Some large breeds do not turn on until eighteen months to two years. The AKC will not register a litter sired by a dog under seven months. The average dog is ready to embark on a limited breeding program at one year. This is a good time to have a complete physical, including tests for heritable defects if the dog is to be used at this age.

A submissive dog can be intimidated by a bossy bitch—or a dominant owner. A spoiled house pet might also refuse to breed. Work up the male's eagerness by removing him for a few minutes or separating the upsetting human influence from the duo during the mating. Rarely, a male who has bowed to the superiority of another male peacefully accepts the position of eunuch or low dog on the totem pole. If the above suggestions don't stimulate the juices, the only alternatives would be to remove him from the subordinate circumstances—or find another stud.

If the temperature's sizzling while passion is fizzling, curtail exercise and rest the male in an air-conditioned room prior to the attempt. Conserve your dog's energy by avoiding fruitless jabs. If it's too hot to trot and the stud's feeling as wrung out as a damp dishrag, plan the interlude for the cooler evening hours rather than the heat of the day.

Dogs with a lack of hormones and very low libido may have to be stimulated by the handler conducting the breeding. Press the sheath right behind the bulb until swelling occurs, at which time Nature should take over. The bitch that does not radiate an attractive hormonal scent will not be appealing. Both parties should be examined for abnormalities and hormonal deficiencies if this is a recurrent problem.

Crybabies are a turnoff for some males, especially those who are new at the game. So is a low-throated growl or the sound of teeth clicking together close to a precious body part. Avoid these with timing tests, control of the bitch and enthusiastic cheerleading.

The main reason for a bored male, however, is poor timing—simply being too early or too late in the season. Experienced stud dogs will not touch a bitch until the right day(s). The stud yawns; owners panic; the bitch flirts. He watches everyone pirouetting in front of him, inviting him to participate in the fun. He's thinking, "Not tonight, dear. Maybe tomorrow." Relax. Try again.

LOVE?

The song goes, "Love, love, hooray for love!" And who says dogs don't fall in love? Ask any frustrated breeder whose two painstakingly selected prize-winners want *nothing* to do with each other. Along comes a scroungy, nondescript, downright unattractive type and Zap! Breeders can stand on their heads trying to make the bitch attractive to the male or trying to convince the bitch that the male they've chosen for her is the best. Don't despair.

Few dogs mate for life. But, occasionally, a rare Romeo (more often, a Juliet) opts to breed to a kennelmate and turns up his nose at the ripe little beauty wiggling her furry hips and preening in front of him. The proof of this is the Irish Water Spaniel that ignored the designated bitch in the following tale: "We put her [the hopeful bitch] in the run next to the stud. He kept looking over the top and wailing for a seedy-looking bitch in season on the other side. My bitch enticed him by flagging and flirting, but he stood on his hind legs and whined for the other bitch. We tried breeding them. He gave a quick lick and strained to get back to his run. After three days, we used another stud, and while we were busy, someone left a gate open and we came back to find the other two tied. Who says dogs don't fall in love?"

The logical explanation is that in a case like this, the rejected female does not have an attractive hormonal essence about her. Also, it may be bad timing or a false heat.

Size difference.

Separation from siblings at too young an age and lack of contact with other dogs is destructive to a canine's normal sex life. The dogs simply don't think they're dogs and don't develop natural instincts.

When your Scarlett refuses her Rhett, she may not be simply flirtatious or coy; she may rather be shy and reserved with unfamiliar dogs. One German Shepherd bitch absolutely *refused* to breed to a stranger. If forced, she did not conceive. She allowed, it seemed, such privileges only to a male of long-standing acquaintance.

If you are determined the breeding *will* take place, and the dogs are just as determined it will *not*, introduce the couple to each other a few days in advance. In humans, distance makes hearts grow fonder, but in dogs, it's proximity. If nothing else succeeds, breeding may be consummated with AI. And next time, try cologne.

"UP, PLEASE!"—SIZE DIFFERENCE

Dog owners are not all the same size, and neither are their dogs. It's hard to understand how a neighbor's Affenpinscher and Doberman Pinscher could possibly have gotten together. Determination is amazing. When it comes to the breeder's plans, however, it's a different story. The male aims forever and is off a foot or two. If it's just poor aim, a little guidance benefits (see Poor Aim in Chapter 4).

If the male is too short or tall, slip a large catalog or phone book under the rug, or fold the rug. In some breeds, this situation is common. For instance, the smaller the better in some Toy breeds, such as Yorkies or Pomeranians. For show purposes, the males are minuscule. The bitches, however, must be of moderate size in order to carry and whelp a litter.

Rig up a platform or ramp for the shorter partner to be elevated. The males quickly adapt to such a device; in fact, they become ecstatic at its appearance. An ingenious Chihuahua solves his tiny problem himself by climbing on the bitch's hocks, thereby raising his sights.

Some breeders of unwieldy, uncooperative and/or unmaneuverable breeds build a breeding rack. In fact, one owner was thrilled at finding one at an antique sale! Fancier models can also be raised or lowered to fit the stud.

If the male is uneasy about the contraption, other methods can be substituted. If the bitch is slightly taller, it helps to spread her rear legs. Doing this lowers the objective.

On the other hand, if the target needs to be raised, a hand under the groin area might suffice. More elevation can be gained by placing a knee under the loin, raising and lowering the bitch as necessary. These situations are all important reasons that the male should be accustomed to performing at your command.

UNATTRACTIVE SEASON

Some seasons are unattractive to males. Whether the problem is lack of hormones, a false season (no ovulation), a vaginal infection, or other influences is difficult to diagnose.

A heat could show bleeding with no swelling, or swelling with no discharge—or occasionally both—but the bitch is not alluring. You think she's ready, and *she* thinks she's ready, but the male's sleeping on the job. Despite your efforts and hers, she simply isn't putting out her usual intoxicating siren scent to the male. Have her checked by a veterinarian to determine if the problem is treatable, particularly if this is a recurrence.

Thyroid or other hormonal ailments may cause an abnormal season. Sometimes these can be treated to keep the abnormality in abeyance until a breeding is accomplished. *These as well as other infertility problems are often hereditary, and the question of whether to breed the bitch at all should be reconsidered.*

Breeders have occasionally found that only every other season is fertile when a bitch cycles more than twice a year. In this case, proper planning is sufficient.

A false season may precede a normal one. The smart breeder takes advantage of smears and progesterone tests before going to the expense and the trials and tribulations of a long drive or shipping the bitch to an aborted affair.

MUZZLING

Prospective mates should always be introduced on leash. If the bitch—or, rarely, the male—is snappy or growly, don't take any chances. Use a muzzle. A leash, belt, adhesive tape, or even pantyhose may be used in lieu of a muzzle. Loop the leash around the dog's muzzle twice; then cross it behind the head and tie it. Don't risk injury of the male if the bitch is resistant or in pain, or is just naturally a "bitch."

This surliness can surface when the mating is poorly timed or forced a day or two early or late. Some bitches, however, never agree to losing their maidenhood, and a muzzle is a safety device. They are often more cooperative on the second breeding or after whelping a litter.

TOO MUCH OF A GOOD THING—EXTENDED TIE

The breeding is finally accomplished, and the dogs have tied. You wait patiently, switching from knee to knee. Then you wait more, not quite so patiently, checking your watch, rubbing your aching back. As the dogs become annoyed with this monotony, you struggle to keep them still so no one is hurt.

The bitch squirms around, whimpers and tries to sit. The male finds a sensitive part of himself dragged painfully to the floor and screams in objection.

80

Place an ice pack on the male's testicles.

It goes on . . . and on . . . and on. When it extends beyond an hour, all of you have had as much as you can take.

Actually, the phenomenon occurs when two powerful forces are counteracting each other like a Chinese finger puzzle. The dogs become anxious to separate, pulling against each other, causing greater discomfort. The vagina grips tighter, and the glans penis stays swollen. So the pressure must be counteracted.

Try placing an ice pack on the male's testicles. As the skin cools, so does the male's ardor. Intending to do this, one breeder grabbed the first package in the freezer, and frozen corn was substituted for the mundane icebag.

Another suggestion is to move the male back into the original mounting position. Push on his rear and hold for a moment, releasing pressure on the swollen penis. The dogs should relax, with the result that the partners are freed.

You would think the stud would roll over and snore, once parted, or opt for a rousing ball game. No sooner does a dog separate from the bitch, however, than once again he is eager and lusty. How fast they forget!

PROLAPSED PREPUCE

Prolapsed prepuce is a rare occurrence in which the sheath everts during erection. The penis is constricted in such a way that it cannot return to normal size. This was discovered to be the quandary of a stud that, after a three-hour tie was finally untied, still maintained a painful erection. When cold-water immersion failed, he was taken to the vet. The condition can be manually or surgically corrected under anesthesia.

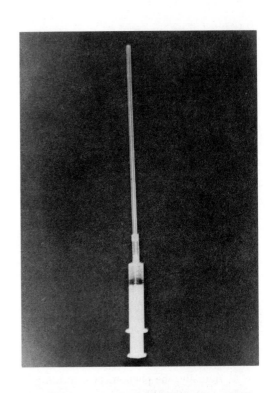

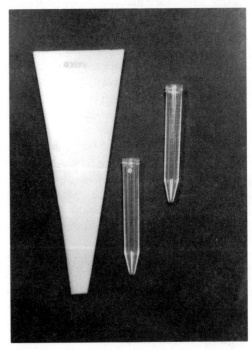

AI kit: artificial vagina, receptacle,
syringe, pipette. Photos courtesy of
International Canine Genetics, Inc.

ARTIFICIAL INSEMINATION

Although it might not be as much fun for the dogs, AI is fairly simple. AIs are often performed by vets, but many breeders also are adept at the procedure. A novice can ask for a demonstration by a vet or another experienced person. Carelessness or improper procedure might cause injury to tender tissues. Most bitches are inseminated by vaginal AI. However, the semen can be inserted directly into the uterus by a veterinarian by means of an endoscope and a catheter under anesthesia.

An AI kit should contain a 12-c.c. syringe, an inseminating pipette, a capped tube, an artificial vagina (for collection) and a latex surgical glove. Measure the approximate length from the bitch's vulva to her cervix, and mark the pipette. (Some come premarked for small, medium or large dogs.) Your stud will appreciate, and perform better with, the perfume of a prime-time bitch filling the room.

The semen is collected with the artificial vagina attached to the tube, then deposited in the bitch by means of the pipette. Sterile equipment is a must, or an infection will result rather than a pregnancy. Some breeders use a paper cup or other receptacle, but the stud much prefers the artificial vagina!

This procedure is an aid when breeding aggressive partners or when a juvenile vagina, low libido or obstructions present themselves. It is also the answer when the stud has arthritis or is injured, too large or advanced in age. Some breeds are just not built to breed naturally anymore, and AI is commonplace. Many handlers, particularly those with top-winning males, refuse to take a chance on exposing the dog to injury or disease.

Sealyham breeders note that show-conditioned males are often bred artificially, because of their short legs and heavy weight. A 50 to 75 percent success rate is reported with AI in a kennel of Sealys, Miniature Schnauzers and Scotties. When accompanied by tests to pinpoint timing, AI has a conception rate nearly as high as that of natural breedings.

When AI Can't Help

If the reason for lack of interest or outside ties is a false heat, AI does not help. Undertaking artificial breeding should not be a poorly timed, last-minute effort. When a natural breeding is not proceeding successfully, tests should be performed to make sure ovulation is occurring. If the procedure is properly handled and timed, success in conception with AI is good. Depending on the reason for the AI, *insemination can be interspersed with attempts at normal matings.*

The Collection

Allow the male to mount the bitch, or grasp the sheath just behind the glans penis (about halfway). Apply pressure, and, as erection begins, quickly

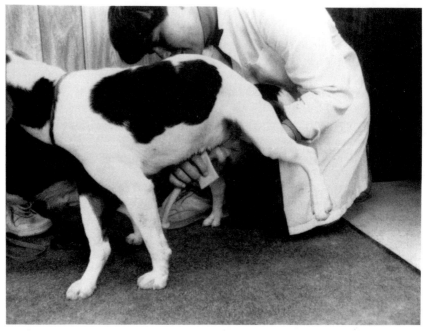

Collecting from a male, using the artificial vagina. Photo courtesy of International Canine Genetics, Inc.

slide the sheath behind the bulb. Fit the artificial vagina (with the tube attached) over the erect penis. If you're slower than he is, walk him around, allowing the swelling to subside.

When the male is ready, he will begin pelvic thrusts; so have the receptacle in place, and continue applying pressure, as though he were fitting snuggly into the bitch's vagina. As pelvic thrusting subsides, you will still be able to feel the ejaculatory pulsations through the sheath. If the male wishes to step over your arm, simulating a tie, allow him to do so. Hold the artificial vagina in place, waiting until all three parts of the ejaculate—i.e., the clear lubricant, the cloudy semen and a final clear prostatic fluid—are collected. Examine a small amount of the ejaculate for motility, number and form. Cap the vial and keep it warm until you are ready to perform the AI as follows:

1. If possible, place the bitch on a table so that you're working at eye level.
2. Draw the ejaculate into the syringe, followed by 3 or 4 c.c. of air.
3. Feed the tube carefully into the vagina, aiming first upward toward the tail and then forward toward the head, until it is near the cervix.
4. Roll the pipette to ease the insertion—*never* force it. Sometimes gentle downward traction in the vulva facilitates insertion.

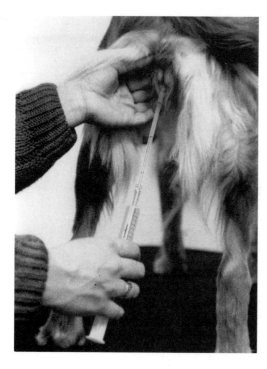

Artificial insemination of a bitch in season. (Note position of pipette.) Photo courtesy of International Canine Genetics, Inc.

5. Attach the syringe to the pipette, and push the plunger gently.
6. Fill a syringe or two with air, and push the plunger, to clear the pipette and speed the sperm on their way.
7. After withdrawing the pipette, put on a surgical glove, and feather (stroke) the upper vaginal wall to stimulate contractions. If the timing is right, the vaginal muscles will clamp down on your finger—an artificial tie!
8. Elevate her rear for about ten minutes; then crate her for approximately two hours.

While you are handling the insemination, have someone walk the male until the swelling diminishes. Or, to speed the process, use a pan of cool water or a cool compress.

You can always tell a male that has participated in surrogate fatherhood. He's the one that bounces into the vet clinic with joy and anticipation, rather than the submissive posture of most canines entering the door. Some males begin their gleeful courtship dance when the glove or AI kit appears. Any port in a storm.

Clean the equipment with a mild soap and water. Rinse it three times with tap water and three times with distilled water to remove any spermicidal substances, and allow it to dry.

Multiple sires.

MULTIPLE SIRES

Once you're pregnant, you're pregnant, and there's no need to take precautions . . . except with dogs, because they can be impregnated by more than one sire. You might take your bitch to the stud, come home, and expose her to other males, assuming that's that. It's not so. A female should be kept away from other suitors throughout her entire season, whether a breeding takes place or not.

Even though the mid-cycle days are usually the best for conception, bitches ovulate over several days. They may continue ovulating even after one breeding, releasing many more eggs. With sperm living up to four days and the eggs being viable for two days, mating with more than one sire creates a giant crapshoot, with possible multiple winners. No matter who wins, YOU are the loser.

The American Kennel Club states this is a no-no. "It is the position of the American Kennel Club that for a litter of dogs to be eligible for registration in the Stud Book of the AKC, the dam of the litter must not be mated with more than one sire during her season."

It is conceivable (pun intended) that a litter of five could have five different sires. Fertility differs in individual dogs, as it does in humans. One bitch may be fertile for several days and conceive easily. Another might release her ova at

Sperm race.

one time and be fertile only for hours. The victorious sperm in this race could belong to dog #1 or dog #5, or #1 *and* #5.

Restrain your tempting lass from consorting with males during her season unless you are positive of her fertile days. Even then, you may stand helplessly by and watch toothless old Grandma mating with her great-grandson on the twenty-third day.

Mismating.

MISMATING / MESALLIANCE

Sometimes the bitch makes her choice without consulting you. You may not know about that selection until it's too late. She surprises all by proudly presenting eight squirming, squeaking all-Americans in the middle of the Persian carpet.

If, however, you observe the male beast putting his paws on your Precious, you can do something about her poor choice of a mate. Don't bother with a bucket of water or the hose. It doesn't matter if the icy dousing does separate the lusty twosome. The deed is done, and you're left with a sopping bitch, and most likely a pregnant one, because you can be darned sure that the same bitch who misses every time you drive halfway across the country and spend megabucks to orchestrate an exquisite breeding will definitely take when the neighborhood Lothario does his thing.

Instead, talk to your veterinarian about the alternatives. The treatment of choice for the pet owner is to spay. The surgery is relatively safe in the first two to three weeks of gestation but becomes more dangerous as pregnancy advances past thirty days. If there are no plans to breed the bitch or show her in the conformation ring, this is the best choice.

A mismating injection can also be given. This must be done within two days to be effective, and preferably within twenty-four hours. The injection of estrogenic hormone prevents the ova from implanting in the uterus by upsetting the estrogen/progesterone balance. The heat is extended, and she may be bred again. But you've learned your lesson. *Never* trust a bitch in season. Some

DNA probes can help identify canine paternity.

breeders fear that the mismating shot may cause conception difficulties during later breedings. This should be a consideration with a valuable producing animal.

Estrogen injections also create a uterus more likely to develop endometriosis, a precondition for the pyometra complex. The most dangerous side effect is potential myelosuppression of the bone marrow. This shutdown of the blood-forming tissue is fatal. Myelosuppression is dosage-dependent, so minimum dosages should always be used, and there should never be a second mismating injection in the same heat.

If you already made plans for a honeymoon, forget it. The ship is sunk for this cruise (see Multiple Sires in this chapter). Contrary to the old wives' tales about miscegenation, however, the elopement has absolutely no effect on subsequent litters.

One thing is certain—steps must be taken to control the urges. When a breeding is not desired by the owner, it will be by the concerned parties. If breeding is planned, the dogs may refuse the choice. Nothing is more frustrating than selecting a stud, then finding your bitch has settled on her own—the Heinz fifty-seventh variety next door.

PATERNITY LAND

Now and then a sneak breeding occurs. Two owners watched with dismay as their Pembroke Welsh Corgi's portliness showed signs of life. They felt their male had to be the guilty culprit, but they had kept one or the other of the dogs confined during the season. Still, with kids, surprises happen, and there was that hound next door who gazed expectantly through the chain-link fence. . . .

A new technology called DNA testing probes can help identify canine paternity. A blood sample is taken from each of the pups, the dam and the suspected sire(s). The genetic fingerprinting matches fragments of genes, proving paternity in at least 95 percent of the cases. Inbreedings make the match more difficult. For instance, in a scenario where two brothers are suspected (particularly if *their* mom is the expected litter's mom), more genes would match anyway.

Should a planned breeding be complicated by an accidental mating, each pup can be matched with the correct sire. The test takes time and is expensive, although not as much as raising a litter only to find homes for unregistered pups. Nevertheless, AKC's Registration Department should be contacted to discuss whether registration of the brood is possible before trying to find a solution.

Some people think dogs can handle everything by themselves. But even the great Itzhak Perlman sometimes needs an accompanist. When dogs perform a cappella, they're more likely to have Jack Benny results than those of a master. When *we* become involved *with* our dogs, we can create a classic.

Is she or isn't she?

6

Is She or
Isn't She?

NOW THAT the breeding is a *fait accompli*, all you can do is wait and wonder. Published charts show dates of mating, followed by your gal's due date. We find it easy to count off nine weeks on the calendar.

Usually, a bitch begins showing about the fifth week. The loin area puffs out and is no longer concave when she is lying on her side. Breast enlargement begins about that time as well. When the abdomen becomes greatly distended, many bitches exhibit discomfort, grunting as they lie down and shifting about frequently. As their time nears, they cannot find a comfortable position. Most nest.

If the litter is small or the bitch is large, well-muscled or deep-chested, evidence may not appear until the end of gestation. The same can be true of a maiden or one with a profuse coat.

One owner wrote that her bitch did not look pregnant until the eighth week but presented her with ten puppies. She isn't the only one who's been fooled. Many owners delight in speculating on due dates and number of pups. One family even has a lottery, or as they call it, a ''littery.'' Experience has no advantage over the six-year-old's guess.

A fun method of guesstimation is suggested by Erlene, who measures her Bulldogs just behind the last rib on the day of breeding. An increase in girth at forty days indicates pregnancy. She measures daily during the last week, counting one pup for each inch gained. We have found the inch does not hold true for all breeds, but measuring (or weighing) can suggest pregnancy.

Personality change.

Milk does not appear until the last week of gestation and, occasionally, not until after whelping. Movement of the pups cannot be detected until the last week to ten days. To feel movement, place a hand on the belly near the loin. A slight pressure to this area can cause the pups to move. Soon, watching the tiny kicks and swimming motions serves as an evening's entertainment. Which one will be a champion? Will one be a guide dog or a High in Trial winner?

But what about the bitch that keeps her hourglass figure, holding in her tummy just to drive her owner nuts? Some preparation is necessary, so subtle signs must be recognized, and a few tests can show proof positive.

NATURE'S INDICATORS

With a maiden, the easiest sign to note is nipple enlargement. The nipples widen, sometimes to a half-inch or more at the base (next to the body). They often darken in color as well. Brood matrons, too, show evidence of impending motherhood in the nipple size.

Appetite increases, even in the most picky eater. This might also be true, however, of those that only think they're pregnant. Some become droopy, sleeping an unusual amount, as though saving their strength for impending motherhood.

Personality change is another clue. A future mother that has enjoyed playing with other dogs might become cranky and grumpy, grumbling "Leave me alone" at erstwhile pals. The same bitch might demand attention from her owners, as if to say, "You got me this way. Now show me you love me. Right now!" Darby, a Beardie, and Frosty, a Westie, are just two that beg to have their swelling tummies rubbed.

The vulva often stays slightly enlarged, rather than shrinking up to its preseason (anestrus) state. In many cases, a string of crystal-clear mucus is seen, particularly during the last half of pregnancy. The backbone stands out near term, much as it does on an extremely thin animal. These are all considered positive, but not definitive, signs.

ULTRASOUND

Patience gives the same rewards as tests, but most breeders are too impatient to wait for Nature. This is especially true with long-planned litters, titled dogs or bitches who have a track record of infertility. It's also helpful when you have deposits from families eagerly waiting.

When medical complications arise, it is not only curiosity that asks, "Is she or isn't she?" A more aggressive treatment may be prescribed if the bitch is not carrying a precious bundle. In addition, breeders might have to make plans to take time off from work or to plan a trip around the expected event.

Some practitioners with state-of-the-art machines and lots of experience offer ultrasound pregnancy diagnosis as early as eighteen days. Cost is moderate. A definite conclusion can be made by twenty-three to twenty-five days. This is a noninvasive procedure requiring no sedation and with no side effects, allowing breeders to make a giant step forward in canine obstetrics.

One Standard Poodle showed a green discharge about midway through gestation, causing great concern. Pregnancy had been confirmed by palpation the previous week. Fetal death and/or placental separation was feared, with impending loss of the litter and subsequent metritis. Prostaglandins, along with antibiotics, were the treatment of choice but would cause abortion if viable fetuses were still present. If there were none, hormones would be used to cleanse the uterus and to prevent more serious infection, possibly necessitating a spay.

An ultrasonogram showed pups dog-paddling contentedly in each horn of the uterus. Because this bitch was in good health otherwise, a more conservative approach was elected. Specific, fetal-safe antibiotics cleared the discharge.

Although the owner says her vet would have proceeded differently had the discharge recurred or had other indications of general illness appeared, she welcomed the opportunity of making an informed choice concerning a valuable dog and litter. Seven healthy pups were whelped normally.

PALPATING

Palpation is easiest when it's a small dog carrying a large litter, but talented fingers can be successful on large dogs with small litters too. The bitch should be relaxed and not overweight. The optimum time to palpate for pregnancy is from twenty-five to thirty days.

By grasping the entire belly in one hand, you can feel the uterus through the abdominal wall. As you move your hand from the rib cage toward the hips, the fluid-filled vesicles (fetus, placenta and fluid) slip through your fingers, like a water balloon with knots tied at intervals. At this stage, they are about the size of ping-pong balls.

This procedure takes a fine touch, and many veteran breeders (including the authors) find this a difficult task. Soon your bitch may be showing other signs, and you will feel little kicks rather than lumps.

PREGNANCY TEST

A pregnancy test is now available from International Canine Genetics (ICG). It is based on changes in blood proteins that occur in pregnant dogs by the fourth week. Your veterinarian can draw a blood test between twenty-eight and thirty-seven days and send it to ICG for evaluation. By that time, most pregnancies have been confirmed by ultrasound, palpation or eyeball. But it can be helpful for an owner who does not have access to a sonograph and whose bitch is still questionable by four to five weeks. It is moderate in cost.

Another test, based on hormone changes, is under development for veterinary office diagnosis. At this time, there is no at-home test or Early Pregnancy Test for canines. But in the future, who knows?

If you are still in doubt about the diagnosis, an X-ray can be taken around the eighth week (or after forty-five days), when bones have calcified. At that time, no damage occurs to the fetuses from radiation.

Some expectant mothers leave no doubt of their condition near term; they lie obscenely on their backs in all their rotund glory.

FALSE PREGNANCY

Either you're pregnant or you're not. But your bitch might fool you and herself. Dogs can experience false pregnancy, or pseudocyesis, which is caused by postestrus hormones.

The hopeful mother believes in every way she is in a maternal state. She may exhibit a distended tummy and enlarged nipples and breasts and may produce milk. Some nest, pant and even suffer contractions.

If thwarted in their motherly instincts, a few bitches adopt another small dog, a kitten or a stuffed toy in lieu of their own pups. While this seems sweet to owners, the condition can be uncomfortable for the bitch. Severe cases bring cramps, caked breasts and mastitis. Temperaments can change to out-and-out crabby when they are protecting their den.

A few bitches adopt a stuffed toy in lieu of their own pups.

This curiosity is caused by a secretion of hormones following estrus and ovulation. Although all bitches go through this period of increased hormone secretion to prepare for pregnancy, most do not show exaggerated symptoms. Scientists do not know the exact causes of pseudocyesis, although they suspect prolactin, an anterior pituitary hormone, is a major factor.

For those owners who have planned a breeding, it is a major disappointment when they—and she—tried so hard, all to no avail. The owner who has not bred a bitch is horrified to watch her blooming with the supposed evidence of her unbridled, albeit sneaky, passion. She can't help it. False pregnancy can develop whether or not she has been bred.

One hypothesis on the reason for this condition maintains that dominant females in the wild prevented others from mating and having pups. The more submissive females would be forced to play nanny or even nursemaid to the boss lady's kids. What alternative would a poor girl have but to imagine she was pregnant?

Indication of false pregnancy begins about six to ten weeks after the heat period (during normal "gestation" time), which is another reason an owner assumes the bitch is indeed pregnant. The episode usually ends within a few weeks.

No treatment is necessary for mild cases, though symptoms may be diminished by reducing food and liquids. Great discomfort may be treated with hormones like mibolerone. This drug is very effective, but since it can cause fetal

An expectant mother can and should have normal exercise for the first weeks of her pregnancy.

abnormalities, it is essential to be sure it is a false pregnancy. If the bitch's breasts are very full or uncomfortable, use hot packs, followed by cold packs, or pat with camphorated oil.

A normal litter may be conceived and whelped during the next cycle. Lowered fertility and smaller litters were noted in a Golden Retriever following a false pregnancy. Actually whelping a litter sometimes ends recurrences. If the condition is chronic, it is best to have the bitch spayed after the symptoms have subsided. During pseudocyesis, organs are enlarged, and a danger of hemorrhage exists.

MORNING SICKNESS

Some bitches suffer all the symptoms of their human counterparts. They are nauseated and refuse to eat during early pregnancy. Yellow bile is vomited from licking the mucous secretions.

Morning sickness is not harmful. Feed small meals of bland food, and call your veterinarian if it continues for more than a week, is voluminous or occurs more frequently than once or twice a day.

At four weeks, the uterus enlarges to the point where it begins folding on itself. During that time, appetite might wane. Make sure your expectant mom is receiving all the nourishment she needs through a premium food or her normal diet with an additive, such as ICG Stress Formula™, which will aid in maintaining appetite, nutritional balance and coat condition. If necessary, coax her with delicacies until she feels like eating again.

TOUCH YOUR TOES

An expectant mother can and should have normal exercise for the first weeks of her pregnancy. Strenuous exercise, such as jogging or high jumps, during this period is not a good idea, unless she is accustomed to it. Caution should be taken during her chores, herding, field trials or other Performance Events to avoid injury to her precious cargo.

Continue her usual routine until her bulk becomes unwieldy. Most bitches themselves know when they should slow down. If yours doesn't curtail her own activity when her girth increases, you must. Continue moderate activity, such as walking.

Some bitches will use any excuse to escape exercising. In the words of a Bloodhound owner, "Inactivity leads to whelping problems. We use a treadmill for walking daily to ensure exercise and have natural whelpers."

FEEDING EXPECTANT MOTHERS

After breeding, bitches should be fed their usual menu until the fifth week of pregnancy. Then offer them two meals a day, gradually increasing the total intake by 20 to 40 percent.

With the fully nutritious, high-quality foods available today, it is not necessary to supplement them with megadoses of vitamins and people food. If it excites her appetite (which will probably need no such incentive) or it makes you feel better to offer additional goodies, such as liver, yogurt, hard-cooked eggs or cottage cheese, use small amounts.

Excesses and imbalances can actually be harmful. Too much liver can cause diarrhea. More seriously, an overabundance of vitamin A, for example, can actually prevent implantation of fertilized eggs. Surpluses of calcium or vitamin D can cause abnormalities in the developing pups, and *excess calcium may lead to eclampsia during nursing*.

The best choice is to feed a premium-grade dog food during a brood bitch's entire life or to upgrade your usual choice of good food, during gestation and lactation, to food or a formula specifically geared for dogs in stressful situations. Some breeders feed the dam puppy or growth dog food.

Some breeders firmly believe in the advantage of *raspberry tea leaves* to assist in easing labor. Brew tea with water to pour over her meal, or add a small amount of dried leaves, for the last four weeks.

RESORPTION

A bitch's breeding pattern has been normal; it is followed by actual signs of pregnancy; then suddenly . . . poof! It's all gone, and you wonder if the pregnancy was wishful thinking. No wonder this phenomenon is pegged a "phantom" pregnancy. In such cases, the possibility of resorption should be considered.

A school of thought says all bitches conceive many fertilized eggs and resorb fetuses as a matter of course until the size of the litter is within her ability to carry and whelp. If something goes wrong, the process could continue until the entire litter is resorbed. No discharge or outward sign is apparent.

Resorption can be caused by injury, illness, medication or hormonal problems. It usually occurs before mid-term, so an owner may not even know for sure whether the dog is pregnant.

A veterinarian should determine whether the bitch did conceive and, if not, what the cause of resorption may be. If the complication is diagnosed as low progesterone, treatment with repositol progesterone, administered four weeks after breeding, may be recommended. Low thyroid levels can be boosted with replacement *l*-thyroxine.

Thought should be given to removing such bitches from a breeding program since the condition could be hereditary. Nevertheless, resorption does not happen as often as breeders believe. Most times, a miss or false pregnancy is the actual cause of disappointment.

ABORTION

Canine miscarriages are rare. Infection, injury, malnutrition or hormone imbalance may cause the loss. Abortion can occur any time from mid-term to the fifty-sixth day.

The bitches suffer little discomfort, because abortions usually occur before the fetuses reach full size. But they grieve and fret, looking for their pups. If you see bleeding or colored vaginal discharge before term, call your veterinarian.

Take the bitch's temperature for about a week. An elevated temperature can indicate retention of fetuses or afterbirth.

THE LABOR ROOM

Your gal is blooming with the blush of approaching motherhood. You may have despaired of reaching this point, but suddenly you realize D-day is fast approaching, and you'd better have a place ready.

Choose an area away from the hubbub but convenient and comfortable for you and the dam. Although some people select a corner of the kitchen or family room, most find it less than appetizing to have puppies—clean as you and Mom may keep them—performing their latrine duties as you bite into the lasagna. It's also more private for the mother and her brood to be away from the eye of the hurricane.

Many bitches still possess a den instinct, which telegrams, "Find a cubby-hole, get in and nest like crazy." To forestall a poor choice on her part (e.g., your closet or an open drawer), select a place that pleases all of you. A spare room, a corner of the basement or the garage might be good choices as long as they're clean, handy and warm. If she prefers a cozier environment, rig up an enclosure within her box—a removable partition—or a roof with hinges. You can also set up a den ambiance by putting an ex-pen around the whelping box and draping it with sheets or blankets. Remember that you might have to join her in the box, and it should be possible for you to maneuver within the confines of her nest.

Once she starts the real business, she will likely forget about where she is. It is during her stewing and fretting beforehand that she eyes your water bed or the soft carpet under the dining-room table.

The Box

Breeders of Toys often use a crate for the birth and the first few weeks. Some owners use a plastic kiddie swimming pool for good footing and easy cleanup. Commercial whelping boxes can also be purchased, but the majority of owners build a sturdy box. There is no more use of yesteryear's cardboard refrigerator box or nest under the porch.

The whelping box should be in place at least two weeks before the due date. Paint the box with a lead-free paint, which can be disinfected and repainted between litters. Take time to install her and convince her this is her family's new home. Feed her in the box. Encourage her to sleep in it. Pad it with cozy blankets and newspapers, and let her mess it up to her pleasure.

The box should be large enough for her and you during the birth and for the mother to stretch at full length. It should be roomy enough for a large litter. Unless you plan to move the litter by three weeks of age (or less), it should also be high enough for older pups and sturdy enough for exuberant playtime. It is amazing how quickly the tiny, blind babes turn into rowdy, romping rascals.

The floor of the box should be raised on two-by-fours or put on a pallet so that the litter will be protected from chill and dampness. Plywood makes a good base. The plans that follow are for a box adequate for large breeds until pups begin to clamber out around four to five weeks of age. The box may be scaled down according to the size of the breed and your setup.

1. The box measures five by four feet. Each side has two pieces of lumber, one on top of the other, each one being one inch thick and nine inches wide.
2. These pieces are screwed onto two one-and-a-half-inch braces.

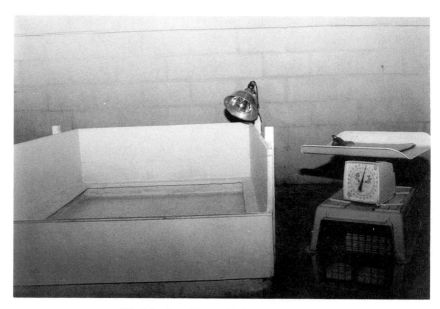

Whelping box. Photos by Chris Walkowicz.

3. Hinges are secured between the two pieces of lumber at the front of the box, in order to lower it for the dam to come and go with ease (though an anxious mother can scale astounding heights).

The top board at the front can be left down until the first pup begins exploration, which can be as early as two-and-a-half to three weeks. At this time, it can be raised and secured to the sides by hooks so that all sides are eighteen inches high.

Inside the box, place a rail three inches above the floor on all sides. The rail is about one inch thick and two-and-one-half inches wide and is screwed to the sides from the outside. This serves as a guardrail for the pups, preventing them from being crushed against the sides by the mother. Dams are usually careful about stepping around the pups and lying down, but with a large litter of helpless, fragile newborns, accidents can happen.

Now sit back and wait.

Labor Day.

7

Labor Day

WHEN THE BIG DAY arrives, you should be where the action is, not dashing around gathering equipment. As soon as you suspect you're expecting the patter of little paws, start building the box and collecting the necessities. Remember to keep complete records of the breeding and whelping, as required by AKC. Send for the proper forms for registering the litter and for record keeping.

WHELPING KIT

The basic whelping kit should include:

1. hemostats or clamps
2. dull scissors
3. latex gloves
4. alcohol for disinfecting
5. a thermometer
6. petroleum jelly
7. your record book
8. a watch or clock to record births and labor time
9. dental floss

White thread is often suggested for tying cords. We recommend dental floss. Practice tying a wet noodle with plain thread, and you'll see why: the waxy floss doesn't slip.

Other helpful items are:

- a nasal aspirator
- a penlight for looking into mouths
- a feeding tube or baby bottles
- iodine or Betadine[R] for cords
- Vetrap[R] bandaging, which is helpful to push in an "outie" navel and to keep dams from worrying at the umbilical cord

Obtain Dopram[R] from your vet to stimulate a sluggish newborn. Other newborn stimulants are Pediatric Stat and Pet Nutridrops. If you don't have anything else available, a drop of whiskey will do. Styptic powder, along with the clamp, works wonders to halt bleeding from a cord. Ask your vet about the advisability of using oxytocin, and, when recommended, have some on hand with syringes. Pedialite[R] can be used for treating dehydration.

This might seem as if you'll need a suitcase instead of a small kit, but we don't want to lose even one precious babe. Actually, a tote bag or overnight case can contain everything. A plastic storage box can double as the puppy crib during labor. Although you may not use all of these things, it's better to be like every good scout and be prepared.

OTHER ESSENTIALS

Stack plenty of newspapers for the actual whelping beside the box. You'll also need a trash bag for soiled papers, a heat lamp or other heat source, and nonskid flooring for the pups when all is done. Gather twice as many clean towels as you think you will need. We find hand towels to be the perfect size and not as cumbersome as a bath towel. You'll use them all. Have a spare box handy to move puppies into when the dam begins thrashing about in labor.

Beg, borrow or buy a baby scale. A loss of weight is one of the first alarms of danger.

Prepare a pick-me-up for Mom, such as weak tea, beef broth or chicken soup. Add a portable phone to call your vet for assistance or your friends to share the joy.

The polls show that running neck and neck for top contender in time passers are choosing names and figuring the first show possible for the as-yet unborn pups. At this time, a friend makes good company and offers an extra pair of hands. If no friends are available, a spouse will do.

Ask old-timers in your breed about predispositions or breed abnormalities (see Appendix I). If you own Chinese Cresteds, ask a fellow breeder or a Papillon enthusiast, rather than a Borzoi lover.

If you haven't already done so, prepare the future mom. Trim long tresses away from the nipples and vulva. If you don't wish to cut away a glorious coat that took her two years to nurture and you to coif, leave the drape at the side, and tie it back with terry-cloth ponytail bands. Or use the method of one Lhasa

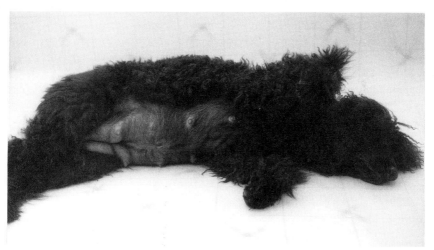

Trim long tresses. Photos courtesy of Tara Darling.

Apso owner—she dresses her gal in a body stocking, leaving the rear exit open and vents for the breasts. Another wraps the tail in a nylon, gauze or plastic wrap. Petroleum jelly helps to keep long hair away from the point of exit.

Some method is necessary for identifying all those squirming, identical little furry Sammy snowballs or golden Pekes-in-a-pod. A few people mark toenails with fingernail polish, but this wears off, and you must be close to determine who is who. The same is true for clipping a wedge of hair against the grain. If you're on the wrong side, you don't see it.

The majority of breeders use a collar ID, and the best dog tag for puppies is rickrack. It's available in a kaleidoscope of colors and widths (wide is best for pups over a pound) and doesn't nestle into the fur. Collars should be changed as needed. They can be checked daily during individual cuddle time and weigh-ins. As an economical plus, they can be washed and reused for future litters, and a rainbow of colors can be bought by the yard at sewing wholesalers. The loops children use for making potholders, available at craft stores, also make good tags.

In a few weeks, these IDs serve for long-distance recognition while pups romp in the yard. When admiring buyers come to pick their bundle of wags and kisses, you can tell them that pink is a girl, green is smartest, orange is spoken for, yellow is the most laid back and purple is the best show prospect.

PACING THE FLOOR—REAL-LIFE PREPARATION

Breeders each endorse their own methods, systems and superstitions, based on their experiences. All, however, agree on one thing. Have a vet you can count on, one who knows you mean it when you holler, ''Help!''

In the fantasy world of commercials and animated features, the dam has no amniotic stains or hanging teats. She is not panting in labor or chomping on a placenta. Nevertheless, she gives birth to pups with open eyes and full coats, appearing to be three weeks old.

In real life, things never go that smoothly. Keep the phone number of your vet clinic handy. Even the most seasoned breeders are more comfortable knowing the whereabouts of their veterinarian, day or night, in case of an emergency. It's wise to have an experienced midwife on alert as well.

Ten days ahead of ETA, *start taking the bitch's temperature to chart her normal range*. The temperature in the evening is usually higher than in the morning, so write down both, recording the pattern for several days ahead of the due date. Although gestation is normally from fifty-eight to sixty-five days, births do occur up to a week early. Large litters often arrive ahead of time, with small litters sometimes a day or two late.

Temperatures are often slightly lower than normal up to one week before whelping. In 98 percent of all births, a sharp decrease of 1 to 2 degrees warns you that the big moment is due within twenty-four hours. At this point, we advise you never to leave the expectant mother alone. Whelping can start at any moment.

The bitch who goes over the due date should be watched closely. Most breeders feel soothed by having the vet check the bitch daily when she is overdue. It seems like a chore, but it's well worth it if even one puppy is saved.

Stocky, short-bodied breeds are physically incapable of aiding themselves during the birth. So are bitches who carry such a large litter that their bulk prevents them from free whelping. There should be no whelping behind the barn for our precious girl! We'll never know how many of those unsupervised dams and babies suffered or were lost.

The owner should be present in case a bitch needs help or comfort. Occasionally, a bitch panics and needs calming. And it's not always difficult deliveries that we need to midwife. Sometimes we have to because the birth is too easy! The dam does not even realize a puppy has been born and neglects to tear the sac. It's been a long time since dogs whelped by themselves in the wild—and *yours never has*. Most first-timers need tea and sympathy.

This is the time to put on a big pot of coffee, chill the champagne, finalize the labor room and nursery, and settle in for the wait with the latest canine magazine. Your hands will be busy soon enough.

Nesting.

NESTING

According to your dog's actions, one of the ecstasies of being an expectant mother must be nesting. She tears and shreds with glee. You can almost see her smile. Her comfy blanket is a lumpy bump in one corner, and the shreds of papers wouldn't soak up a tear in the desert. You change papers, and she starts anew, tossing them into the air, nesting with a passion.

This trait is a natural instinct and a common symptom of impending birth. Some nest with a dogged scratch, scratch, scratch. Others wreak chaos with a vengeance.

Allow her to nest at will, although you should encourage her to do it in her box rather than in the petunia patch or your bed. One breeder learned this lesson quickly after her German Wirehaired Pointer destroyed a bedspread and two pillows. Instead of continually changing papers and straightening her blanket, relax and let her have her way. There's no sense in both of you being frustrated. Have fresh papers ready when the action kicks off. Postpartum, you can replace papers with good nonskid flooring.

Some bitches begin nesting halfway through their pregnancy, others wait until the last day and a few never do. Each is normal in her own way. For the dam who continues nesting in the aftermath, wait a day or two before replacing papers with a carpet. Small pups can squirm out from beneath the paper jungle more easily than from a heavy rug or blanket.

A carry-over from the dam's long-ago ancestors is her bunny-soft undercoat, which loosens near the due date. The bitch pulled out these tufts of fur to line her den as a cozy home for her infants. Nowadays, you should brush it out to avoid hair wafting about your house, your clothes, and the puppies' mouths.

LISTLESSNESS / RESTLESSNESS

As their time nears, many bitches alternate periods of deep sleep with flurries of activity. This means they are preparing for presentation of their babes.

One minute the bitch is sleeping so soundly she does not awaken to the usual temptations—food cooking, car keys rattling, the door opening. The next, she becomes restless, sensing that something is looming, though she's not sure what. She paces, crawls into minute cubbyholes and sticks to you like dog hair.

She wishes to escape from the household bustle and find a quiet place for privacy, yet two minutes later she returns to verify that you're still here should she need you. She wants your reassurance and loving touch.

As time passes, she becomes more urgent in her insistence, nesting and asking frequently to go out. When you exercise her at this point, attach a leash and go with her, carrying a flashlight at night. Pups can be born in the yard and die from exposure. Avoid one breeder's experience: she crawled under the deck of a house to coax out a stubborn bitch during a supposed rest-room break.

Some females have accidents or vomit as pressure builds. A house pet will be mortified if she goofs. Don't scold her, but you may find it easier on your nerves to install the bitch in her whelping box, letting her nest, tear and pace to her content. A well-trained dog is an advantage, as the owner can put her on a "Down. Stay," which should give you at least one minute's peace until her instincts overtake your command. If you do not remain with her, check in every few minutes to assess progress.

SHIVERING

Just before whelping, some bitches quiver like a bikini babe in an arctic storm. Though this might be due partially to discomfort or fear of what is happening, it is probably caused by her lowered body temperature. Reassure her if she is upset. Most often, shaking ceases with the emergence of the first pup. She seems to realize, "Oh, that's what I'm here for."

If shivering continues throughout or after delivery, have the bitch examined by a vet ASAP after whelping. One Pembroke Welsh Corgi quivered throughout the whelping of eight healthy pups. The bitch was uninterested in the litter. During the first week, four puppies died, fading within a day. The dam was belatedly treated with antibiotics for subclinical infection. After a few days, she resumed normal care of the pups. It is also possible to have this marathon shivering reaction from calcium deficiency (see Eclampsia [Milk Fever] in Chapter 9).

CRYING/SCREAMING

Some of us stub a toe and screech and curse. Others burst into tears, crying and sobbing. Otherwise, our reaction might be to moan bravely or to tell everyone about the injury. And a few stalwart folks bear the throes of agony in silence and with clenched teeth.

The same is true of dogs. Of course, we don't have to listen to them cuss and tell us their troubles, but pain might be expressed aloud. As the contractions escalate and the awareness of impending delivery heightens, some bitches cry and whimper their protest against pain and fear. A bitch may share her troubles with you for a couple of days in advance, making you as miserable as she is. A few breeds, Afghans for instance, are admitted screamers. Beardie and Miniature Schnauzer owners say their first-time mothers often yelp at the birth of the first pup. Breeders find that the firstborn is often the largest, and delivery seems to progress more easily after the first whelp has stretched and lubricated the birth canal.

PANTING

Women in childbirth-preparation classes are now taught to do what dogs have known all along: to pant. As delivery nears, huffing and puffing accompanies other symptoms. Increased panting may precede labor by as much as twenty-four hours.

THE GREEN LIGHT

Gestation is nine weeks, or fifty-eight to sixty-five days. The cause of the temperature drop is not known, but scientific speculation involves the decrease in progesterone. Sometimes the dogs fool you—the temperature drops a bit, then rises, then once again goes down, leaving you sitting home two days waiting for the blessed event. At least it's more warning than we mere humans have.

The temperature isn't all that drops. So does her belly. One morning you get up, and so does she, but her distended abdomen doesn't. She looks as though she could use a skateboard, and her backbone shows prominently. This is particularly noticeable with the first litter.

Your bitch might refuse food a day before whelping. A few chowhounds snack midway through delivery, but fasting is a good indication of imminence. The clear, stringy vaginal discharge increases and thickens, and her vulva becomes soft and spongy, often much enlarged. Licking and hard panting accelerate.

REAL LABOR

Reread this book, and then start reading a good mystery. Just about the time you get to whodunit, the bustle invariably starts. It's a sure cure for slow starters. If not, you can be sure she'll have the first one right after you fall asleep.

The future mother tries to find a comfortable position, and none are left, it seems. She whines and shifts her weight. Many bitches peer quizzically at their rear quarters, as though trying to understand what this involuntary action of their bodies may be. Some become upset, fearing that this involuntary action is soiling the house. Calm your bitch with soothing words and caresses. Remain calm—at least outwardly—for the dog picks up her owner's tensions.

Examples of extraordinary rapport between breeder and pet are cases in which the bitch halted her pacing to sit by her owner with a soulful expression in her eyes. The owners swear that when they asked, "Are you ready for your babies?" their bitch ran to her box and began the proceedings immediately.

You are soon able to see contractions. Your bitch strains and grunts as labor intensifies. She may move around and whip her tail (and amniotic fluids) against your nicely painted white box. She might crouch, as though passing a stool, or she might stand with a roach back. There is also the treasure who lies quietly on her side, calmly waiting.

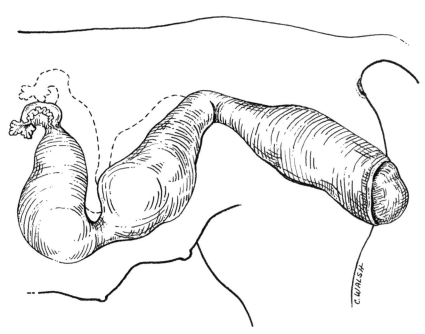

The placental bubble appearing at the vulva. Note other puppies still in uterine horn. Second uterine horn is indicated by dotted lines.

SIMPLE WHELPING

The first visible sign of a pup is usually a bubble that appears at the vulva. Sometimes the pressure bursts the sac, lubricating the birth canal, helping to pass the first pup. Most times the puppy remains within the membranes. Some bitches produce pups as easily as passing a stool; others must strain.

As each pup is born, weigh, tag and record it, and check each one for normalcy as well. Some births leave little time for doing this, though.

An Irish Water Spaniel can spew her pups out with remarkable force. The midwife had better be prepared to catch the whelp, as must the breeder whose bitch delivers from a standing position. Experienced matrons frequently sit with hips to one side or lie quietly.

When the sac arrives intact, the bitch's first instinct should be to tear it open and lick the pup clean, rousing it to cry and move. Bitches normally consume the placenta, then lick the pups clean and dry, stimulating the passage of the meconium plug (first stool).

If she does not act quickly, *you must. Tear* the membrane away from the head, and *wipe* the liquid from the mouth and nose. Vigorously *rub* the whelp as the dam would, to encourage it to gasp and cry. Don't worry about cutting the cord yet. *The first item of urgency on the agenda is to remove the sac and stimulate breathing.*

111

Clamp the cord and cut it on the other side of the clamp.

The bitch then crushes and shreds the **umbilical cord** with her teeth. A few dams tear it much too close, and in such cases, the breeder should take over. If you must sever it, squeeze the blood in the cord toward the pup, and clamp the cord about one inch from the pup's belly. Tear the cord with a dull instrument or fingernails, rather than making a clean cut with a sharp knife or scissors. Using this method causes less bleeding. The cord should be severed on the placenta side—away from the whelp, with the hemostat in between. Iodine may be used for disinfecting and cauterizing.

After the puppy emerges, the placenta might remain inside the dam. If she is quiet—don't worry. It will pass before the next whelp. Some dogs thrash about with the imminence of the next birth, however, and could injure the attached pup. If the dam is restless, clamp the cord twice with hemostats, and cut it between the two. The hemostat next to the pup prevents bleeding, and the one next to the dam prevents the placenta from retracting.

Discourage the dam from continued pulling and tugging at the whelp's navel; doing this could cause damage or hemorrhage. If bleeding does continue, apply a hemostat, or tie the cord with floss or thread. When a pup's tender tummy was torn because of the bitch's fussing at the cord, the inventive owner grabbed Super Glue[R] and a paper towel to hold the pup together. It worked! Although a hemostat would have been preferable, this story shows what people in desperate circumstances can accomplish.

To stanch persistent bleeding, apply styptic powder. The powder stings, but it not only stops the bleeding quickly but also dries the cord.

Pups jostle into position.

Healthy pups cry and sniff for a nipple with heads raised and wobbling back and forth, like dog statues in car windows. The sucking reflex is surprisingly strong. One vet tells of a pup nursing on a back teat when only half out of the birth canal!

Normal presentations include both head-first or rear-first at about a 60/40 percent ratio. In head-first deliveries, both front feet are extended forward along the neck and show soon after the head is apparent. Normal rear-first deliveries have the rear legs extended, followed by hips, body, then head. In both cases, the puppy is oriented just like the dam, backbone upward and belly underneath, not upside down.

If the emerging pup has the pads of its feet down, it will be born head-first; if pads are up, rear-first. A greenish discharge appears after each placenta. The dark reddish placenta may not appear until the next pup, but there should be one-to-one issuance. *If the bitch does not object, move the pups to another box during each birth so they are not injured in the process.*

"**Dry**" **births**, caused when membranes rupture before delivery, are also common. When this happens, it is imperative to work quickly so that the pup does not smother in the birth canal. Often a pattern of one pup emerging soon after another, followed by a rest between these and the next pair, is seen. This is thought to be caused by release of a pup from each horn of the uterus, with a pause as the next two jostle into position.

Have water available throughout the labor, though few bitches will touch it. Some lap once or twice at water or broth during the birth of a large litter.

Dams commonly rest between puppies. Thirty minutes is the average length of R & R, but it may last up to as much as six hours or even longer. One Dalmatian bitch who whelps large litters sensibly takes rests of two hours between pups. Records show she takes as long as thirty-two hours to whelp eight pups. Don't act rashly or rush into hastening a normal delivery. The thing to watch for is straining. If she exhibits none, there is no immediate alarm.

Most breeders would call the vet, however, if the break lasts longer than three hours, in order to determine whether oxytocin would help or if a Caesarean section is indicated.

Breeders must learn to distinguish between mild and hard contractions. If intermittent hard labor continues for more than one-and-a-half to two hours—or sooner if distress is apparent—a trip to the vet is demanded. Continual hard contractions should never last longer than fifteen to twenty minutes without being productive.

The new mother indicates the conclusion of the birth by relaxing and nurturing her babies. She curls protectively around the pups and takes a well-deserved nap. Her abdomen looks collapsed for the first time in several weeks.

POSTPARTUM

Now offer your proud dam a pick-me-up of beef broth, bouillon or eggnog. We've heard of some lucky Salukis who receive ice cream! After a rest period, take the mother out to relieve herself, wipe her up a bit with a damp towel and clean the messy box. You might have to attach a leash to force her away from her brood.

Adjust the **heat lamp** to the proper height. Move it to one side of the box if the dam is too warm. Mom and littermates add body heat, and if needed, the pups seek out more warmth. A clever Bulldog breeder operates her heat lamp with a dimmer switch, controlling the amount of warmth needed at the moment.

Indoor-outdoor carpeting is a popular choice for lining the box, as are fake lamb's wool rugs. They're washable and easily replaceable. Do not use straw. It is prickly and irritating to pups' delicate skin and causes allergies. Infant puppies have strangled from inhaling cedar chips.

The bitch should be taken to **the vet** within twenty-four hours of whelping for an exam and an oxytocin shot. Palpation or a radiograph of deep-chested breeds and suspicious cases will determine whether all is clear.

After a few deliveries, many breeders feel confident enough to administer the purified oxytocic principle (POP). Oxytocin should *never* be given before the first puppy has dilated the cervix, however. Either a puppy *must* be born, or at least a portion of the body must be visible at the vulva. It is the practice of several breeders to give a shot (subcutaneously) midway through a large litter as a boost. Many give a shot two hours after the last pup is born. This should expel any retained placenta—and, in some cases, one more pup! The dose is variable according to the breed size and brand of drug. *Have your vet discuss usage of the product when you purchase it—ahead of time*, please.

Anyone who plans to breed more than once should consider learning how to give subcutaneous injections, for it is sometimes necessary to do so when a vet is not available.

Write all statistics in your record book: sex, time of birth, color, markings, weight, activity level and ID.

Remember: The most important requirement for a breeder—other than a good bitch—is common sense. You can do almost anything if you have to. A teen-ager tells of whelping her first litter when her parents were gone. She woke up to find the bitch nesting under her cot in the whelping room, a week before the due date. She flipped on the light switch and discovered the electricity was out because of a thunderstorm raging outside. She managed to help a litter of seven come into the world by candlelight and kept the pups warm until the heat and lights came on.

CONSUMING PLACENTAS

Although some bitches turn up their noses at the placenta, most take to it as though it were a deluxe pizza. The slippery sac containing the pup is torn, and the baby is licked and cleaned. Then the dam turns to the task of eating the placenta. Others eat it first, chomping and slurping, before they tend to the pup, while *you* break the sac. It may also be consumed as the pup is delivered, without your ever seeing it, particularly if the dam's long coat hides the birth from clear view.

Consumption of the placenta, with its hormones, stimulates the milk flow, facilitates delivery of the following pup and aids reduction of uterine size after delivery. Before domestication, bitches ate the evidence of a fresh birth to hide the litter from predators.

Opinions concerning placentas differ. Some breeders allow the bitch to consume all of them; others let the dam have two or three and dispose of the rest. A few people gag at the thought and do not want the bitch to touch the placentas, preferring to handle the entire process themselves (in the trash bag, not in the manner of the dam).

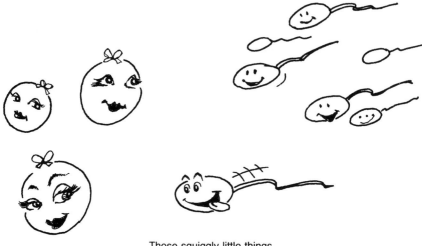

Those squiggly little things.

The wisest course is to allow the bitch to follow her instinct. Don't upset her by starting a tug of war with the placentas. If the situation can be managed calmly, let her consume a few. Too many increase the discharge or result in diarrhea or indigestion. It is better to cope with diarrhea, however, than a frantic bitch that has been thwarted in her efforts to do as Nature is telling her.

NUMBER AND GENDER OF PUPS

If you're mad at the sire because there was only one pup, your anger is misdirected. It's the dam that determines the number of pups—it depends on how many eggs are released during ovulation and how many are carried to delivery.

On the other hand, all those kings that divorced or, worse, beheaded their wives for presenting them only with girls were off base. It's the sperm that determines the gender of offspring. You know—those squiggly little things with the X's become the girls, and the ones with the Y's become the boys. Overall, the number of males and females whelped pretty much evens out, although some sires seem to produce a preponderance of males . . . or the reverse.

It's been suggested that breeding early produces more girls because the XY sperm live longer than the XX sperm. Other tongue-in-cheek, profemale superstitions include facing the dogs toward the moon or bringing a pink blanket to the vet's for a Caesarean section. One breeder said with an almost straight

The birds and the bees—how do you tell a boy from a girl?

face, "If you want boys, face the dogs to the north in the morning; for girls, it's south in the evening."

The important point to consider is not how many females or males you have but how healthy and sound they are.

THE BIRDS AND THE BEES

How do you tell a boy from a girl? In adult dogs, it's rather simple. *He's* the one who marks every tree, post and fireplug as his territory. *She's* the one who attracts every male for three males around to your front door.

With short-coated breeds, the reproductive organs and nipples are obvious. They aren't hidden by Calvin Klein jeans or Izod shirts. Even a long-coated dog may be rolled over on its back for closer inspection.

Newborn puppies, however, are dogs of a different sort. Even veteran breeders have been embarrassed at discovering that one of the "girls" wearing pink rickrack should have been wearing blue. It's best to double-check before forwarding the registration application.

Remember the childhood game of "Button, button, who's got the button?" Male and female puppies both have buttons, but the location tells the story. The tinier the dog, the tinier the button, but it's always there. The male's is a minuscule penis, directly behind the umbilical cord. The tiny vulva is between the rear legs of the female, under the anus.

Even though their owners are sometimes confused, the dogs themselves never are, and that's what the sniffing is all about.

8

Dilemmas
and Difficulties

$\mathbf{D}$ON'T SELL yourself short. If you've bred for any length of time, you've probably seen a lot more normal births than your veterinarian. But when whelping difficulties and emergencies arise, you'll appreciate a professional working relationship with your vet(s). In the vein of professionalism, be ready with facts when you call for help.

Record the time your bitch's temperature dropped and when the first contraction occurred. Your vet will also need to know: the current temperature, the color of mucous membranes (gums), the mental attitude (depressed, indifferent, hysterical), the interval between pups (if any have been born), the pattern and current status of uterine contractions, the approximate number of pups left unborn (is she still huge, or do you think she's almost through?) and the results of a careful vaginal exam. A short history of prior whelpings can also prove helpful.

Assessment of all the data by phone helps you and your vet decide if you're just worrying a bit early, whether you can do something to help or whether the bitch needs immediate veterinary attention.

VAGINAL EXAM

Constant or unnecessary exams only serve to introduce trauma and infection. A vaginal exam may be necessary, however, during an abnormal whelping. The exam is done with an index finger, or (in cases of large hands and/or small bitches) a little finger may suffice.

Dilemmas and difficulties.

Scrub the hands thoroughly, and trim back the nails—they hurt! You can use surgical gloves or do it barehanded, but in either case, a bit of K-Y Jelly^R makes digital insertion into the vagina smoother. Gently introduce your finger into the vulva, and proceed slowly upward (toward the backbone). At the level just below the anus, the vagina becomes horizontal. Thus, your path is first upward and then forward toward the head.

If the bitch were not in labor, you could not proceed this far. The tract would be narrow and tight, and the bitch would protest vigorously. During labor the vagina is dilated, and although the bitch's head might still have to be held to keep her still, there is less resistance.

As your finger advances, you might detect nothing or bump into a puppy. Most commonly, you'll feel a head, nose first. The nursing response is so strong, sometimes a pup will begin sucking the end of your finger!

Once you've encountered a pup, gently probe to establish its position. Can you feel both feet next to the head? Is the forehead above or below the nose? Sometimes all you encounter are the legs. Remember that feet with pads up are hind feet, and feet with pads down are front feet—and here's the exception to the rule—unless the pup is upside down.

Now you are able to tell your vet the presentation.

PRENATAL LOSS OF FETUSES

If a colored discharge appears prior to the due date, let your vet know immediately. When it is too early for live birth (before the fifty-sixth day), an abortion may be in progress. A greenish-colored discharge or a foul odor before the first delivery suggests a dead pup. You must act quickly to save the others. If birth does not commence, call your vet.

A Caesarean section or manual delivery of the dead fetus might save the remaining littermates if the bitch is close to term.

PREMATURE PUPS

Breeders tell of puppies that were born up to one week in advance of their due date but grew to normal adulthood. Premature puppies (from a later breeding), given the misnomer "runts," are sometimes whelped as part of a term litter. *Since gestation is only nine weeks, breedings spaced one week apart can cause a large size difference.*

If the puppies are normal but small, supplemental feeding, warmth and TLC should save them. Eventually, they will catch up to—and perhaps surpass—the others.

INFLUENCE OF LITTER SIZE

Two or fewer puppies might not exert enough influence for proper cervical dilation or for adequate uterine contractions. If you have charted temperature, however, you are aware of the time lapse before labor is expected. When a small litter is suspected, X-rays can confirm the number during the last week. On the other hand, if the litter is large, primary or secondary inertia may occur. Careful observation is imperative, as well as making sure *all* pups are born.

When labor does not proceed normally to delivery of a fetus, the condition is called dystocia. Dystocia can be fetal in origin (the pup is dead, too big or improperly positioned) or maternal (the mother has uterine torsion, primary or secondary uterine inertia, incomplete cervical dilation or a narrow pelvis).

ASSISTED DELIVERY

If the pup is in normal position but is just stuck, assisted delivery can be lifesaving. This is common with the first pup in the litter.

Extracting a pup is not for the meek and mild. Owners are terrified of pulling off a leg or a tail. This is extremely unlikely unless the pup is already dead and partially decomposed. (Pups are sturdier than you think.) Besides, allowing the pup to remain wedged in the birth canal not only causes the death of that one but also can cause the death of the others and extends the pain of the bitch.

If legs are protruding, time is of the essence. Should the pup survive, there may be other consequences. Lack of circulation during delivery can lead to gangrene, which in one case resulted in the loss of a Sheltie's ears and half a foot at one week of age. Prolonged delivery can also cause brain damage and/or epilepsy.

Stand the bitch or lift her abdomen, taking advantage of gravity. This is when two people come in handy. Give PIT (pitocin or oxytocin) if contractions have slowed. Use a rough cloth or towel—pups are slippery. Pull toward her hocks in time *with* the contractions. Do not jerk. Exert pressure firmly and evenly downward, continuing to hold on to the whelp but letting up on pressure between contractions. Rotate the pup as you pull, first to one side, then to the other side with the next contraction.

ENORMOUS PUPS

Extremely large puppies may lodge in the vagina—assuming that they can even pass that far. It is frustrating and urgent when a pup is wedged and birth is delayed.

Sometimes a little elbow grease—combined with petroleum jelly—is all that is needed (see Assisted Delivery, above). At the same time, you may need a third hand to hold the bitch or to aid in the birth. Exert downward pressure on the pup through the perineal area (between the anus and vulva). Peel the tight vulva back around the pup, allowing more of it to slip out of the vagina so you can grasp the pup to pull on it.

As you might expect, this is painful, and even the most docile bitch might snap at the hand that is helping her. A very understanding partner to aid you at this time is helpful. Nondoggy people may not feel that the life of a pup is worth the pain of a bite. Your assistant can muzzle the bitch if necessary. Act quickly, and everyone's agony will be over shortly.

If you are unsuccessful in dislodging the whelp, it will be lost, and a Caesarean section might be necessary to save the rest of the litter. The wedged pup may be dead before you can get to the vet. This is another urgent situation and a reason that it is very important for you to diligently try delivery at home.

PLACENTAL PROBLEMS

An entire placenta should pass before the delivery of another pup. Often, when Mom appears to be only licking herself, she's actually slurping up the placenta. True failure of an afterbirth to pass can block the passage of a pup beyond it. Even if all the pups are born, a shredded placenta left inside will putrefy and soon cause metritis. This is another reason for using your handy thermometer.

Placentas that separate before the fetus is ready to be born can cause normal-term pups to be born dead. Once the placenta separates from the uterus, the pup must breathe air within a reasonable time or drown in fluids. The cause of this separation is not always known and can sometimes be congenital. In one case, four live pups were born, followed by five not breathing. Two of the last five were revived with lifeguard techniques. Tissues sent to a pathologist identified viral inclusion bodies, indicating that a viral infection had been present and had caused placental damage—although the dam had shown no signs.

MALPRESENTATION

Puppies who somersault to the cervix in other than the two normal positions might need assistance. Malpresentations may include head-first with one or both front legs tucked back or tail-first with rear legs folded under (true breech). In these cases, attempt to snare one of the trapped legs and pull it into the correct position.

Sometimes gentle retraction, pushing it back in the direction from which it came, allows the offending part to come into place. If you feel that a pup is upside down (the forehead below the nose or the nose with the foot, pads up), you can attempt rotation of any part that can be grasped. Upside-down whelps

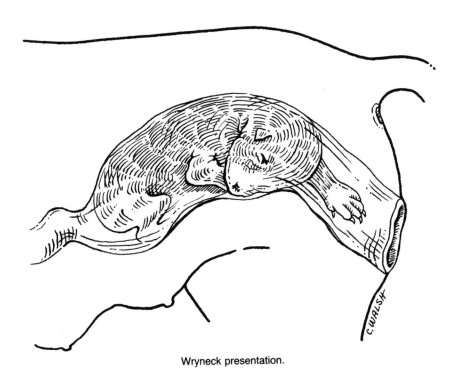

Wryneck presentation.

123

are difficult to deliver because the pup's body doesn't bend in the same direction as the vaginal canal.

One or both front feet showing (pads down) with no head adjacent is an indication of a "wryneck" pup (as shown on page 123). The head is turned back, and the bitch is attempting to deliver both body and head side by side. These whelps are usually impossible to deliver, and the pup is dead from asphyxiation or a broken neck. A sideways presentation of back or belly is likewise unrectifiable.

A malpresentation that is not remedied in one or two attempts is a signal for vet attention and a possible Caesarean section. *Do not pull on a pup until it is in a normal delivery position.*

PRIMARY INERTIA

If the delivery date arrives but puppies don't, be alert for *signs of primary inertia (PI). The cervix dilates, but no hard labor is in evidence.* Mild, unproductive uterine contractions may be felt in the body wall from time to time but with no abdominal press. No puppies are born. When a water sac breaks, it might appear as though the bitch has wet herself. Labor should begin within one hour.

The bitch does not always exhibit signs of distress. More than likely, she'll do nothing more than nest, pant and wonder why you're so worried. Follow your instincts. This is just one example of why rapport between animal and owner is so important. *Do not leave a bitch while labor is impending.*

Once a notable temperature drop occurs and stays down, labor should begin within twenty-four hours. When it does not, an examination is vital to ascertain whether the cervix is dilated. If it is not, then you and your girl must suffer another day of nail biting. A Caesarean section is vital when your vet finds her fully dilated. This is an Emergency, with a capital E, and cannot wait until morning. Hesitancy spells the difference between live and dead pups.

PI is fairly common in Toys but can also occur in single-pup litters and bitches over five years of age in any breed. This condition can also be the result of obesity, hormonal deficiency or lack of exercise, any of which could result in a lack of muscle tone or degenerative changes in the uterine wall. Overstretching, caused by uneven distribution or too large a litter, has also resulted in PI.

In a rare case of hydrops amnii, accumulation of more amniotic fluid than normal, a Caesarean section was necessary to salvage the Giant Schnauzer pups. A bitch incurring this malady is obvious. She enlarges soon after conception, her abdomen becoming immense and unwieldy. The uterus is too overstretched for contractions to be efficient.

PI can also be the result of hypoglycemia and/or hypocalcemia. These conditions can be treated by your vet when specifically diagnosed, and labor may then proceed normally.

Of course, not every dog that goes over her due date is a PI case. We know of a Min Pin that refused to do *anything* until the breeder joined her in the box. Then she settled down to business and free-whelped a normal litter. Most bitches

... bitch held out three long days ...

prefer having their owners present, as in the case of the out-of-town owner whose bitch held out three long days, having her first contraction just about when the key turned in the lock.

But don't gamble on dam moods. Have your bitch checked when she is over term unless you know from past history that this is protocol for her.

SECONDARY INERTIA

When the uterus tires and labor ceases or weakens before the entire litter is whelped, the condition is called secondary inertia. During a large litter or in an older bitch, the uterus may become fatigued before delivery of the entire litter. This condition is common in many giant breeds or with dogs that routinely whelp very large litters.

Secondary inertia can also be caused by extremes—too long a labor, too large a fetus, too small a pelvis. Prolonged straining with a malpresentation or a dead puppy lodged in the birth canal can cause uterine exhaustion and effective cessation of labor.

Manual removal of the impediment helps, but if contractions have weakened, they might have to be recommenced with oxytocin. This can intensify labor within ten minutes to help prevent loss of pups or the necessity for a Caesarean section. *Remember the proper usage of this drug.* If it is given before the cervix is open or when the impediment is still present, the uterus can weaken further with unproductive labor or even rupture. It will only intensify existing contractions.

A Scottie breeder reports some success with a "lazy" whelper. Wearing sterile gloves, she feathers (strokes) the inside of the vagina, which can have the same effect as PIT in strengthening contractions. The user should apply the motion firmly against the upper wall, pulling the finger back toward the exit.

Some secondary inertias, even without physical blockage, will not respond to oxytocin. When labor does not resume or is still unproductive, veterinary attention is required.

PROLAPSED VAGINA

Although prolapse can occur in any dog, it is most common in the mastiff-type breeds, which are prone to vaginal hyperplasia. Just prior to or during whelping, part of the vagina everts, presenting a rather gruesome red ball of tissue at the vaginal opening. Although this is easily put back into place by your vet, swelling may not recede enough to allow vaginal delivery of the current litter, thereby necessitating a Caesarean section. In at least one case of vaginal prolapse that we know of, the bitch whelped normally in a subsequent pregnancy.

Vaginal hyperplasia in another bitch was corrected with surgery. Caesarean sections were necessary after the surgery because of postsurgical adhesions.

PROLAPSED UTERUS

A prolapse of the uterus is an extremely rare condition in which prolonged straining continues after all pups have been delivered, perhaps because of a retained placenta and/or weakened pelvic ligaments. If this is allowed to go on, the flaccid organ can turn inside out.

A long, gory mass extends from the vagina, often to the hocks. It may be Y-shaped if both uterine horns are involved. Wrap the organ in a clean, damp cloth, and transport the bitch to the vet clinic. Using anesthesia, the surgeon will reinsert the tissue where it belongs. Depending on the degree of damage to the uterus, immediate or subsequent spaying probably will be recommended.

UTERINE TORSION

The term "torsion" strikes fear in most dog owners' hearts. Although less common than the gastric variety, uterine torsion should be treated as an equal emergency. *This results when part or all of one or both horns of the uterus twist. The path to delivery is shut off, as are the blood vessels of the uterus.*

Either delivery never begins at all, or, if the twist occurs during labor, everything can shut down. Labor might start and stop, and the bitch could appear depressed and in discomfort, often with abnormal crying or moaning. Partial torsion might have no symptom except inertia, but complete torsion is more dangerous. With a full twist, the gums might be a dark, muddy red or white with shock. If you are in doubt, compare her gums with these in other dogs' mouths. The bitch can exhibit a mental vagueness or even become comatose.

Should the situation not be rectified, infection from decayed fetuses usually requires spaying or can even prove fatal. The pups and the dam will die unless the breeder is alert to the trouble and acts swiftly, seeking veterinary help.

Complete uterine torsion in a German Shepherd bitch was reported in our survey. When the bitch braked in midlabor, the novice breeders listened to poor advice and waited three days for delivery to resume. The end result was dead pups, causing a ruptured uterus, peritonitis and eventual death of the bitch.

One breeder lamented keeping watch and consulting with her vet on an overdue bitch. When no labor had begun on the sixty-eighth day, she insisted on a Caesarean section. A partial torsion of the uterus had lowered blood supply for the last two weeks of gestation, retarding development of the fetuses and resulting in the belated birth. The pseudopreemies weighed seven to thirteen ounces less than normal and had no hair or nails.

In another instance, an Akita had delivered four live pups when labor ceased. During a Caesarean section, torsion was found high in one horn, trapping one whelp. Two pups that were in birth positions were already dead, but another and the trapped pup were alive. Prompt intervention saved the pups and the bitch.

RUPTURED UTERUS

A rupture can be the result of an overanxious, misguided breeder who administers oxytocin inappropriately. Abdominal injury could also cause traumatic rupture of the uterus. Infection or prolonged contractions—usually with dead pups or putrefying afterbirths—cause tissue death in the uterine lining, leading to a weakened wall and rupture.

Symptoms are shock, pale mucous membranes, a rigid abdomen and/or an extremely high temperature, up to 106° F (41.1° C).

CAESAREAN SECTION

Breeds with large heads and/or small pelvises are commonly given Caesarean sections. Owners of those prone to inertia also should be prepared for the possibility of a Caesarean section. If your dog falls into these categories, talk to other breeders beforehand. Alert your vet, rather than calling in the middle of the night or during a busy clinic day. Of course, some surprise birthdays can't be helped. Ideally, your vet clinic has a high success rate with Caesarean sections. One breeder drives three hours to a vet who handles the surgeries by the method she has found to be most successful with her Bulldogs.

While Caesarean sections should not be routine, they are accomplished swiftly and are often lifesavers for both pups and dam. For most surgeries, a wide variety of reliable anesthetics exist, and your veterinarian uses the ones in which he or she has confidence. Unfortunately, some commonly used anesthetics cross the placenta during a Caesarean section, resulting in groggy, depressed, weak or even dead pups.

Anesthesia

If your bitch is facing a Caesarean section, your veterinarian should be willing to discuss the choice of anesthetic. Familiarity with the drug and safety for your bitch are desirable, but with a valuable purebred litter, the puppies' viability should receive equal consideration. After all, the pups are why you bred her in the first place, aren't they?

In Caesarean sections where the bitch is still fresh and live puppies are anticipated, several good choices exist. Probably the best, although the most expensive, is isoflurane gas. Small dogs can be masked and anesthetized, while larger ones need to be asleep first to pass the endotracheal tube through which the gas goes to the lungs. Several good, safe ultra-short-acting injectable gases can accomplish this. An advantage of gas is the ability to shut it off when surgery is nearly completed. After several breaths, all anesthesia is gone! Isoflurane requires a specific machine.

If isoflurane is not available, one of several narcotic or dissociative drugs can be used in low doses, followed by a novocaine block along the incision line. These create a stage of relaxed sleepiness without pain in the mother and minimize the degree of depression in the puppies. A specific antidote to the narcotic agents (Nalline[R], from the Merck Company) can be given following surgery. But doing this is not always wise; it's already too late to reverse the effect on the puppies, and it eliminates the dam's pain control.

Breeders extol these newer methods, saying their bitches are nearly awake after surgery and can go home immediately. In at least one case, the bitch actually walked out to the car, following her owner and the box containing her squealing litter! Dams often are caring for their lively brood in a few hours.

After Surgery—At Home

When a Caesarean section is scheduled, prepare a box to transport the litter home. Line it with several layers of newspaper, covered with a towel or blanket, and bring an additional cover to keep the pups warm. A hot-water bottle helps ensure warmth. As soon as they are out of danger, mothers and pups should go home, where continual observation is possible, rather than staying in a hospital cage.

After a Caesarean section, the pups could be a little sluggish for a time, and the new mother may seem uninterested in them. The natural birth process stimulates the hormones and the maternal instincts, especially in primipara bitches.

Introduce the pups to the mother cautiously and with constant supervision. You might have to wait until she's completely awake to leave her alone with them. Heed the warning of a breeder who lost two pups when the confused dam snapped at and killed them. Unfortunately, at this time, she cannot tell the difference between her babes and a pesky flea. Because many anesthetic drugs are hallucinogenic, she might think they're screaming green monsters!

Reassure your bitch. Keep the pups warm and cozy until Mom is awake. Rub a bit of her own milk on a pup, offer a nipple to one pup at a time, and soon she will respond. Muzzling the dam and staying with her during nursing can avoid tragedies if she takes longer than usual to accept her brood.

Encourage the puppies to nurse the mother and drink the colostrum (earliest milk). Hold them to the nipple, and extract the first milk into each one's mouth. Usually doing this is enough to stimulate interest. Otherwise, wait a few hours and attempt it again.

Depending on the reason for the surgery, bitches may deliver subsequent litters naturally. If surgery is needed a second time, serious thought should be given to the question of further breedings. When the cause is primary inertia or too narrow a pelvis, your bitch's daughters could be inheriting the same tendencies. The exception would be certain breeds (see Appendix I, Breed Specifics and Predispositions) where a planned Caesarean section is the norm.

MUMMIFIED FETUSES

Mummified fetuses are startling to those who have never seen them and have no reason to expect dead puppies. Mummies are dead and dehydrated

Mummies.

Lifeguard techniques.

fetuses retained within the uterus. They are undersized and withered and can be delivered as part of an otherwise normal litter.

A breeder of large dogs said, ''I knew it was tiny [about three ounces]. In breaking open the sac, the skin started to peel off the fetus. I was horrified and sick. The rest of the litter produced another mummy, three pups that expired during the birth and five normal pups.'' An occasional mummy in an otherwise normal litter is no reason for concern.

LIFEGUARD TECHNIQUES

When pups remain in the birth canal too long or inhale fluid, revival techniques may turn the situation from disaster to celebration. Resuscitation procedures also aid in rousing surgically delivered pups.

Various methods are helpful to stir vitality: the gag reflex, a tug on the tail, artificial respiration, vigorous rubbing, respiratory stimulants, removing secretions from the mouth and nose, and the shakedown or swing method.

Insert a finger into the pup's mouth. **Gagging** can cause a gasp that may rouse the breathing reflex. An ear bulb syringe can be used to suck fluid from the mouth and nose.

Mouth-to-mouth resuscitation can be accomplished by blowing into the nostrils. Gentle compression of the rib cage helps breathing as well as stimulating the heartbeat.

A **respiratory stimulant** called **Dopram**[R] is enthusiastically recommended by some breeders. One states she would not be without it during a delivery. One

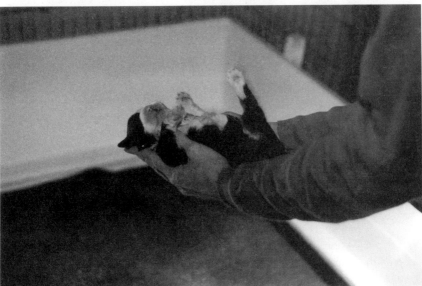

To shake down a pup, cushion the puppy's neck and back in your hands with its head down (belly up). Photos by Ed Walkowicz.

Makeshift incubator. Just cover with a towel. Also doubles as a warming box during labor. Photo by Peggy Bommersbach.

drop on the tongue of "blue" pups (pups suffering from lack of oxygen) gets them going. Your vet will probably use it in a similar way on pups delivered by Caesarean section. For those who do not have it on hand and need a substitute, a drop of brandy can help—or you can make a glucose solution: a tablespoon of honey or corn syrup plus a dash of salt in one cup of boiled water. These solutions should be administered a couple of drops at a time from the fingertip or by eyedropper.

To **shake down** a pup, cushion the puppy's neck and back in your hands with its head down (belly up). Vigorously swing the pup in a wide downward arch from your head through your legs. Gravity dislodges fluids and encourages circulation. Use a washcloth or small towel to hold the slippery little tyke. An overenthusiastic swinger launched a puppy into flight when he slid out of her hands. Fortunately, he survived. Intersperse swinging with aspiration of fluids and brisk rubdowns.

An ingenious breeder of Irish Water Spaniels taped a failing puppy to a bread board, which left her free to tend the rest of the litter. She put a heating pad on the board, taped the pup's hind feet and slanted the board at a 45-degree angle, with the pup's head hanging down. She said: "I sort of batted him around a bit until he squirmed. When he stopped, I would nudge him some more. I really annoyed that pup for about a half-hour. His nose ran and I wiped. He squawked a bit too. I didn't think he had any fight in him, but he must have. It cleared his lungs. After that, I gave him some honey and boiled water and put him back, feeling I had done all I could. In a day I couldn't tell which pup it was!"

When pups are chilled, warm them before giving them any food or stimulant. Chilled pups cannot digest food, and doing this may kill them. A hint for warming puppies is to put them close to your skin, in an inner pocket, a T-shirt, or even a bra! Another way of warming them is by holding them in lukewarm water. Don't just leave them under a heat lamp, since a weakened pup cannot squirm away if it becomes overheated or burned. Body warmth is best to heat a chilled pup. If you don't have time for these things or you're squeamish, you shouldn't be breeding.

Try any and all of the above, or use your imagination to provoke a lusty cry. The sweetest sound a breeder can hear is a bawl of protest from the whelp, signifying that the lungs are clear and he is ready to join the fight for his life.

How much is too much? Although most of us hesitate to give up, brain death occurs when the pup has not been breathing for five minutes. Check the gums. If they are pale and cold, usually there is little hope of a healthy survivor.

When your struggle to assist a weak pup continues for more than a couple of days without progress, pups often have to be put away later. Some of our own experiences of extreme methods used to keep puppies alive include those used on one still at birth weight at four weeks, another diagnosed as having a bone deformity at ten weeks and another discovered to be suffering from patent ductus arteriosus at eleven weeks. All were euthanized. Sometimes Nature knows best.

INCUBATOR

Many owners whose breeds need frequent Caesarean sections purchase an incubator just like those used for human babies in intensive care. These have covered openings through which to insert your hands so that you can handle and move the puppies as necessary. They also have a clear top for easy viewing. A Bulldog breeder keeps her puppies in an incubator in between chow times for six to ten days. She can easily hook up oxygen, if needed, and can regulate heat and humidity.

When it first became apparent that an incubator would be helpful, she rigged up a cardboard box (some use a baby bassinet) as temporary headquarters for the infants. If you do this, you should put in towels first for insulation, followed by a heating pad on one side. Doing this allows the puppies to wriggle on and off the pad as they want. The pad should be covered thoroughly so that tender skin won't be burned through contact. Hot-water bottles cool too quickly for use in an incubator, but a regular light bulb can be attached or suspended away from the pups and substituted for the heating pad. A good thermometer is required to make sure the isolette does not become too warm. You can adjust the temperature by covering the box fully or partially.

An incubator can be a lifesaver whenever pups need an extra boost—if they are underweight, need extra warmth, have a respiratory or other illness, or simply have a drowsy mom that has had a Caesarean section.

BE PREPARED

Although we wish, for the sake of all dams and their owners, that you would never need this chapter, the likelihood is that if you continue breeding, you will. If an owner is prepared for any circumstances, realizes what is happening, has this handbook nearby and knows when to call the vet, then this chapter has served its purpose.

9

For Females Only

As YOU WATCH the roly-poly puppies tumbling about, you reap the rewards from your bitch's labor. In return, she deserves the best postpartum care.

Check her temperature twice a day; it is commonly elevated one degree the first day or two. Trouble, such as an infection of the uterus or mammary glands, is usually preceded by a temperature of 103° F or higher (39.4° C or higher). Fever can occur twenty-four hours before any other symptoms are apparent. Your vet should be consulted quickly so that the appropriate antibiotics and other therapy can be initiated. Aspirin helps reduce fever. Encourage consumption of liquids.

Postwhelping discharge is greenish black or dark red immediately following delivery. This sometimes lasts for a day or two, then turns to brownish red for one to three weeks. If it lasts longer, contains fresh blood or pus, or is discolored, take the dam to your vet. The normal odor is musty; any putrid odor should be checked.

Carrying the newborns around for the first week or two is not uncommon behavior, especially for those dams who seek the smallest nook in the room. This tends to make owners nervous. It is possible, of course, for the pups to be injured. See if you can calm her. She might cease the pacing if you can make her den cozier—cover it with a blanket, make it smaller or darker, or eliminate traffic and noise in her room.

Keep a close eye on a nervous mother. She might need veterinary help or simply your comforting presence. Many breeders sleep near the box for a few nights.

For females only.

FEEDING THE CAPTAIN WHO FEEDS THE CREW

The mother should be given anything that turns her on—and lots of it. The usual fare—decked out with broths, liver, yogurt or cottage cheese—is appealing. She should be eating at least twice as much as she normally does, and more if she wants it. For the first day or two, feed her wet and sloppy food, encouraging her to chow down.

Make sure you are feeding her a high-biological-quality dry food. Cheap food cannot be consumed in sufficient volume to provide adequate nutrition. Cutting costs here can increase veterinary expenses and decrease the thriftiness used for Mom and her pups.

136

Catering to Mom.

Use whatever tricks you need to entice her. Warm the food, sprinkle it with garlic powder, cook a stew, stir in your leftover goodies, use gravies— anything that works. This is the one time you should cater to her tastes in whatever way is necessary. Her caloric need while nursing is immense. Without TLC, she—and her dependents—will deteriorate.

LACK OF MATERNAL INTEREST

A spoiled bitch who thinks of herself as a person rather than a dog might not behave maternally. This pampered princess begrudges being shut away from the family. All these yammering, pesky little creatures have brought her pain and trouble . . . and jail.

Her people are insisting that she do all types of disgusting things, such as bathing puppies (with her tongue yet), feeding them (when she's so doggoned hungry herself) and, worse yet, "potty-training" the little pests. She didn't ask for this; her people did. But she's the one doing the work. Well, she'll just show them—she won't.

So the owner has to break the sacs, clean the pups, put them on the nipple, hold Mama still while the babies eat and take over the latrine duties. It's time-consuming, and owners wonder why on earth they planned this. The mother acts totally bored, and the minute her human family leaves the room, so does she. A dam with this attitude should be watched for animosity toward the pups.

An immature dam might behave this way with her first litter and improve with subsequent ones. Sometimes just a few days suffice until the new mother discovers she's a dog and these little beings are really kind of sweet. There are exceptions who are genetically lacking in maternal instincts.

Warnings abound from our survey that spoiled "only dogs" are the worst mothers and exhibit a lack of interest. Kennel dogs and those in multidog households seem to be more instinctive. To avoid this problem, treat the dog like a much-loved *pet* rather than like a human.

In a couple of instances, breeders found that surrounding the box with an ex-pen helped. The dam could escape infantile demands and lie outside the box but still was confined to an area with the puppies.

Some females think that if they ignore their pups, they will go away. Unfortunately, they might. If the dam won't care for them, the *owner must*, or the pups will die.

Lack of interest also might signal infection, eclampsia or other postpartum problems. Watch for abnormal discharge and unusual symptoms, as well as using your trusty thermometer.

A dam who has undergone a Caesarean section, particularly a first-time mother, might not show interest in her litter. Encourage her by rubbing her milk and scent on the puppies. Be patient. If she is not ready to yield to motherhood, keep the puppies warm in a separate box, giving them small doses of glucose. Wait a bit. The colostrum is present for up to twenty-four hours after birth. Their immediate vital need is warmth.

Should a dam appear hostile, do not force her to stay with the pups except during feeding. Stay with her, seeing that she does not harm them. Some breeders of Rottweilers caution that some dams literally must be muzzled to allow pups to nurse. Hostility is not unique to this breed and can be true of others as well.

If the room is kept warm and the pups are gaining weight, the dam does not need to be with them constantly. Socialization can be provided by you. Temporary tranquilization of an extremely nervous mother may be called for in *extreme* circumstances. Ask your vet about such treatment.

When only one puppy is rejected, the breeder must warm and feed the pup if it is to survive. The rejection might be due to a pup's undetected illness or congenital defect (see Chapter 10). This is the dam's dormant survival-of-the-fittest instinct.

LOSSES

Though they are not common, it remains a sad fact that neonatal deaths do occur. If owners absolutely cannot face the possibility of casualties, they should not breed.

Puppies are sometimes stillborn. Fatalities in neonates can occur through disease, congenital abnormalities or accidents. Preemie or weak puppies often succumb. Some dams seem to be able to count and know if even one pup is missing. Hide your own disappointment, and comfort her by directing her attention to the surviving littermates. Quickly wrap the body in a towel or newspaper, and remove it from the room. Talk to your vet about the advisability of an autopsy on the dead pup to determine whether the cause of death was a hereditary defect, physical trauma or an infectious agent that could threaten the remaining pups.

Under tragic circumstances, when the entire litter is lost, special care for the mother includes soaking the breasts with cool, wet towels to help dry up milk. Cut back on food and water to hasten the process, which should be over within a week. Do *not* strip out milk. This stimulates production of more milk. The owner must be alert to caked breasts or other signs of mastitis. Emotional support is also necessary for the grieving mother.

Even worse than infant loss is the heartbreak of losing a much-loved female. A breeder's worst nightmare becomes true when dams die because of birth complications, leaving orphan pups. While mourning, a breeder cannot become incapacitated. Otherwise, the tragedy will be magnified by further loss.

INFANTICIDE

Whether it is accidental, is an overreaction to fear, or comes from a distorted sense of protection, perhaps nothing is more shocking to the breeder than infanticide. Prevention of this is just one more reason that someone should be present during whelping. During consumption of the placenta or chewing of the cord, the whelp can be accidentally injured or even killed.

Care should be taken to ensure that the dam has privacy and is not uneasy about her new family. If she is upset in any way, find the cause. At the least, a jittery mother will incite her pups to be skittish; at worst, she might injure or kill the pups in her nervousness. One new mother tried to move the pups from one spot to another and dropped a puppy in her water dish. It later died from the inhalation of fluids into the lungs.

Some bitches become overprotective and do not want anyone but their human family around their babies. A few don't want even their own people handling the pups. If this is the case, humor the new mother. Do any necessary handling while the dam is out relieving herself. Keep the peace. Usually, within a day or two, she mellows and becomes her normal self, proud of her whelps and happy to have you help out. An unruffled owner helps the situation. *A neurotic owner makes a neurotic pet.*

Other dogs around the mother's territory are Intruders, with a capital *I*. Even the best of canine friends occasionally become enemies when another dog, particularly another female, becomes curious or challenges the new mother for dominance. In one instance, a fight resulted in a laceration on the dam's breast, forcing a mastectomy.

Survey reports showed two unhappy stories in which kennelmates burst into nursery areas. In each case, the litter was destroyed. Owners were unsure which dog killed the pups, but it made no difference.

The dam of one litter carried a single pup outside, dug a hole, put the pup in the hole and sat on it, perhaps for protection. This bitch remained nervous while in the whelping box with subsequent litters.

If the dam wishes to leave the pups and be with her people, allow her this freedom. Spoiled pooches do not understand the seeming imprisonment of being excluded from their human family.

Infanticide may be provoked by a physical cause. The dam should be checked by a veterinarian to eliminate any uterine or breast infection, high temperature, hypocalcemia or other problem. A reported incident of infanticide showed the dam to have a raging 106.5° F (41.4° C) fever. Do keep a temperature chart and check with your vet. He or she may recommend antibiotics to control even a low-grade infection. When the dam feels better, she behaves better.

Should the bitch be truly uninterested in her pups or even antagonistic, steps must be taken to avoid injury to them. Muzzle her or remove her from the litter. If the dam is aggressive, a foster mother might be introduced, but she often needs as much supervision as the reluctant birth mother. The nursery period doesn't last long. If necessary, pups can be weaned as early as two weeks. After so many months of planning, any less-than-perfect situation can be tolerated for two weeks for the safety of the babies.

ECLAMPSIA (MILK FEVER)

Eclampsia appears most often during the first three weeks, although it occasionally develops before delivery or up to six weeks after birth. It is caused by a deficiency in serum (blood) calcium due to a malfunction of calcium metabolism. Small dogs are cursed with this problem. Symptoms are salivation, rapid breathing, restlessness, nervousness and whining. A victim staggers or has stiff limbs. A pinched look shows around the face, exposing the teeth. Muscle twitches might be seen or felt. The bitch will shiver and be glassy-eyed.

Breeders report other weird behavior, such as bitches attempting to climb walls, hide under furniture, or maul or even kill pups. Since the depletion of calcium comes through giving milk, early, mild symptoms often are controlled by removal of the pups.

If not treated, eclampsia can lead to convulsions and death. Persistent symptoms constitute a true veterinary emergency. After diagnosis of the exact level of serum calcium, a solution is administered intravenously or subcutaneously. Careful medical supervision of these treatments is important since an overdose or too rapid administration can cause cardiac arrest.

The difficulty is caused by *inadequate parathyroid hormone* (which mobilizes body calcium), complicated by the increased draining of calcium supply by the pups. It is untreatable by adding calcium-rich milk, dairy products or pills to the diet. In fact, *high amounts of calcium fed during pregnancy might actually increase the risk* by convincing the parathyroid gland that it doesn't have to work as hard as it should. This condition often recurs with each litter. In a few cases, bitches that have a history of eclampsia are routinely given calcium injections prior to and following birth. Pups must be removed and hand-fed. Spaying and retirement may be recommended.

MASTITIS

Breast infections can occur as secondary problems in dams that have weak, small litters or in a bitch who had pups that died, leaving her with some breasts engorged. One bitch with inverted nipples had only two glands from which pups were able to nurse. The remaining breasts had to be milked to avoid caking, which can predispose a dam to mastitis. Mastitis can also occur if mothers have an overabundance of milk or if puppies scratch breasts, allowing infection to enter.

Inflammations are red, hot and painful. The breast might appear bruised and be hard or caked. Mammary glands should remain soft, though full. Compare one with another to check. The dam often has a fever, refuses to eat and is depressed or restless. She may vigorously resent the pups' nursing.

Milk from affected glands may be blood-tinged, discolored or stringy with pus. Healthy milk appears like that bought in a store. Use a glass to test the color and texture. Normal milk runs clear down the glass; "bad" milk clots.

Mastitis can also happen during false pregnancy, usually in the two heavy rear breasts. Infection can follow bruising as well. Prevent a heavily uddered bitch from running and jumping—these activities invite injury.

Do not allow pups to nurse from an affected breast. Either wean the pups, or cover the infected faucets. Antibiotics are necessary to treat the dam. Warm packs help; aspirin eases the pain. If the condition is untreated, the skin and mammary tissue can die and slough, with permanent loss of the breast. Infection from mastitis can be spread via circulation to create a life-threatening septicemia. Pups should also be dosed with antibiotics if they show signs of discomfort from ingesting infected milk. If the decision is to wean the pups, reduce the food and liquid intake of the mother.

To help prevent mastitis, see that pups nurse from all breasts, or hand-strip the breasts yourself twice a day.

ACUTE ENDOMETRITIS

An abnormal discharge after whelping, accompanied by a fever, indicates a possible uterine infection called endometritis (inflammation of the uterine lining). Rather than a slight reddish tinge, the discharge can appear to have the consistency and color of tomato soup. A foul odor is often present. Your vet will find the cervix still dilated, and improper uterine involution may be present. Vaginal discharge contains pus cells. The mother may not be eating and may seem depressed, and her milk production often is inadequate.

In severe cases, the bitch becomes toxic. She might vomit, be unusually thirsty, have diarrhea and suffer a painful abdomen. Dehydration can result. The mucous membranes have a brick-red, muddy appearance. Temperature above 103° F (39.4° C) is dangerous. Whether caused by retained fetuses or placentas, or by infection acquired during whelping, medical attention is essential. Uterine rupture can be a sequel.

The bitch is treated with appropriate antibiotics and other therapy, such as Ergot or prostaglandins, to empty putrid uterine contents. The pups should be watched for adverse reaction. Check the milk. Mastitis is often a sequel to endometritis.

Puppies that have acquired the infection will cry from cramps and have diarrhea. They, too, must be dosed with antibiotics and hand-fed. Give lactobacillus to the pups.

In some cases, hospitalization of the dam might be required for fluid therapy and injection of medication. Without aggressive treatment, spaying may be necessary to save the bitch's life. If untreated, endometritis leads to spaying or to death.

PYOMETRA

Endometriosis (appearance of the uterine lining in places where it is not normally found, such as in the ovaries) can be a cause of misses and resorptions. Chronic endometrial disease can lead to pyometra, a uterine infection that appears in two types. The open-cervix form, showing discharge, is more obvious and more easily treated. The discharge is sticky reddish pus, often appearing up to three months following heat or after birth. It usually is foul-smelling.

Closed-cervix pyometra contains pus sealed within the uterus. The symptoms are increased thirst and urination, fever and a tender abdomen, which may be bloated. Vomiting might occur. White blood cell counts are high, and bloodwork shows other signs of chronic infection and toxemia.

Although pyometra once led to certain spaying or death, other treatments for open-cervix pyometra are now available. Attempts can be made to clear the infection of a valuable producer by treating it with prostaglandin injections and appropriate antibiotics. If prostaglandin treatment is used, the bitch should be bred on the next heat. The underlying endometriosis ensures that the disease will sooner or later return.

This disease is most common in bitches over the age of six years and can be prevented by spaying once the bitch is retired from the breeding program. Bitches with recurrent pyometra should be spayed.

BREAST CYSTS, MASSES AND TUMORS

Intact bitches are much more likely to have cysts and tumors of the mammary glands than their spayed sisters are. Cystic disease appears as a firm breast

Promotion to Grandma status.

lump soon after a heat. It usually disappears before the next season. Lumps and masses that do not regress should be checked and removed if advised, then sent to a lab for histopathology. Repeated mammary tumors would be an indication to retire the bitch and have her spayed.

RETIREMENT AND SPAYING

Your brood bitches are like precious gems—they're very valuable. As they age, they become more and more dear to us. Their health insurance comes from years of our loving care and from retirement while they're still in good health.

Reproductive careers must have a limit. To make genetic progress, we need to move on to the next generation. Whether early (because of dystocia, eclampsia or whatever) or after a few nice litters, promotion of the bitch to Grandma status is a must. She should be spayed to relieve the stress and irritation of seasons, as well as the health risks of pyometra, mastitis, breast tumors and so on.

Breeders occasionally retire a brood bitch to a home where she can be the center of attention, rather than one of many in a kennel. Although it's difficult to say goodbye, her welfare must be utmost in your mind. After giving you so much, she deserves the best. And you can see that she receives it—warm, loving care, whether in your home or another's, for the rest of her life—just like anyone's grandma.

The nursery.

10

The Nursery

AT LAST, at last, you breathe a sigh and figure the worst is behind you. And most times, it is. The pups have been safely born, and now you can just sit back and let the mother do the work. Right? Wrong! You still have to act as a watchdog. Nearly three-quarters of puppy losses occur during the first three weeks, most within seven days.

As you watch these little bundles of hope squirming around the whelping box, notice that they move almost constantly. Blindly, they follow their noses to the source of their warmth and full tummies. Pups demonstrate a homing instinct, equal to that of the best pigeon, piling up together for warmth and homing in on Mom's Café as soon as she enters the box. Even when they are sleeping, their muscles quiver; then the head moves, followed by a kick of the rear leg.

They squeal now and then, showing the power of their lungs, when the dam bumps them, when they're stuck on the wrong side of the chow line or when you weigh them. But overall, the sounds are murmurs of contentment, similar to the sounds of a swarm of bees.

You should note the consistency of stools; an anus that appears red and swollen is a sign of diarrhea even if you see no stools. Cleanliness is highly important. Scratches or sores contaminated by feces can lead to infection or gangrene.

Certain chores are inescapable even during this tender age. Trimming off the tiny hook on the end of each nail should be done weekly. Don't forget dewclaws. Sharp nails can injure the dam's breasts, as well as the extremely vulnerable eyes of their littermates, and bring infection to both. Minor scratches on the dam's breasts can be soothed with petroleum jelly or ointment.

Newborns.

One breeder covers three-quarters of the box with washable carpet and puts newspaper on the other end. Within a couple of weeks, the pups toddle to the far end for their latrine. Shredded paper or seemingly useless tear ends from computer paper help keep the area cleaner. Pit stops are covered as the puppies stir up the shreds.

NEWBORNS

Activated sleep is normal in newborns. It develops the muscles, since at this stage, 90 percent of the pups' time is spent sleeping. In fact, when a puppy is ill, the first sign is cessation of the active sleep. Breeders realize fulfillment of their dreams when watching the puppies "chasing bunnies."

A puppy in danger is listless and shows little interest in nursing. The body is limp when you pick it up, and the pup does not protest, nor does it nuzzle in a vain attempt to find a food source. Or a sick puppy might be hyperactive, frantically moving about, often away from the others. The cry is either a weak, pitiful sound or a constant wail.

Not surprisingly, the other 10 percent of the infants' time is spent eating. Healthy pups squirm eagerly to the breast, latching tightly on to a nipple. Their back legs and tails stretch straight back when they're eagerly nursing and satisfied. Should a pup appear to be listless or weak, place it on the nipple. If necessary, remove the other pups for a few minutes, allowing the weaker ones to nurse without being elbowed aside. Squeeze his cheeks to make him accept the nipple, and coax some milk into his mouth. If this is not sufficient to encourage nursing, supplement the breast with hand-feeding.

Many Toy breeders administer a drop of glucose solution at birth (see the formula under Lifeguard Techniques in Chapter 8). This mixture can be used every hour or two to increase energy. If the puppy has not perked up after a few doses, see your vet.

Normal puppy temperature is 94° to 97° F (34.4° to 36.1° C) during the first week. It's important to remember that a chilled pup should be warmed first before offering it food. A temperature below 94° F (34.4° C) means serious trouble.

Warmth is critical for the pups during these first few days. As soon as they are born, towel them dry. Keep their area warm and cozy. Pups warn you by crying and panting if they are overheated. During the first two weeks, their temperature reflects that of their environment.

Keep track of weight (this is especially important with Toy breeds). Pups that weigh less than 75 percent of the average birth weight suffer a higher mortality. Although it is not unusual for pups to have a slight weight loss the first day, supplement the feed if the decrease is more than 10 percent of the birth weight or continues for more than one day. Birth weight should double in about ten days.

Put the weakest and smallest pups on the rear breasts with the most milk, or let them nurse first while the chubbettes wait their turn. If necessary, supplement the nursing. As they grow stronger, they'll mix it up with their siblings and fight for prime position. The big ones can take care of themselves.

Right from the beginning, these blind, deaf babes react to touch, nuzzling your hands and clothing when you pick them up. Eyes open in ten to sixteen days. Ears begin their duty at thirteen to seventeen days. The needle-sharp temporary teeth erupt around eighteen days. Shortly after, the dam's enthusiasm for round-the-clock nursing and maid service subsides. By three weeks, they're galloping to the chow line, rather than squirming.

They might even become frisky with their littermates, pawing and mounting each other, no matter what their sex. About this time, the pups begin to relate to humans. Although they've been accustomed to your touch, now it's even more important to give plenty of gentle cuddling and attention.

As they grow, acclimate the pups to noise. We live in a noisy world, and seldom do our dogs live in deserted areas where nothing is heard but an occasional word. Our lives are filled with roaring cars, slamming doors, banging pots, children's shrieks, video games and vacuum cleaners, as well as other animals. Therefore, the pups will have to learn to live with this commotion, unless you're selling them to hermit shepherds. Even then you'd better practice baaing.

COLOSTRUM

The dam's milk during the first twenty-four to thirty-six hours is called colostrum. It contains a high level of antibodies that provide temporary immunity for the pups. Newborns can absorb these complex proteins for a day; after that time, antibodies are broken down and digested like any other food source. The amount of passive immunity they receive depends on the bitch's titer—the concentration of antibodies dissolved in her milk, indicating how much immunity she has. Titer is an unknown factor. The way to ensure the highest level is to inoculate the dam prior to her breeding. Of course, if the dam has not been immunized within the last year, the colostrum isn't likely to protect her pups against those diseases. Zero equals zero.

It is vital for newborns to receive colostrum. If the whelps do not suckle on their own, squeeze the milk onto their tongue, or milk the breast and give it to the pups by bottle or tube. The colostrum milk looks different from later milk—it is thicker and yellowish.

If the pups do not receive the colostrum (for instance, if they are orphans), they should be isolated from other dogs and people until inoculated. Extra precaution should be taken that no germs are transported on hands or clothing. Their immune systems are too immature to respond to vaccines until the age of five to six weeks.

ORPHANS

Loss of the mother means that the puppies must be fed by other means. They must also be massaged to stimulate urination and movement of the bowels. Orphan puppies should be handled and caressed frequently. You'll need to fill them first, then empty them, all the while keeping everyone clean and dry. Absence of a furry mom means that extra warmth and nurturing must be provided by the breeder.

Owners who are too frantic or fastidious to help their puppies will soon have none left to help. Pups cannot relieve themselves unaided until about two weeks of age. Rub the genitals with a Baby Wipe^R or similar product until the urine flows, and the anus until the stool is passed. A cotton ball or rag soaked in warm water or baby oil can also be used. This should be done each time the pups are fed. Most puppies pass two or three stools a day. Jot a note to yourself so that you know whether each puppy has moved its bowels. The formula might have to be adjusted if stools become loose or the puppy is constipated.

The infant wipes are also super for cleanups. During the grooming session, use a clean, moist cloth to cleanse the eyes. The dam bathes her puppies' faces each day, helping the eyes to open.

Rig up an incubator, using a box, a well-insulated heating pad turned on low, and a cover (see Incubator in Chapter 8). Exposure of the pups to any potential contamination should be avoided even more conscientiously, particularly if the colostrum was not received.

Foster mother.

Satisfying the Instinct

When the sucking instinct is unsatisfied, pups sometimes turn to littermates. If you are tube-feeding, try switching to a bottle for one feeding. A pacifier coated with a yummy substance, such as sugar water or formula, might help allay the desire. If not, they should be carefully watched or even separated. Once the teeth come through, damage can be caused to others. This sucking has made more than one owner wonder whether the pups would grow up with normal ears—and other vital protruding parts.

You can try a routine of feeding every two hours or when the puppies cry. Demand feeding is particularly appealing at night. Thankfully, puppies are more cooperative than human infants and sleep through most of the night by the age of one week.

FOSTER MOTHERS

In the event that puppies are orphaned or the mother is unwilling or unable to feed them, a foster mother can be an alternative to bottle- or tube-feeding. Choose a dam that has a small litter, has pups that are ready to wean or has lost her own litter. Bitches with a great maternal instinct may welcome the adopted pups. (Some supermoms even adopt animals of other species!) Not all will be eager, however. Let the foster mother's milk accumulate until she is uncomfortable; then rub the pups with her scent or with her milk.

Your greatest challenge may be trying to find a wet nurse. Unless you or a close friend has an appropriate canine substitute, hand-feeding is the choice. If none is available, a retired matron is sometimes willing to assist with cleanup

Pup Weight		Formula Quantity		Feeding Schedule
lbs	ozs	cc's*	ozs	hours
	3-7	1 per oz		3
	8	12		4
	10	15		4
	12	18		5
	14	21		5
1		24		5
1¼			1	5
1½			1½	5
1¾			1¾	6
2			2	6
2¼			2¼	6
2½			2½	6
3			3	6
		*(30 cc's = 1 oz)		

Hand-feeding chart.

chores and maternal bonding. In at least one instance, the sire, a German Shepherd Dog, took over everything except nursing!

Introduce puppies to the foster mother with care. The breeder should watch closely to see that rejection or injury does not occur. If you see any animosity, switch to hand-feeding.

HAND-FEEDING

Each feeding method has its own advantages and advocates. When nursing from the bottle, the pup makes the decision on how much it eats. This makes the puppy work for the food (some people believe tube-feeding can produce lazy eaters), and it satisfies the nursing instinct. It's the only method of choice if you're timid about pushing a tube down a tiny throat.

Hold the pup in its natural nursing position, belly down and head raised to the nipple; otherwise, milk can be inhaled into the lungs. After bottle-feeding especially, hold the pup on your lap, and rub its back until it burps. Bottle-feeding is time-consuming, and you will spend most of your waking (and some of your sleeping) hours feeding and making formula. If you choose this method, rub the nipple with a bit of formula; then wiggle the nipple around when introducing the pups to it, encouraging them to nurse. Once they are accustomed to this

150

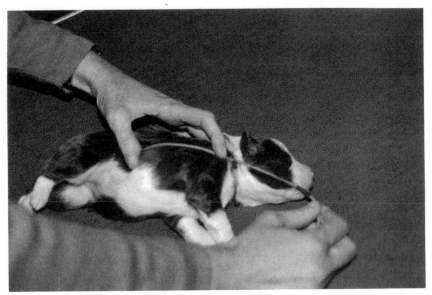

Measuring the tube for hand-feeding. Photo by Ed Walkowicz.

strange latex mother, they become eager. They're adorable curling their paws around the bottle.

Assistance must be solicited, or the results will be as frustrating as feeding quintuplets. One session is barely finished, and it's time to start again.

The main advantages of tube-feeding are time efficiency and the ability to feed the puppy any amount you choose. Experts suggest the schedule shown in the table at left.

Obtain a sixteen-inch soft-rubber Number 8 French catheter and a 35-cc syringe from your veterinarian. Spread clean cooking oil around the inside of the syringe and the plunger to lubricate them. Equipment should be washed in hot, soapy water, rinsed thoroughly and enclosed in a plastic bag between each use.

Measure the distance from the pup's mouth to the last rib (the approximate position of the stomach), and mark the tube with a tiny piece of tape, changing the mark as the puppy grows. Insert the syringe into the formula, and pull back on the plunger, filling the syringe. Now attach the tube and push the plunger enough to move formula to the tip of the tube.

The easiest place to tube-feed is on the floor. Kneel, placing the pup on a towel between your legs. The pup should be facing in the same direction that you are. If you are right-handed, grasp the head lightly with your left hand and the tube with your right. Using your fingers at the corners of the mouth, gently force it open.

Place your index finger and thumb on the tube about three inches from the end. Insert the tube straight into the mouth toward the back of the throat, moving

151

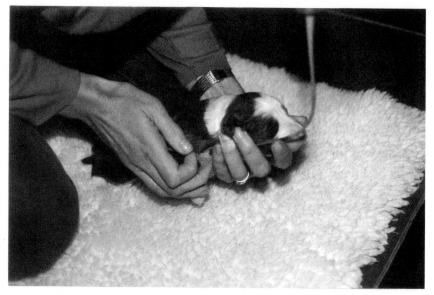
Kneel, placing the pup between your legs. Photo by Ed Walkowicz.

it over the tongue about two inches. Slide your tube hand back a couple of inches, pushing gently down the throat. Repeat in short strokes until the tube stops or the mark is reached.

The syringe can be placed on the floor during insertion of the tube. To double-check the location, insert the tube in a cup of water to see if there are any bubbles, which would signify the lungs rather than the stomach. Hold the syringe straight up, forcing any air to the upper part of the syringe, and depress the plunger steadily.

Remove the tube quickly. The procedure is over before either one of you knows it. If you give the pup too much, a safety valve will make it vomit or snuffle a bit out through the nose.

Older pups can also be fed by this method if they are too ill or weak to eat. Care must be taken that they do not push the tube out. Healthy pups resist the tube after two weeks of age, but pan-feeding can be introduced by then.

Goat's milk or commercial substitutes for dam's milk can be used, but the following recipes are nutritious, inexpensive and easy to prepare.

Almost like Mom's
- 1 lg. (15 oz.) can evaporated milk
- 2 egg yolks
- 1 (8 oz.) carton plain yogurt with active cultures
- For bottle-feeding, add 6 oz. boiled water.

Supplement or Supper
- 1 lg. (15 oz.) can evaporated milk
- 2 cans water

- 2 packages unflavored gelatin (Dissolve in cold water, heat and blend.)
- 2 beaten egg yolks
- 1 tablespoon cream (or half-and-half)
- 1 tablespoon honey (Reduce if stools become loose.)

Both formulas can be mixed in a blender, stored in the refrigerator and heated to body temperature for feeding. Soon you'll be greeted with as much glee as though you had long, floppy ears and a wagging tail.

DEWCLAWS

We have five toes on each foot, and so do dogs—always on the front and sometimes on the rear (except Lundhunds, but that's another story). The teeny excuse for a fifth toe is located above the foot on the inside of the leg. According to breed Standards, some breeds should have the rear dewclaws removed, some are born without them, and others demand that they be retained. A few breeds—the Briard, the Beauceron and the Great Pyrenees—require not one but two dewclaws on each rear leg!

The front dewclaws are removed in most Terriers and Sporting dogs, as well as many others. This is done for grooming ease, a clean look to the front leg, and avoidance of accidents in the field. If dewclaws are to be removed, the preferred time is between two and five days of age. When pups are older, it becomes a major operation, requiring anesthesia to amputate the toe. Your veterinarian, using surgical skill, can do it neatly in a few minutes and leave less chance of scarring. Some suture and some don't. A few veteran breeders handle removal themselves. Whoever does it, however, must be careful to take the second joint out to prevent the toe and nail from growing back. The tiny hook of a pair of suture-removal scissors works well for this job.

If not removed, dewclaws should be trimmed along with other nails. Otherwise, the nail grows in a circle, eventually piercing the pad. Dewclaws might also snag and tear, causing pain, bleeding and infection.

Tail docking.

TAIL DOCKING

Several breeds have their tails docked (see Appendix I, Breed Specifics and Predispositions). The surgery is done at two or three days of age and should be done only by a veterinarian who is experienced and knowledgeable about breed Standard requirements—or at least is willing to listen to someone who is! Many vets ask the client where they would like the tail docked. Length requirements vary greatly from breed to breed, from the nub of the Schipperke, Old English Sheepdog and Welsh Pembroke Corgi to the longer span of the Vizsla and Cavalier King Charles Spaniel.

Tails are usually sutured to promote rapid healing without scarring (no hair grows on scars). Dams sometimes worry at stitches, doing more damage than if the wounds were not sutured. Therefore, some vets do it without sutures, using styptic power to control bleeding and antibiotic ointment to promote healing.

Although docking can be performed later, it then changes from minor to major surgery. After one week of age, it must be done with anesthesia. If the tail was cut too short, that's the end of the tale. There are no tail transplants.

In some parts of the world, humanitarian legislation has outlawed amputation of healthy canine parts, including tail docking and ear cropping. Originally, one of the main reasons for these surgeries was to avoid injuries. Breeders often have strong opinions pro and con on this controversial subject. We are accustomed to seeing many breeds with shortened tails and/or erect ears, and injuries can occur, particularly with working dogs. Yet some owners argue that most dogs are companions now and rarely venture into the woods or the field, and they wonder whether fashion is a valid reason for surgery. More and more veterinarians have ceased ear cropping, feeling it is cruel and unnecessary; some breeders also admit they dread having healthy pups cut. Even the American Veterinary Medicine Association is beginning to question the process. Unless the AKC takes a stand against docking and cropping, these procedures are likely to continue.

NEWBORN EYES

Eyelids begin opening at about seven to fourteen days. If the puppies were born prior to the due date, it may be a corresponding number of days later. One day a teensy crack appears, with a glint from the eye. Do not expose newly opened eyes to bright light. At three weeks, recognition begins.

If the eye area is swollen and painful prior to opening the eye or a stickiness appears around the eye as it opens, wipe it gently with cotton soaked in warm water, and apply ophthalmic ointment.

RUNTS

While one puppy might have a birth weight less than other littermates, a true "runt" is not as common as laypeople believe. With proper care, the smallest pup can mature to become the largest adult. The runt of the litter is not necessarily the worst pup. This is especially true if all the other pups are oversized!

Sometimes, however, a puppy is greatly undersized in proportion to the rest of the litter. Positioning in the uterus, particularly in a large litter, can cause insufficient nourishment. The small pup might be the result of a much later breeding, though parturition has begun on the due date of the first one. Poor nourishment of the bitch can also cause runts. Puppies that suffer congenital defects, such as heart disease, are usually born at average weight, losing ground in the neonatal period. In some breeds with a wide variation in adult size (e.g., Shelties or Toy Poodles), one pup may have just inherited all the "tiny" genes.

Supplemental feeding helps in some circumstances. Most breeders do not want to give up easily on any puppies as long as they appear healthy and they gain. Too many stories are told about Best in Show winners or at least Kings-of-the-Household who are hale and hearty because their breeders exerted extra effort to aid survival.

If these methods do not help the little one catch up and thrive (as evidenced by daily weight gain), or if he loses or remains the same weight, an inborn (congenital) defect is likely the cause. Have your veterinarian confirm your suspicions, and then you can better make the difficult decision to have the pup humanely euthanized before he/she starves or suffers. One breeder reported tube-feeding a pup for four weeks when the pup was still almost birth weight. His eyes opened much later than those of his littermates. When bigger brothers and sisters began bullying him, the breeder made the tearful decision to let it go.

FADING PUPPY SYNDROME

This phrase is a catch-all name applied to puppies that begin fading and dying. Individual pups—even entire litters—can succumb within a day or two. Many times the cause is one of the ailments in this chapter or can also be the consequence of stress, drugs, disease, prematurity or bacterial infections, as well as congenital or genetic defects. If the breeder is alert and prepared to combat the problem, contacting the vet with the first symptoms, the pup(s) may be saved. A diagnosis is paramount, and lost pups should always be autopsied, with tissues sent for a histopathological exam.

This often yields important information, not only for your breeding program but also for your breed as a whole. As more and more rare and unusual congenital conditions are identified (see Appendix II), fewer sick pups are lumped under this umbrella term of "fading pup."

COLIC

The painful tummyache called colic is caused by gas and cramping due to toxic milk, GI infection or other causes of poor digestion. The affected pups cry constantly and have swollen abdomens and/or diarrhea. If the problem is discov-

155

ered to be the mother's milk, the pups must be taken away and hand-fed by tube or bottle. An attempt at identifying a specific diagnosis should be pursued. Both the mother and the litter may have to receive antibiotics. Taking the pups off milk and switching to a corn syrup–water mixture or a 5 percent glucose solution taken orally may help ease symptoms. A breeder of Saint Bernards recommends Lactinex^R for colicky pups to restore normal intestinal flora.

DIARRHEA

True diarrhea, liquid feces at increased volume and intervals, can be life-threatening to infants. Loss of fluids, salt imbalances and reduced nutrient absorption all contribute to a potential crisis. Babies don't have much reserve. Diarrhea can result from a variety of problems, and it's important to identify and correct the underlying cause. But it's even more urgent to first stop the diarrhea.

Initially, take the pups from the dam to stop all milk intake. Pups can be bottle-fed lactated Ringer's solution (Pedialyte) or a 5 percent glucose solution every couple of hours (or on demand) to maintain hydration. Meanwhile, the vet can examine a stool sample, the pup and/or the bitch to try to pinpoint the cause. The vet may recommend an oral binding agent (such as Kaopectate^R), injectable antibiotics, gut regulators, weaning or whatever else it takes. Causes of diarrhea range from viruses to parasites, toxic bacterial infections and so on.

Antibiotics given to the pups or the dam can cause diarrhea as a side effect. If antibacterials must be given, don't wait for problems to appear. Lactobacillus, contained in unpasteurized yogurt, buttermilk or Lactinex^R (from a health-food store), restores the natural intestinal bacteria that have been destroyed by the antibiotics. A little of any of these products never hurts.

Loose stools (usually not more frequent or voluminous) in otherwise vigorous pups also result from pigging out. Some mothers are very heavy milkers, and greedy little ones eat more than they can digest. This condition disappears when they start walking and work off some flab.

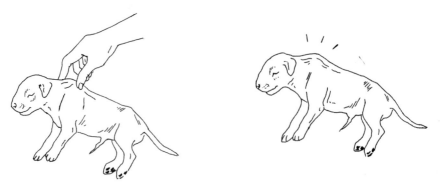

Dehydrated pup. Skin stays up and returns slowly.

Parasites are common in pups even in the cleanest nursery, presided over by the most careful Mary Poppins. Roundworms and coccidia can occur even when the dam tests negative. So routine stool checks on the litter are important, especially if stools have been loose off and on.

DEHYDRATION

Dehydration evolves through infection or disease and is caused directly by fever, vomiting, diarrhea or failure to take nourishment. It is one of the most frequent causes of neonatal death.

If a puppy is not eating eagerly or is sickly, beware of dehydration. The easiest way to discern the problem is to pluck the skin at the back of the neck, then compare that pup's skin with that of its littermates. Skin that springs back quickly shows normal hydration, but if the skin is inelastic, stands in a ridge or returns slowly to position, the puppy is in trouble. Sunken eyes are also a clue.

Fluids must be replaced by supplemental feeding, subcutaneous injections and/or intravenous fluids at your vet's. If still eating, the pup should be encouraged to consume more liquids by feeding a salty food, such as beef bouillon.

Fluids can be replaced orally as long as there is no vomiting. But in very weakened infants, parenteral (subcutaneous or intravenous) fluid replacement is imperative. Obtain a bag of sterile lactated Ringer's solution from your vet, along with appropriate syringes and equipment. Many breeders learn to administer fluids subcutaneously to sick pups. Otherwise, the frequency of dosages would necessitate moving everyone to the vet's clinic for the duration. Large volumes, based on the pup's weight, can be given under the skin. The huge lump that develops disappears quickly as the parched bloodstream siphons it away.

Constipation can occur in a dehydrated pup. If stimulating the anus with a wipe doesn't work, try a small piece of an infant suppository.

NAVEL ILL

Bacteria can enter the navel opening, then travel through the bloodstream to any part of the body. Joint, liver and general infections have been known to develop in victims.

To prevent germ entry, treat the open umbilical cord with iodine or another antiseptic at birth. Upon any indication of swelling or oozing at the umbilicus, bathe the area with bacteriocidal soap and rinse twice daily. If no progress seems to be made, see your vet. A generalized infection must be treated with parenteral antibiotics.

HERPESVIRUS

Herpesvirus is a highly contagious virus that causes few, if any, symptoms in adult dogs. But if a nonimmune pregnant bitch is exposed, herpes can attack the pups, with 50 to 100 percent mortality. If pups are infected in utero, abortion, stillbirths or quickly fading puppies result. Pups contracting the virus from Mom's urogenital tract during birth or prior to three weeks of age can die from the disease. By the fourth week, they seem able to mount an immune response.

The virus attacks the kidneys and liver, causing internal hemorrhage. Affected puppies are restless and shiver; then they suddenly become limp, refuse to nurse and cry pitifully. Symptoms can include below-normal temperature (see Newborns in this chapter), yellow-green diarrhea and a tender abdomen. Most die within twenty-four hours. Take one of the dead pups to your vet so that a specific diagnosis can be made.

The only hope of saving any of the infected pups is good nursing care, antibiotics to prevent secondary infection and fluid to forestall dehydration. Remove the dam and hand-feed the pups. Cleanse the nursery with a diluted bleach solution and raise the pups' temperature to above normal by keeping the environmental temperature high.

Surviving pups sometimes have kidney failure between eight and ten months of age because of viral damage. The one bright spot is that subsequent litters are not affected because of developed immunity in the dam. The best prevention is to avoid contact of a pregnant bitch and/or neonatal puppies with other dogs.

BIRTH ABNORMALITIES

Carefully examine all pups at birth for any abnormalities or malformations. It is usually unproductive to try to save these babes. Most do not survive anyway. Others usually have to be euthanized eventually, so it is heartless to extend their suffering. Extremely rare conditions occur, as they do occasionally in human births, such as a lack of front legs, reversed rear legs or no head. Others are mentioned in Appendix II.

Schistosoma Reflexus

The condition called schistosoma reflexus is a developmental accident in which the intestines and other organs are not contained within the body cavity but are on the outside. Breeders often call these cases "toothpaste-tube puppies" because the intestines pour out of an opening in the abdomen, much like toothpaste out of a squeezed tube. Unless these are born in a sterile atmosphere, such as during a Caesarean section, any attempt to stuff the organs back in and stitch the opening would be unsuccessful. Contamination from the birth canal would almost guarantee peritonitis. These pups should be euthanized immediately.

Umbilical hernia.

When we had a puppy with this affliction born in the middle of the night, our hearts ached, but we knew what had to be done. The kindest and swiftest way to euthanize a newborn is to wrap it in newspaper and place it in the freezer, where the puppy will momentarily become comatose and die in its sleep. Another method is to place it in a sealed plastic bag. Unless this is done quickly, these pups will die in agony. This is not an easy decision for someone who loves dogs.

Umbilical Hernia

A puppy with an "outie," a lump appearing at the navel, has an umbilical hernia. Although this can be corrected surgically in a fairly simple procedure, it is not always necessary to do so.

Hernias can be inherited or developed. The tissues surrounding the umbilical area may be genetically weak, causing the hernia. A hereditary predisposition can be determined by investigating the pups of an affected dam. Pulling on the umbilical cord at birth by the dam or an excited owner can lead to an umbilical hernia, even if there is no inherited tendency. Of course, the predisposition toward tugging on the cord could also be hereditary (in the dam)!

Pushing the navel in each time you pick up the puppy sometimes helps. Breeders have also had some luck with belly bands, taping a piece of gauze over the protrusion. This can be further contained by wrapping a product such as Vetrap^R around the belly. Often the hernia becomes proportionately smaller as

159

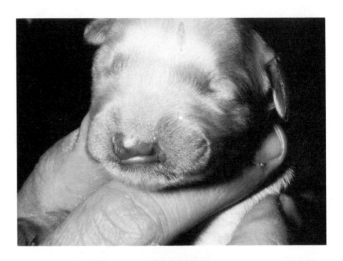

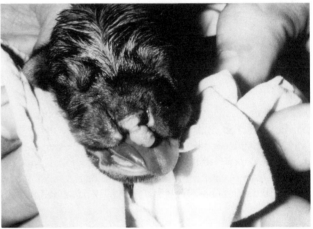

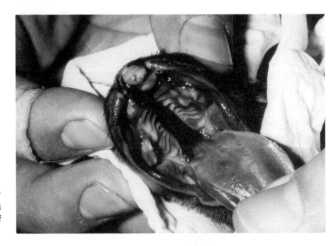

Cleft palate. Courtesy of Dr. Patricia Olson, University of Minnesota.

the puppy grows. It seldom causes difficulty unless it is very large. Before breeding a bitch, an examination of its severity should be conducted, with discussion of possible surgical correction.

Cleft Palate / Harelip

A harelip is very obvious: the upper lip is split, sometimes through the nose. A cleft palate forms a crack in the roof of the mouth. Check the puppy by looking into the mouth with a penlight and feeling the roof. Some clefts are far back in the throat. Neither defect is unusual, and they often appear together.

Nursing is hampered by either condition; bubbles of milk appear from the nose. Death results from starvation or pneumonia when milk is inhaled into the lungs. Mild cases can be saved by tube-feeding. Surgical corrections can be performed but are not practical in most cases.

Anasarca

Pups with the condition anasarca are aptly called walrus pups from their grossly swollen bodies. You might also hear breeders talk about water, monster or rubber puppies. They can weigh more than three pounds at birth! Often a cause of dystocia, they are delivered surgically. This condition is caused by a defect of lymphatic circulation, which may be associated with congenital thyroid disease. Severe cases are fatal. Some breeders, following the advice of their veterinarians, have treated mild cases of edema with a diuretic at birth, followed by another dose twelve hours later.

Atresia Ani

A puppy suffering from the rare defect called atresia ani bloats and cries within the first four to six days. The anal opening is missing, or there is an internal gap between the bowel and the anus.

One breeder who lives near a well-known soft-tissue surgeon opted to have reconstructive surgery done on a ten-day-old Bernese Mountain Dog pup. She did this knowing the puppy might need lifelong care to maintain proper bowel function. If breeders are courageous enough to make these choices, they must be totally selfless in committing themselves to long-term care. Reconstruction is not an inexpensive procedure or a chore you can foist on a buyer. This condition is not always immediately noticeable since Mom handles the cleanup chores at first. All pups should have a rectal thermometer inserted in the first few days to ascertain a proper anal opening.

Swimmer pup. Note flattened chest. Photos by Chris Walkowicz.

Swimmer Pups

Most dogs are natural swimmers, but they shouldn't display this skill in the whelping box. A wide, ventrally flattened chest is easily detected, particularly by someone who has seen swimmers before. The puppy moves crabwise, with legs extended out to the sides, as in a breast stroke. Or the legs might extend straight back, with the pup seeming to move like a seal. Thus we gave the term "swimmer." Although this condition can develop because of improper footing or other environmental factors, some cases are obvious at birth because of congenital weaknesses.

The legs do not function under the body, as the other pups' do, no matter how wobbly. If this condition is not corrected, the puppy will never walk normally and, in fact, might be so crippled it would have to be euthanized. In addition, because of decreased chest capacity, swimmers may suffer from difficult breathing and heart failure. This is one condition, however, that usually can be successfully corrected. If the pup can learn to stand and walk, the chest will re-form into a more natural state. But if the chest is left flat, the body weight compresses it more. By this point, the condition is even harder to correct, making the chest more compressed—a discouraging circle of events.

Treatments offered by breeders include handling the puppy daily, gently pressing the soft, pliable ribs into the proper shape. Also, place rolled towels or rugs under the nonskid flooring, forming hills and valleys to exercise the pup in the proper method of walking. It won't hurt the rest of the litter to build up muscle either!

One breeder of Sussex Spaniels and Bulldogs—both heavy-bodied breeds prone to swimmers—raises her puppies on an "egg carton" convoluted foam-rubber pad. She covers it with a washable casing. The pups must continually work to squirm over to Mom and build up the proper muscles.

Another recommendation is dangling the puppy in a basin of water. Ironically, swimming with proper use of the legs and expansion of the lungs aids correction of the swimmer syndrome. Attempt to keep the puppy lying on his side rather than on his tummy, which flattens the chest even more. Every time you enter the room, place him on his side.

In severe cases, the owner should tape the pup around the front elbows, pulling its legs into the proper position until it improves. If the rear legs are also incorrectly positioned, they should be hobbled as well. Watch the puppy so that it does not become overweight. The earlier the treatment, the more likely the recovery.

Hydrocephalus

The malady hydrocephalus becomes more noticeable as time goes on. If the unfortunate pups that have this are not euthanized, the pressure on the brain causes retardation or death. Toy and brachycephalic breeds are afflicted more than others.

Roll up towels and place under carpet for swimmer pups to crawl over. Photos by Chris Walkowicz.

The skull is large and domed. There is a tendency for the eyes to bulge and turn outward (strabismus). An open soft spot may be present, although open fontanel is not associated with hydrocephalus. Pups are slower in coordination, often appearing clumsy, awkward or retarded.

Heart Defects

A certain small percentage of puppies are born with congenital heart abnormalities or malformations. Some with minor defects show absolutely no signs. Others, more drastically affected, can exhibit a variety of symptoms.

The pup might suffer breathing difficulties and, when older, an intolerance of exercise. Breathing may be rapid and labored, with short rather than deep breaths. This is easy to spy, because when breathing is normal, you do not notice it. Remember your last cold? Pups may cough, and in severe cases, the pads and mouth have a bluish cast. When the puppy is picked up, the heartbeat, murmur and/or abnormal rhythm may be felt through the chest wall or in the throat.

All puppies should have a veterinary physical, including stethoscopic examination of the chest.

Some heart defects are surgically correctable, and dogs may be able to live with minor defects or can even outgrow them, but affected animals should never be bred. Even if the ailment is not hereditary, the stress of pregnancy and raising pups is too much for a dog that is not in peak condition.

Deafness / Blindness

Hereditary deafness is sometimes seen in white-headed dogs and double merle-colored lines. Puppies can be tested starting at two weeks and weekly thereafter. Do not make noises that cause air waves (such as clapping of hands). Instead, bang a pan, ring bells or blow whistles.

Deaf pups do not move their ears or bark as often or in the same way as their littermates. In breeds with known incidences of hereditary deafness, all pups should be Baer-tested at weaning. Unilateral pups can be sold on a spay/neuter contract and live a full life as pets. Auditory evoked response testing is available at veterinary schools.

Early causes of blindness include congenital juvenile cataract and microphthalmia (very small eyes). Pups can be checked by a canine ophthalmologist for some diseases as early as eight weeks.

CULLING

Any malformed pup, particularly with a life-threatening deformity, should be quickly and humanely euthanized. In addition, any pup that begins fading after birth and does not respond to special attention likely has an internal congenital defect and will have to be culled. You should take the defective pup away, distracting the dam with the rest. Some mothers seem to know when even one is in trouble. The vet can painlessly euthanize the pup to curtail suffering.

The law of nature—survival of the fittest—dictates that handicapped puppies do not survive. Such puppies need a great deal of care, time and, often, money to help them. With so many healthy, normal puppies available, it is difficult, if not impossible, to find homes to adopt these cases. Unless you are willing to raise and keep the pups in comfort, it is most humane to euthanize them.

Sometimes the mother culls a puppy herself by repeatedly rejecting or removing a sickly pup or one that is subnormal in temperature. In the latter case, warm the puppy. If the mother does not accept her pup after survival techniques are used, take it to the vet for an exam. Small doses of glucose solution (see Lifeguard Techniques in Chapter 8) or a few tube feedings often tip the odds, and the dam will then accept her fledgling.

Imperfect but healthy pups can be sold on a Limited Registration, with spay/neuter contracts. If pups are removed from the gene pool, they are effectively culled. "Culling" does not always mean killing.

WEANING

If possible, we like to allow bitches to control the weaning process. A few simply kiss them all goodbye, leave the nursery and never look back. Some regurgitate their food, as wild animals do, so that their young can eat the partially digested mush. Disgusting to us, this is yummy to pups. Other dams grumble a low warning when the greedy little sharp-fanged monsters become too much to bear.

Once in a while, Mom continues to allow her brood to nurse, standing and gritting her teeth while the little piranhas scratch and nibble their way to a sagging, depleted breast. When this occurs, the breeder must take the reins. It's back to Waist Watchers for the dam.

Cut her rations back to normal proportions once a day, and restrict water for the first day. Confine her away from the pups for twelve hours, then twenty-four and, finally, forty-eight hours. After this program, her milk should be dried up.

Gruel

Pan food can be introduced at about three weeks to decrease the demand on Mom. Buy a "flying saucer" feeder, or use a muffin pan. Mix rice baby cereal with a bit of milk and yogurt—or use one of the recipes given earlier (Hand-Feeding in this chapter). To start with, it should be runny enough to lap. Gradually, firm it by adding more cereal. If stools become loose, use less liquid. Some pups dive in feet first; others have to be coaxed with a dab of cereal on their noses or on your finger. Work up to four meals a day.

When the cereal reaches the consistency of your morning oatmeal, switch

Chow time around the "flying saucer" pan. Photo by Peggy Bommersbach.

to a high-quality puppy food by soaking it or using a blender to grind it. Add enough liquid to make it mushy. A few goodies, such as yogurt, egg yolks, scrambled eggs, meat, baby food or crumbled hamburger now and then offer a menu tempting enough to whet the appetite of the pickiest mama's boy or girl. With this method, you can eventually change the pups from creamy to chunky food by the time they're ready to leave your nest.

As they become able to eat more at one time, *increase* the *size* of the meals, and *decrease* the *number* to three. After complete weaning, allow the mother to play with her youngsters if she wishes. Don't be surprised if she doesn't. Many dams wear a martyred look. Some gems, however, continue the education of their brood.

Two weeks after weaning, the shedding process begins. Just about the time when buyers come to look at the pups and ask to see the dam, she looks like a bag lady, with shriveled teats and a shabby coat.

CHANGING OF THE GUARD

As the bitch ends her duties, your work is only beginning, but so is the fun. In the next few weeks, pups grow like campaign promises. Individual

The End.

characteristics begin emerging. The pecking order becomes established; pups enter into tough-guy fights, with the more timid littermates submitting to the more dominant ones.

Pups are awake more and play, toddling about on gelatin legs and trying out their barks. A breeder can spend hours sitting beside the pen, watching in delight when a puppy discovers the intrigue of a ball for the first time or startles itself with a bark, tumbling over backwards.

Acting as a canine nanny is a labor of love, indeed, with its scary moments, its awesome responsibility and its many rewards.

BITTERSWEET MOMENTS

You've heard them all: "You have to take the bad with the good. Every cloud has a silver lining. If you didn't have sorrow, you couldn't know joy. Gray skies will turn to blue. April showers bring May flowers. There's always somebody worse off. Make lemonade out of lemons." Clichés don't make problems any easier, but perhaps this book will.

Although many of the lemons have been presented, you may never experience them. If you do, perhaps you will now be able to overcome them. Dog breeding is a bittersweet experience. It's up to you to make the sweet outweigh the bitter.

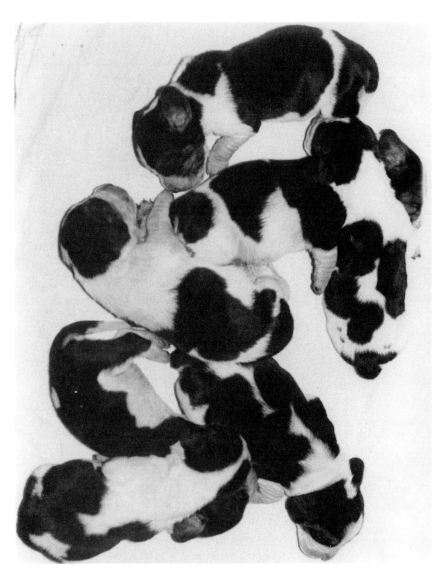

Successful Dog Breeding. Photo by Peggy Bommersbach.

APPENDIX I

Breed Specifics and Predispositions

Breed: AFFENPINSCHER
Female: normal
Male: normal; eager breeders
Litter Size: 2–4
Birth Weight: 3–5 oz.
Motherhood: breeches a problem w. large head size; may require C-sec.
Dewclaws: Remove all.
Tails: docked; leave ⅓
Ears: cropped at 12–16 wk.; short w. bell
Standard Deviations: retained puppy teeth
Reported Disorders: 8, 12, 27, 46, 50, 59, 75, 174, 212

Breed: AFGHAN HOUND
Female: puberty as late as 2 yr.; thrash, scream &/or bite during matings; never allow unattended breeding
Male: puberty often 18–24 mo.; normal breeders
Litter Size: 7
Birth Weight: 10–18 oz.

Motherhood: large litters; normal but slow, may scream & can be lazy; if overassisted, may let you do it all
Dewclaws: Remove all.
Standard Deviations: light eyes; hypersensitivity to anesthesia & insecticides
Reported Disorders: 5, 28, 45, 74, 103, 115, 172, 262

Breed: AIREDALE TERRIER
Female: puberty 15 mo.; normal; eager; sometimes must muzzle
Male: normal
Litter Size: 8–12
Birth Weight: 12–15 oz.
Motherhood: nest vigorously; small litters may cause problems; good moms
Dewclaws: Remove rears.
Tails: docked; leave ⅔ of tail (upright tail even w. top of head)
Ears: Set ears during teething.
Standard Deviations: soft coats; drop ears; malocclusions

Reported Disorders: 29, 31, 32, 45, 78, 87, 115, 126, 173, 200, 208, 226, 251, 262

Breed: AKBASH DOG
Female: cycle once/yr.
Male: normal; early puberty but late maturity
Litter Size: 8
Birth Weight: 30–36 oz.
Motherhood: free whelpers; good moms
Dewclaws: singles and doubles in back common; don't remove
Ears: cropped in Turkey but not in USA
Reported Disorders: 77, 115, 121

Breed: AKITA
Female: false seasons common
Male: discriminating; only on right day; may have to fall in love
Litter Size: 6–10
Birth Weight: 16–24 oz.
Motherhood: often no outward signs of pregnancy; normal whelpers but slow, w. long intervals between pups; occasional eclampsia; supermoms
Dewclaws: Remove rears.
Ears: tape ears if not up by 4 mo.
Standard Deviations: long coats; large ears w. heavy leather
Reported Disorders: 55, 78, 103, 115, 126, 150, 174, 208, 213, 260

Breed: ALASKAN MALAMUTE
Female: early puberty; normal breeders
Male: easy breeders; like to play
Litter Size: 6–8
Birth Weight: 12–22 oz.
Motherhood: free whelpers; good moms
Dewclaws: Remove rears.
Standard Deviations: poor pigment; missing teeth; malocclusions
Reported Disorders: 28, 36, 76, 78, 85, 87, 89, 103, 112, 115, 126, 143, 175, 208, 259

Breed: AMERICAN ESKIMO (STANDARD, MINIATURE AND TOY)
Female: normal
Male: normal
Litter Size: 6 (standard), 4 (miniature), 2 (toy)
Birth Weight: 8–10 oz. (standard), 5–8 oz. (miniature), 3–5 oz. (toy)
Motherhood: free whelpers; good moms; some minis & toys slow to come into milk
Dewclaws: Remove rears.
Reported Disorders: 8, 67, 82, 113, 115, 117, 151, 208, 244

Breed: AMERICAN FOXHOUND
Female: normal
Male: normal
Litter Size: 8
Birth Weight: 16 oz.
Motherhood: almost no problems; large litters; dam may lie on pups or have trouble feeding all
Dewclaws: Remove all.
Reported Disorders: 50, 55, 167, 177, 241

Breed: AMERICAN PIT BULL TERRIER
Female: normal; some aggressive bitches
Male: normal
Litter Size: 6–9
Birth Weight: 8–12 oz.
Motherhood: free whelpers; good moms
Tails: NEVER DOCK! (show disqualification)
Ears: cropped or uncropped
Standard Deviations: variations in size and type; poor temperaments
Reported Disorders: 13, 38, 115, 174

Breed: AMERICAN STAFFORDSHIRE TERRIER
Female: aggressive breeders
Male: eager; sometimes aggressive
Litter Size: 7–8

Birth Weight: 12 oz.
Motherhood: free whelpers; good moms
Dewclaws: Remove all.
Ears: natural rosed or cropped short & straight (no curve)
Standard Deviations: crooked or partially missing tails; malocclusions
Reported Disorders: 27, 34, 38, 47, 50, 55, 115, 146

Breed: AMERICAN WATER SPANIEL
Female: some cycles irregular or once/ yr.; may be aggressive & need muzzling
Male: normal
Litter Size: 6–8
Birth Weight: 8–10 oz.
Motherhood: usually free whelpers (some C-secs.); dams may be nervous & harm pups if other dogs or too many people around
Dewclaws: Remove all.
Standard Deviations: yellow eyes; poor (nonmarcelled) coats; missing teeth; malocclusions; poor temperaments
Reported Disorders: 3, 28, 38, 50, 82, 113, 115, 126, 130, 174, 208, 210, 251

Breed: ANATOLIAN SHEPHERD
Female: ovulate late in cycle; often difficult to breed
Male: normal
Litter Size: 7–9
Birth Weight: 16–24 oz.
Motherhood: free whelpers; good moms
Dewclaws: Remove rears.
Ears: cropped in native Turkey but not in USA
Standard Deviations: hypersensitivity to anesthesia & insecticides; malocclusions
Reported Disorders: 78, 115

Breed: AUSTRALIAN CATTLE DOG
Female: normal
Male: normal; eager

Litter Size: 3–6
Birth Weight: 12–16 oz.
Motherhood: free whelpers; don't interfere; pups born white; roan comes in later
Dewclaws: Remove only rears.
Standard Deviations: body patches of color
Reported Disorders: 55, 103, 115, 139, 208

Breed: AUSTRALIAN SHEPHERD
Female: normal
Male: normal; some lines lack libido
Litter Size: 5–10
Birth Weight: 8–16 oz.
Motherhood: free whelpers; good moms
Dewclaws: Remove all.
Tails: If not born tailless, dock to stub.
Standard Deviations: malocclusions
Reported Disorders: 28, 38, 69, 82, 103, 115, 151, 208, 223

Breed: AUSTRALIAN TERRIER
Female: normal
Male: normal; eager
Litter Size: 4–5
Birth Weight: 5–7 oz.
Motherhood: easy whelpers; 59–61-da. gestation
Dewclaws: Remove all.
Tails: docked; leave a generous ⅔
Ears: Clip hair or tape if not up by 3 mo.
Reported Disorders: 12, 13, 38, 50, 62, 208

Breed: BASENJI
Female: one heat/yr. (in fall); lasts 4 wk.
Male: normal
Litter Size: 5–6
Birth Weight: 6–8 oz.
Motherhood: easy whelpers; good moms
Dewclaws: Remove all.
Standard Deviations: malocclusions
Reported Disorders: 39, 45, 69, 93, 130, 144, 165, 182, 201, 208, 251

Breed: BASSET HOUND
Female: normal but may use breeding rack
Male: difficult bec. of size & weight; often AIs
Litter Size: 8–9
Birth Weight: 6–16 oz.
Motherhood: can be slow whelpers w. large litters; occasional C-secs.; X-ray since hard to tell when done
Dewclaws: removal optional; usually left on
Standard Deviations: long &/or wire coats; malocclusions
Reported Disorders: 3, 34, 59, 72, 77, 78, 82, 101, 103, 130, 139, 166, 174, 203, 208, 241, 251, 252, 262

Breed: BEAGLE
Female: normal
Male: normal
Litter Size: 5–6
Birth Weight: 8–16 oz.
Motherhood: 13-in. often have pups too large to deliver naturally
Dewclaws: Remove all.
Standard Deviations: short or crooked tails; size differences; malocclusions
Reported Disorders: 13, 26, 29, 35, 38, 50, 51, 55, 69, 75, 82, 83, 88, 89, 103, 104, 115, 126, 131, 134, 135, 171, 196, 197, 198, 201, 205, 208, 210, 223, 260

Breed: BEARDED COLLIE
Female: may cycle longer than 6 mo.; 8–12 mo. not uncommon; maidens often fight deflowering; some inverted vulvas
Male: very lusty; mount at 3 wk. in whelping box; sometimes overexcited, w. poor aim; some sterility, usu. in later years
Litter Size: 7
Birth Weight: 10–12 oz.
Motherhood: enthusiastic nesters; first-timers may be vocal w. first pups; free whelpers, but large litters and long

bodies can make aiding nec. w. first pups
Dewclaws: removal of front optional
Standard Deviations: mismarks; smooth or woolly coats; fading pigment (nose and eye rims); late descent of testes; malocclusions
Reported Disorders: 13, 18, 27, 38, 82, 115, 122, 126, 157, 182, 208, 210, 212, 232, 236

Breed: BEAUCERON
Female: normal
Male: normal; eager
Litter Size: 10
Birth Weight: 14–18 oz.
Motherhood: free whelpers; good moms
Dewclaws: Double rear dewclaws required.
Ears: cropped; "rustic" (short & wide) or "elegant" (like pet Doberman Pinscher)
Reported Disorders: 115

Breed: BEDLINGTON TERRIER
Female: normal but w. long intervals
Male: normal
Litter Size: 4–6
Birth Weight: 6 oz.
Motherhood: good moms; often injure pups' very long tails
Dewclaws: Remove all.
Standard Deviations: missing canines
Reported Disorders: 27, 44, 67, 78, 136, 168, 205, 208, 210

Breed: BELGIAN MALINOIS
Female: normal
Male: normal
Litter Size: 8–11
Birth Weight: 12–13 oz.
Motherhood: easy whelpers; pups born black, lighten w. age; pups need socialization
Ears: tape if not up by 12 wk.
Standard Deviations: malocclusions; shyness
Reported Disorders: 27, 82, 115, 126, 173, 208

Breed: BELGIAN SHEEPDOG
Female: normal
Male: good; eager
Litter Size: 8–11
Birth Weight: 12–13 oz.
Motherhood: easy whelpers; good moms; pups need socialization
Dewclaws: Remove all.
Ears: Tape if not up by 12 wk.
Standard Deviations: silver coat (not silver muzzles); malocclusions; shyness
Reported Disorders: 27, 43, 82, 115, 126, 142, 173, 208, 261

Breed: BELGIAN TERVUREN
Female: normal
Male: slow to mature
Litter Size: 8–11
Birth Weight: 12–13 oz.
Motherhood: easy whelpers; pups born black, lighten w. age; pups need socialization
Ears: Tape if not up by 12 wk.
Standard Deviations: malocclusions; shyness
Reported Disorders: 27, 82, 115, 126, 142, 173, 261

Breed: BERNESE MOUNTAIN DOG
Female: regular cyclers but notoriously hard to settle
Male: some uninterested
Litter Size: 8–10
Birth Weight: 16–24 oz.
Motherhood: slow whelpers; C-secs. common; if more than 1 hr. betw. pups, intervene w. POP or surgery; low birth-survival drive
Dewclaws: Remove all, including extra rears.
Standard Deviations: mismarks; blue or partially blue eyes; malocclusions
Reported Disorders: 27, 38, 78, 97, 101, 115, 116, 122, 124, 208

Breed: BICHON FRISÉ
Female: cycle irregularly; silent heats; annular rings common
Male: normal; macho

Litter Size: 4–5
Birth Weight: 3.5–4 oz.
Motherhood: sensitive to pain, but usu. OK; may need manual or surgical assistance
Dewclaws: Remove all.
Standard Deviations: 10% color OK; bad teeth w. age
Reported Disorders: 27, 82, 87, 115, 174, 208

Breed: BLACK-AND-TAN COONHOUND
Female: normal
Male: normal
Litter Size: 7–10
Birth Weight: 12–16 oz.
Motherhood: free whelpers; good moms
Dewclaws: removal optional
Reported Disorders: 27, 72, 87, 115, 207, 208

Breed: BLOODHOUND
Female: fairly normal; hard to diagnose pregnancy
Male: awkward bec. of size; some AIs
Litter Size: 7–8
Birth Weight: 16–18 oz.
Motherhood: long, slow deliveries; occasional C-secs; a few poor moms
Dewclaws: removal optional
Standard Deviations: malocclusions
Reported Disorders: 35, 50, 72, 78, 101, 115, 182, 193, 252

Breed: BORDER COLLIE
Female: normal
Male: normal
Litter Size: 5–8
Birth Weight: 16 oz.
Motherhood: easy whelpers
Standard Deviations: malocclusions
Reported Disorders: 27, 29, 33, 45, 50, 55, 69, 115, 139, 166, 207, 208

Breed: BORDER TERRIER
Female: can have silent or irregular heats & small tracts but usu. settle once bred

Male: normal
Litter Size: 4–7
Birth Weight: 8–12 oz.
Motherhood: usu. free whelpers, but primary or secondary inertias occur in large litters; may strongly resent owners' help
Dewclaws: Remove all.
Tails: born naturally short; DO NOT CUT
Standard Deviations: wry, kinked or bob tails; malocclusions; late descent of testes
Reported Disorders: 23, 44, 108, 180, 195, 240

Breed: BORZOI
Female: puberty often not until 24 mo.; settle better if bred more than once
Male: puberty may be at 2 yr.; not very eager; easily discouraged; more than one person needed during tie
Litter Size: 8–10
Birth Weight: 12–16 oz.
Motherhood: free whelpers, but, bec. of deep chest, routine X-ray nec. to be sure they're done; first pups may require assistance
Dewclaws: Remove all.
Standard Deviations: missing premolars; hypersensitivity to anesthesia & insecticides
Reported Disorders: 19, 27, 88, 101, 115, 208, 210

Breed: BOSTON TERRIER
Female: dry seasons; no bleeding or swelling even on right day; may bite, fight &/or scream during breeding
Male: lack of interest; use studs of other breeds or progesterone testing to discern timing; need help w. breeding; can become "stuck" w. outside tie
Litter Size: 3
Birth Weight: 7–8 oz.
Motherhood: primary inertias, large pups & prolonged labors lead to 90% C-secs.
Dewclaws: Remove all (protects eyes).

Tails: docked just to cover anus, if not born w. natural "screw" tail
Ears: may be cropped for show appearance (no length removed) but rarely done today
Standard Deviations: mismarks; blue eyes; wry mouths; "cocked" eyes
Reported Disorders: 1, 2, 8, 28, 31, 32, 35, 38, 45, 46, 47, 55, 61, 67, 75, 103, 117, 118, 146, 163, 174, 175, 183, 199, 208, 223, 234, 259

Breed: BOUVIER DES FLANDRES
Female: irregular estrus; cystic ovaries; endometritis
Male: normal
Litter Size: 1–15
Birth Weight: 8–24 oz.
Motherhood: dystocias common bec. of very large or small litters
Dewclaws: Remove all.
Tails: docked; leave ⅝ in. at 3 da.
Ears: cropped moderately short & straight, w. wide base
Standard Deviations: malocclusion
Reported Disorders: 27, 38, 78, 101, 103, 115, 126, 138, 151

Breed: BOXER
Female: late puberty; normal breeders; vaginal hyperplasia & prolapse common
Male: normal
Litter Size: 5–6
Birth Weight: 20 oz.
Motherhood: freqent C-secs. since 1 or 2 pups often much larger; hard to tell when done; supermoms
Dewclaws: Remove all.
Tails: docked; leave ¾ in. at 3 da.
Ears: cropped long and gracefully curved, w. narrow base
Standard Deviations: whites; mismarks; unpigmented haws; extra incisors; "wet mouths"; some hypersensitivity to anesthesia
Reported Disorders: 1, 14, 22, 27, 38, 46, 50, 51, 53, 55, 60, 67, 72, 75, 78,

79, 82, 92, 89, 101, 102, 115, 131,
142, 146, 163, 166, 174, 198, 199,
207, 226, 232, 239, 257, 262

Breed: BRIARD
Female: normal
Male: normal
Litter Size: 7–13
Birth Weight: 12 oz.
Motherhood: free whelpers
Dewclaws: double rears required;
removal of front optional
Standard Deviations: yellow eyes;
white spots
Reported Disorders: 21, 101, 115, 126,
207

Breed: BRITTANY
Female: normal
Male: normal
Litter Size: 7
Birth Weight: 6 oz.
Motherhood: free whelpers; good moms
Dewclaws: Remove all.
Tails: docked, leaving width of finger
(¾ in.) at 3 da.; some born tailless
Standard Deviations: malocclusions
Reported Disorders: 7, 50, 72, 85, 115

Breed: BRUSSELS GRIFFON
Female: normal, although puberty up to
18 mo.
Male: normal; sexy
Litter Size: 4–5
Birth Weight: 5–6 oz.
Motherhood: difficulties due to large-
headed pups; many problems in bitches
less than 5 lb.
Dewclaws: Remove all.
Tails: docked; leave ⅓
Ears: cropped at 3 mo. (like Miniature
Schnauzer's) or left in natural drop
Standard Deviations: chocolate or blue
(disqualifying colors); webbed feet;
wry mouths
Reported Disorders: 9, 27, 38, 46, 67,
115, 117, 174, 208, 219, 255

Breed: BULL TERRIER
Female: easy breeders, although some
very aggressive (use breeding rack);
may cycle only once/yr.
Male: normal but too aggressive; lots of
AIs for handler convenience
Litter Size: 5–7
Birth Weight: 11–13 oz.
Motherhood: prolonged, hard deliveries;
may need oxytocin or calcium; 60% C-
secs.; frequent eclampsia; nervous
moms may mouth pups or clumsily lie
on them; some pup mortality
Dewclaws: removal optional
Ears: do not crop; tape if not up by 10
wk.
Standard Deviations: retained baby
teeth
Reported Disorders: 4, 13, 22, 35, 38,
78, 130, 139, 146, 205, 232, 251

Breed: BULLDOG
Female: normal, but hard to detect right
day bec. of lack of tail
Male: bec. of body weight & shape,
very few ties; hold dogs together; AIs
very common
Litter Size: 4
Birth Weight: 14 oz.
Motherhood: less than 10% free
whelpers; poor muscle tone, small
pelvis & large pups mean planned C-
secs. common to normal; can't reach
vulva to chew cord or clean
themselves; good moms
Ears: Glue ears back if not "rosed" by
8 wk.
Reported Disorders: 8, 9, 27, 35, 38,
66, 67, 72, 75, 78, 85, 134, 146, 153,
163, 198, 232, 234, 244, 245, 246,
257, 258, 259

Breed: BULLMASTIFF
Female: irregular cycles & ovulation;
dry seasons; vaginal hyperplasia
Male: need help; cumbersome &/or low
thyroid; 90% AIs
Litter Size: 5–8

Birth Weight: 16–24 oz.
Motherhood: "lazy" whelpers; need help; frequent C-secs.; often lack milk
Dewclaws: Remove rear or all.
Standard Deviations: yellow eyes; no mask, short or screw tails; extra incisors (slight underbite normal)
Reported Disorders: 8, 29, 31, 34, 38, 101, 103, 115, 208, 252, 257

Breed: CAIRN TERRIER
Female: sometimes short seasons or outside ties bec. of hypothyroid; otherwise normal
Male: normal
Litter Size: 3–5
Birth Weight: 5 oz.
Motherhood: free whelpers; good moms
Dewclaws: removal optional
Tails: DO NOT DOCK.
Reported Disorders: 12, 27, 31, 47, 50, 53, 87, 85, 103, 104, 126, 139, 174, 188, 201, 204, 208, 210, 262

Breed: CANAAN DOG
Female: normal
Male: normal
Litter Size: 4–5 (3–9 possible)
Birth Weight: 12 oz.
Motherhood: free whelpers; good protective moms
Dewclaws: removal optional
Reported Disorders: 82, 115, 208

Breed: CARDIGAN WELSH CORGI
Female: normal
Male: normal
Litter Size: 5–8
Birth Weight: 9–12 oz.
Motherhood: some tendency to dystocia
Dewclaws: Remove rears.
Tails: DO NOT DOCK.
Standard Deviations: mismarks; curled tails
Reported Disorders: 27, 38, 51, 53, 59, 103, 133, 139, 203, 207, 208, 210, 262

Breed: CATAHOULA LEOPARD DOG
Female: normal
Male: normal
Litter Size: 8–9
Birth Weight: large
Motherhood: free whelpers, but like privacy
Tails: some born tailless
Reported Disorders: 27, 55

Breed: CAVALIER KING CHARLES SPANIEL
Female: normal
Male: normal
Litter Size: 4–5
Birth Weight: 5–8 oz.
Motherhood: easy whelpers; good moms
Dewclaws: Remove all.
Tails: leave ⅔ to ¾; must be white on end, so sometimes don't dock
Standard Deviations: underbites
Reported Disorders: 16, 27, 45, 50, 95, 115, 151, 208, 262

Breed: CHESAPEAKE BAY RETRIEVER
Female: usu. normal; some infertility & irregular seasons
Male: normal; some sterility
Litter Size: 8–10
Birth Weight: 12–16 oz.
Motherhood: most free whelpers; some inertias & dystocias; good moms
Dewclaws: Remove all.
Standard Deviations: soft or open coats
Reported Disorders: 16, 27, 67, 78, 82, 115, 208, 262

Breed: CHIHUAHUA
Female: too small; frequent outside ties or AIs
Male: normal; eager; often need assistance, so accustom them to being handled
Litter Size: 2–5
Birth Weight: 3–5 oz.; pups as small as 2 oz. survive

Motherhood: small litters; inertia & C-secs. frequent in some lines
Dewclaws: Remove all.
Standard Deviations: open fontanels common (OK by the Standard); missing canines; retained baby teeth; malocclusions
Reported Disorders: 33, 38, 45, 78, 85, 96, 103, 117, 123, 133, 134, 139, 153, 162, 174, 198, 208, 219, 223, 244

Breed: CHINESE CRESTED
Female: normal
Male: normal
Litter Size: 3–5
Birth Weight: 2–4 oz.
Motherhood: easy whelpers; good moms
Dewclaws: Remove all since they "wash their faces" with their paws.
Standard Deviations: severe underbites
Reported Disorders: na

Breed: CHINESE SHAR PEI
Female: some late-onset puberty & irregular heats
Male: poor libido in some lines, so some AIs
Litter Size: 5
Birth Weight: 14–16 oz.
Motherhood: free whelpers, often at 58–59 da.; good moms; may wean pups early
Dewclaws: Remove rears.
Standard Deviations: too long coats; tongue not black; tongue not solid color; malocclusions
Reported Disorders: 1, 6, 24, 57, 64, 75, 78, 80, 101, 114, 115, 116, 117, 126, 130, 146, 151, 174, 192, 214, 251, 252, 261

Breed: CHOW CHOW
Female: often cycle more than twice/yr; hard to time ovulation & difficult to settle

Male: lack of interest; low libido
Litter Size: 4–6
Birth Weight: 10–20 oz.
Motherhood: hard to diagnose pregnancy; C-secs. common in very large or small litters
Standard Deviations: short tails; poor pigmentation; nonblack tongue; malocclusions
Reported Disorders: 31, 67, 75, 78, 103, 115, 124, 126, 155, 166, 174, 182, 205, 208, 249

Breed: CLUMBER SPANIEL
Female: puberty as late as 2 yr.; irregular cycles common
Male: heavy males w. low libido; AIs common
Litter Size: 4–6
Birth Weight: 12–16 oz.
Motherhood: some C-secs. bec. of secondary inertia; hard conditioning may help w. delivery; zealous moms may mutilate newly docked tails
Dewclaws: Remove all.
Tails: docked at taper; leave ⅓
Standard Deviations: underbites; missing teeth; wry mouths
Reported Disorders: 72, 78, 115, 131

Breed: COCKER SPANIEL
Female: normal
Male: normal; may be shorter-legged than female; use elevation
Litter Size: 4–6
Birth Weight: 6–8 oz.
Motherhood: free whelpers; good moms
Dewclaws: Remove all.
Tails: docked at taper; leave a generous ⅓
Standard Deviations: malocclusions; mismarks
Reported Disorders: 3, 8, 9, 12, 15, 26, 28, 35, 38, 48, 59, 67, 70, 72, 78, 79, 82, 87, 90, 96, 103, 115, 117, 126, 130, 131, 134, 151, 174, 175, 183, 184, 196, 197, 205, 208, 210, 211, 214, 226, 251, 252

Breed: COLLIE (ROUGH & SMOOTH)
Female: easy breeders, although strictures & polyps frequent
Male: normal
Litter Size: 6–10
Birth Weight: 12 oz.
Motherhood: easy whelpers; pups often have low birth-survival drive
Dewclaws: front removal optional; remove rears
Ears: Tape or glue if not tipping properly by 12 wk.
Standard Deviations: malocclusions
Reported Disorders: 27, 29, 37, 38, 45, 52, 55, 58, 67, 69, 78, 85, 88, 102, 115, 151, 157, 165, 175, 186, 207, 208, 251

Breed: COTON DE TULEAR
Female: normal
Male: normal
Litter Size: 5–8
Birth Weight: small
Motherhood: normal; free whelpers
Reported Disorders: na

Breed: CURLY-COATED RETRIEVER
Female: lots of misses; always check thyroid
Male: generally normal; some sterility
Litter Size: 6–9
Birth Weight: 8–14 oz.
Motherhood: free whelpers; pyometras common
Dewclaws: Remove all.
Standard Deviations: light eyes &/or nose (especially in livers); bald spots; coat not uniformly curly
Reported Disorders: 27, 67, 78, 115, 118, 126, 208, 262

Breed: DACHSHUND (SMOOTH, WIREHAIRED, LONGHAIRED)
Female: may have to muzzle; many false pregnancies; retire young
Male: keep males apart; bec. of shape, may need assistance

Litter Size: 2–4 (mini), 5 (Standard)
Birth Weight: 4–6 oz. (mini), 8–10 oz. (Standard)
Motherhood: usu. free whelpers, but inertia frequent; C-secs. more common in minis; good moms
Dewclaws: remove rears
Standard Deviations: walleye; inproper coat texture (esp. in wires); screw or kink tail; malocclusions
Reported Disorders: 1, 13, 28, 33, 38, 45, 51, 53, 55, 59, 62, 67, 69, 82, 103, 118, 126, 131, 134, 139, 146, 151, 170, 173, 174, 182, 190, 191, 205, 208, 209, 226, 234, 246, 251, 252, 259, 261, 262

Breed: DALMATIAN
Female: normal
Male: normal
Litter Size: 8–10 (13 not unusual)
Birth Weight: 11–15 oz.
Motherhood: normal
Dewclaws: may be removed
Standard Deviations: unpigmented eye rims & nose leather; patches (colored spots present at birth); lemon or tri-colored spots (pups are born white; spots appear around 2 wk.)
Reported Disorders: 13, 33, 55, 62, 78, 103, 104, 115, 124, 151, 173, 208, 223, 254

Breed: DANDIE DINMONT TERRIER
Female: fairly normal; some small tracts
Male: late maturity; mostly normal; some AIs
Litter Size: 4–6
Birth Weight: 8–10 oz.
Motherhood: hard to diagnose pregnancy; wt. gain by 35 da. is best indicator
Dewclaws: Remove all.
Standard Deviations: malocclusions
Reported Disorders: 74, 103, 126, 131, 174, 219

Breed: DOBERMAN PINSCHER
Female: normal
Male: normal; some reluctant breeders, so train early
Litter Size: 8
Birth Weight: 16 oz.
Motherhood: easy whelpers, although small litters can create problems; some hysterical moms
Dewclaws: Remove all.
Tails: Dock almost to end of tan, or leave ½ in. at 2–3 da.
Ears: cropped w. moderate length, smooth base & graceful curve; best done at 6–8 wk.
Standard Deviations: malocclusions
Reported Disorders: 27, 34, 41, 44, 47, 55, 57, 63, 94, 115, 126, 151, 156, 172, 189, 190, 191, 205, 208, 225, 260, 261, 262

Breed: ENGLISH COCKER SPANIEL
Female: normal
Male: normal
Litter Size: 5
Birth Weight: 8–10 oz.
Motherhood: easy whelpers
Dewclaws: removal optional
Tails: docked; leave a generous ⅓ (or to taper)
Standard Deviations: retained baby teeth, "short toe"
Reported Disorders: 27, 50, 72, 78, 92, 103, 115, 126, 196, 197, 205, 208, 234, 260

Breed: ENGLISH FOXHOUND
Female: normal
Male: little interest, esp. older pack hounds
Litter Size: 8
Birth Weight: 16–18 oz.
Motherhood: slow; free whelpers; good moms; to develop personality, place pups in homes till grown to hunting age
Dewclaws: Remove all.
Ears: "rounded" (¼ of ear length removed) in some hunt packs

Standard Deviations: malocclusions
Reported Disorders: very few (from practical working stock)

Breed: ENGLISH SETTER
Female: long, excessive estrus flow; irregular ovulation; poor fertility
Male: low libido in some strains
Litter Size: 6–10 (or more)
Birth Weight: 16 oz.
Motherhood: inertia from eclampsia freq.; after calcium injection, may whelp rest of litter; too much milk; caked breasts common even w. large litters
Dewclaws: Remove all.
Reported Disorders: 33, 47, 55, 72, 85, 103, 115, 207, 208, 251

Breed: ENGLISH SPRINGER SPANIEL
Female: normal
Male: normal
Litter Size: 7–8
Birth Weight: 9–14 oz.
Motherhood: easy whelpers, but avoid overweight
Dewclaws: Remove all.
Tails: docked; leave ⅓
Standard Deviations: malocclusions
Reported Disorders: 27, 51, 67, 72, 78, 86, 99, 103, 115, 151, 154, 173, 180, 184, 207, 208, 210, 214, 232, 262

Breed: ENGLISH TOY SPANIEL
Female: late puberty onset as with some Toys (12–14 mo.)
Male: slow to mature; normal breeders
Litter Size: 2–6
Birth Weight: 4–6 oz.
Motherhood: usu. normal; some slow; some C-secs. due to large-headed pups
Dewclaws: Remove all.
Tails: docked; leave 1½ in. at 4–5 da.
Standard Deviations: any white on King Charles or Ruby varieties; open fontanels
Reported Disorders: 28, 45, 62, 130, 151, 174, 175, 208, 251

Breed: FIELD SPANIEL
Female: irregular seasons, often 2 yr.
  apart
Male: normal
Litter Size: 6
Birth Weight: 16 oz.
Motherhood: generally free whelpers,
  but small litters may require C-secs.;
  pyometras common
Dewclaws: Remove all.
Tails: docked; leave ⅔ of tail
Standard Deviations: lack of coat (esp.
  in livers)
Reported Disorders: 27, 115, 126, 200,
  208

Breed: FINNISH SPITZ
Female: normal
Male: normal
Litter Size: 3–4
Birth Weight: 6–8 oz.
Motherhood: free whelpers; good moms
Standard Deviations: white patch on
  chest or toes
Reported Disorders: 28

Breed: FLAT-COATED RETRIEVER
Female: normal
Male: normal
Litter Size: 3–4
Birth Weight: 6–8 oz.
Motherhood: free whelpers; good moms
Dewclaws: removal optional
Standard Deviations: yellows; faded
  pigment (in livers)
Reported Disorders: 27, 67, 78, 115,
  126, 174, 207

Breed: FOX TERRIER
     (WIRE & SMOOTH)
Female: normal
Male: normal
Litter Size: 8
Birth Weight: 11–13 oz.
Motherhood: fairly normal; a few
  inertias
Dewclaws: Remove all.
Tails: docked; leave a generous ⅔ (even
  w. top of head)

Ears: Glue at 7–8 wk. if not tipping
  properly.
Standard Deviations: gay tails;
  malocclusions
Reported Disorders: 1, 12, 28, 31, 34,
  38, 55, 67, 108, 125, 139, 146, 154,
  164, 183, 198, 208, 219, 232, 239

Breed: FRENCH BULLDOG
Female: small tracts; either secure
  female, or do AI
Male: most AIs due to body shape
Litter Size: 4–5
Birth Weight: 6–8 oz.
Motherhood: Small pelvis, large-headed
  pups & inertias result in mostly C-secs.
Reported Disorders: 8, 9, 27, 32, 38,
  67, 75, 78, 85, 87, 131, 174, 226,
  252, 259

Breed: GERMAN SHEPHERD DOG
Female: generally normal; some
  strictures; some 4-mo. cyclers
Male: most normal; a few lazy breeders
Litter Size: 8–10
Birth Weight: 12–20 oz.
Motherhood: generally free whelpers;
  very large pups may require assistance;
  good moms
Dewclaws: remove rear; front removal
  optional
Ears: Tape if not up by 12 wk.
Standard Deviations: long coats; heavy
  ear leathers; whites, blues & livers
  (disqualifying colors)
Reported Disorders: 1, 22, 27, 31, 38,
  50, 51, 53, 55, 56, 59, 63, 67, 69, 77,
  79, 82, 85, 103, 115, 131, 139, 144,
  153, 161, 166, 172, 173, 175, 179,
  183, 186, 205, 208, 220, 226, 232,
  234, 243, 252, 260, 262

Breed: GERMAN SHORTHAIRED
     POINTER
Female: may cycle more than twice/yr;
  ovulation time varies; many false
  pregnancies
Male: shy breeders in some lines
Litter Size: 10

Birth Weight: 9–15 oz.
Motherhood: occasional eclampsia during delivery; good moms; heavy milkers
Dewclaws: Remove all.
Tails: docked; leave a generous ⅖
Standard Deviations: malocclusions
Reported Disorders: 27, 33, 50, 55, 61, 77, 78, 82, 86, 100, 101, 115, 126, 142, 161, 166, 173, 196, 197, 208, 232, 241, 262

Breed: GERMAN WIREHAIRED POINTER
Female: normal
Male: normal
Litter Size: 10
Birth Weight: 9–15 oz.
Motherhood: free whelpers; good moms
Dewclaws: Remove all.
Tails: docked; leave just under ½ of tail
Standard Deviations: wispy, soft coats; long, woolly coats; smooth coats; malocclusions
Reported Disorders: 27, 115

Breed: GIANT SCHNAUZER
Female: don't settle well if shipped
Male: normal but late to mature
Litter Size: 7–9
Birth Weight: 6–16 oz.
Motherhood: frequent secondary inertia; very protective of pups
Dewclaws: Remove all.
Tails: docked short at 2nd or 3rd vertebra
Ears: cropped similarly to Doberman Pinscher's
Standard Deviations: malocclusions; missing teeth
Reported Disorders: 27, 50, 82, 103, 115, 166, 186, 198, 208, 247

Breed: GOLDEN RETRIEVER
Female: some long cyclers; otherwise normal
Male: good, but may not be eager
Litter Size: 6–8
Birth Weight: 16–24 oz.

Motherhood: free whelpers; good moms
Dewclaws: Remove all.
Standard Deviations: mismarks, wry mouths, missing teeth, malocclusions
Reported Disorders: 26, 27, 31, 38, 40, 45, 50, 63, 72, 78, 82, 115, 126, 190, 191, 207, 208, 232, 234, 262

Breed: GORDON SETTER
Female: ovulation variation; otherwise normal
Male: normal
Litter Size: 8–12
Birth Weight: 12–16 oz.
Motherhood: easy whelpers; good moms
Dewclaws: Removal optional
Standard Deviations: red color; too much white; crooked tails
Reported Disorders: 27, 29, 115, 126, 208

Breed: GREAT DANE
Female: many false pregnancies; otherwise normal
Male: normal; eager; height differences in large males; breed downhill
Litter Size: 9
Birth Weight: 24 oz.
Motherhood: most free whelpers; sometimes large litters w. large pups lead to inertia & C-secs.
Dewclaws: removal optional
Ears: cropped long & graceful with clean base; best done at 7–9 wk.
Standard Deviations: mismarks; too much white (on all colors); illegal colors; walleyes; malocclusions
Reported Disorders: 1, 22, 28, 31, 34, 50, 53, 54, 56, 72, 78, 101, 103, 115, 121, 153, 161, 166, 169, 208, 225, 226, 252, 262

Breed: GREAT PYRENEES
Female: regular cycles but erratic ovulation
Male: may need assistance
Litter Size: 6–7
Birth Weight: 16 oz.

Motherhood: most free whelpers; more than a 3-hr. delay requires assistance; good moms; may lie on pups the first day
Dewclaws: double rear dewclaws required; leave all on
Standard Deviations: blue eyes; normal body temperature is low; malocclusions; use care with anesthesia
Reported Disorders: 28, 78, 86, 115, 174, 200, 226, 252

Breed: GREATER SWISS MOUNTAIN DOG
Female: puberty at 8–15 mo.; usu. cycle twice/yr., but some more frequent; may not stand
Male: slow to mature; some AIs
Litter Size: 5
Birth Weight: 8–16 oz.
Motherhood: some primary & secondary inertias require C-secs.; good moms
Dewclaws: Remove all.
Standard Deviations: red base coat; blue eyes
Reported Disorders: 67, 101, 115, 166

Breed: GREYHOUND
Female: puberty 2 yr. or more; cycle 9–12 mo.; may not stand; AIs common
Male: slow to mature; low libido; taller than females; AIs common
Litter Size: 7–10 (15 not unknown)
Birth Weight: 16–30 oz.
Motherhood: dystocias frequent bec. of long, slow delivery of many large pups; may scream during delivery; often lots of blood; X-ray to be sure done; fetal death rate high; good moms
Dewclaws: Remove all.
Standard Deviations: light eyes; hypersensitivity to anesthesia &/or insecticides
Reported Disorders: 1, 22, 50, 51, 73, 85, 101, 139, 173, 183, 208, 218, 223

Breed: HARRIER
Female: normal
Male: normal
Litter Size: 8–10 (13 not unknown)
Birth Weight: 8–10 oz.
Motherhood: free whelpers; good moms
Dewclaws: usually removed for show; optional for field work
Standard Deviations: malocclusions
Reported Disorders: 115, 129

Breed: HAVANESE
Female: normal
Male: aggressive breeders, but don't quarrel among themselves
Litter Size: 4–6
Birth Weight: 6 oz.
Motherhood: free whelpers; good moms
Dewclaws: Remove rears.
Standard Deviations: lack of pigment; malocclusions
Reported Disorders: 27, 126, 174, 208

Breed: IBIZAN HOUND
Female: puberty 2 yr. or more; cycle 10–12 mo.; extreme false pregnancies
Male: normal
Litter Size: 6–12
Birth Weight: 14 oz.
Motherhood: easy whelpers; good moms
Dewclaws: Remove all.
Standard Deviations: sensitivity to some anesthesia &/or insecticides
Reported Disorders: 23, 44, 75, 147, 233

Breed: IRISH SETTER
Female: late puberty; erratic cycles w. false seasons; many false pregnancies
Male: normal
Litter Size: 8–10
Birth Weight: 16 oz.
Motherhood: secondary inertias common; frequent eclampsia; may be hyperactive & step on pups (watch first few da.)

Dewclaws: Remove all, especially field stock.

Standard Deviations: kinked & stub tails; malocclusions

Reported Disorders: 1, 24, 27, 34, 53, 72, 76, 78, 82, 85, 101, 115, 121, 126, 161, 166, 172, 179, 183, 190, 191, 200, 202, 207, 208, 262

Breed: IRISH TERRIER

Female: normal

Male: normal

Litter Size: 4–8

Birth Weight: 8 oz.

Motherhood: easy whelpers; very independent & protective; good moms

Dewclaws: Remove all.

Tails: docked; leave ⅔ to ¾ (to top of head)

Ears: Begin setting if not folding properly by 12 wk.

Standard Deviations: soft coats; bad teeth with age

Reported Disorders: 53, 65, 151

Breed: IRISH WATER SPANIEL

Female: ovulation variation; may not stand; some misses

Male: mostly normal; a few infertile or sterile males

Litter Size: 8–10

Birth Weight: 12–16 oz.

Motherhood: free whelpers; tend to "sling" pups out; good moms

Dewclaws: Remove all.

Standard Deviations: coat problems (lack of curl, alopecia); variations in size; kinked tail

Reported Disorders: 27, 115, 126, 208

Breed: IRISH WOLFHOUND

Female: puberty at 18–24 mo.; cycle 6–9 mo.

Male: some low libidos; if willing, are dignified & easy to handle

Litter Size: 5–6

Birth Weight: 20–24 oz.

Motherhood: long deliveries; secondary inertia & C-secs. often halfway through; may lie on pups (watch carefully first wk.)

Dewclaws: Remove all.

Reported Disorders: 22, 27, 73, 78, 101, 115, 161, 169, 190, 191, 252

Breed: ITALIAN GREYHOUND

Female: normal, but puberty may be at 18–24 mo.

Male: normal; testes late to descend

Litter Size: 3–5

Birth Weight: 6–9 oz.

Motherhood: natural whelpers; a few inertias; mothers orphan pups easily

Dewclaws: Remove all.

Standard Deviations: retained baby teeth; crooked teeth; other dental problems; hypersensitivity to barbiturates & anesthesia

Reported Disorders: 1, 27, 82, 103, 174, 183, 208

Breed: JACK RUSSELL TERRIER

Female: normal

Male: normal

Litter Size: 3–5

Birth Weight: 4–8 oz.

Motherhood: free whelpers; good moms

Dewclaws: Remove all.

Tails: docked; leave ⅔ on an average tail (leave ¾ on a thicker tail)

Standard Deviations: pricked ears; poor temperaments

Reported Disorders: 12, 32, 139, 154, 174

Breed: JAPANESE CHIN

Female: normal

Male: normal libido; need assistance for aim & height differences

Litter Size: 3–5

Birth Weight: 3–4 oz.

Motherhood: pups have large heads, but usually free whelpers; need help w. cords; good moms

Dewclaws: remove rears; front removal optional

Standard Deviations: wry mouths
Reported Disorders: 27, 46, 50, 100, 174, 208

Breed: KEESHOND
Female: often ovulate late in cycle
Male: normal
Litter Size: 5–7
Birth Weight: 8–12 oz.
Motherhood: 70 da. not unknown; free whelpers; good moms
Dewclaws: Remove all.
Reported Disorders: 27, 63, 82, 115, 126, 153, 200, 205, 208, 239

Breed: KERRY BLUE TERRIER
Female: may ovulate early; some small, immature tracts; hard to settle
Male: need some courtship time, but normal
Litter Size: 4–8
Birth Weight: 7–12 oz.
Motherhood: dystocias not unknown, but most easy whelpers; may go early; some do not want to stay w. pups, especially spoiled house pets
Dewclaws: Remove all.
Tails: docked; leave a generous ⅔
Ears: Glue to proper fold position at 8 wk.
Standard Deviations: no fading (staying black instead of fading to "blue"); missing premolars; narrow palpebral fissure
Reported Disorders: 15, 27, 29, 78, 86, 113, 115, 134

Breed: KOMONDOR
Female: late puberty; cycle 5–12 mo.; may ovulate late in heat (up to 18–25 da.)
Male: low libido in some lines; heavy coats may be problem
Litter Size: 5–8
Birth Weight: 16 oz.
Motherhood: free whelpers; good moms; often late to come into milk (have formula ready)
Dewclaws: Remove only rears.

Standard Deviations: faded pigment; light eyes; malocclusions; missing teeth; shy temperaments
Reported Disorders: 27, 64, 78, 80, 101, 115, 126, 251

Breed: KUVASZ
Female: normal
Male: normal
Litter Size: 7–8
Birth Weight: 16–24 oz.
Motherhood: free whelpers; good moms
Dewclaws: Remove rear.
Standard Deviations: yellow in coat; blue eyes; "satin" coats (too long, fine & open); malocclusions
Reported Disorders: 27, 50, 55, 77, 101, 115, 126, 166, 252, 262

Breed: KYI-LEO
Female: normal; may cycle 9 mo.; may ovulate late (15th da.); some spoiled brats
Male: can be a bit shy if not trained properly
Litter Size: 3–4
Birth Weight: 4–7 oz.
Motherhood: free whelpers, but may stop in midlabor bec. of noise, confusion or lack of "their" people; good moms
Reported Disorders: 13, 174

Breed: LABRADOR RETRIEVER
Female: normal
Male: normal
Litter Size: 6–8
Birth Weight: 16–24 oz.
Motherhood: usu. free whelpers; good moms
Dewclaws: remove rears; front removal optional
Standard Deviations: lack of pigment; missing teeth; malocclusions
Reported Disorders: 1, 16, 24, 27, 36, 40, 47, 50, 53, 63, 67, 72, 78, 82, 115, 121, 126, 139, 146, 166, 190, 191, 207, 208, 210, 248, 252, 262

Breed: LAKELAND TERRIER
Female: some lines have late puberty
(20–24 mo.); 12–15-mo. cycles
common in cold kennels
Male: normal; some sterile
Litter Size: 4–5
Birth Weight: 8 oz.
Motherhood: free whelpers if not
overweight; good moms
Dewclaws: Remove all.
Tails: docked to level of top of head
Standard Deviations: liver dogs with
faded pigment; malocclusion
Reported Disorders: 12, 27, 50, 67,
139, 151, 182, 252, 262

Breed: LEONBERGER
Female: normal; some 4-mo. cyclers
Male: normal
Litter Size: 8
Birth Weight: 16 oz.
Motherhood: free whelpers; good moms
Dewclaws: Remove rears.
Reported Disorders: 115

Breed: LHASA APSO
Female: normal
Male: normal
Litter Size: 3–5
Birth Weight: 5–7 oz.
Motherhood: generally free whelpers
Dewclaws: normally remove rears; front
optional
Standard Deviations: smooth coats;
blue eyes
Reported Disorders: 27, 53, 59, 61, 67,
78, 115, 130, 131, 134, 141, 173,
174, 205, 208, 251, 262

Breed: LÖWCHEN
(LITTLE LION DOG)
Female: normal; some cycle just once/
yr.
Male: normal
Litter Size: 3–4
Birth Weight: 5–7 oz.
Motherhood: free whelpers; good moms
Dewclaws: Remove all.

Standard Deviations: wry mouths;
malocclusions
Reported Disorders: 12, 174

Breed: MALTESE
Female: very short seasons; false
pregnancies frequent
Male: normal, but tiny males may
require assistance
Litter Size: 2–4
Birth Weight: 3–6 oz.
Motherhood: show bitches in 6-lb.
range often too small & require C-sec.;
occasional eclampsia; some indifferent
moms
Dewclaws: Remove all.
Standard Deviations: lemon color on
side coat; malocclusion; retained puppy
teeth; open fontanels
Reported Disorders: 38, 50, 55, 78,
103, 117, 123, 174, 208

Breed: MANCHESTER TERRIER
(STANDARD & TOY)
Female: normal puberty; may cycle
only every 12–18 mo.
Male: normal
Litter Size: 3 (Toy), 5–6 (Standard)
Birth Weight: 5–6 oz.
Motherhood: free whelpers
Dewclaws: Generally remove all.
Ears: cropped moderately long &
smooth (Standard); natural, but tape if
not up by 6 mo. (Toy)
Standard Deviations: incorrect size (in
both varieties); retained puppy teeth
Reported Disorders: 12, 27, 38, 51, 82,
117, 139, 208, 251, 262

Breed: MAREMMA SHEEPDOG
Female: may be hard to settle
Male: may be uninterested
Litter Size: 6–8
Birth Weight: 12–24 oz.
Motherhood: free whelpers; good moms
Reported Disorders: 115, 205

Breed: MASTIFF
Female: irregular seasons & ovulation; many resorptions & false pregnancies; vaginal hyperplasia & prolapse
Male: sometimes low sperm count & libido; check for hypothyroidism
Litter Size: 5 (can be up to 14)
Birth Weight: 16–24 oz.
Motherhood: secondary inertia common after first few pups; vaginal hyperplasia & prolapse frequent
Standard Deviations: screw tails; obesity
Reported Disorders: 72, 101, 115, 126, 151, 182, 257

Breed: MEXICAN HAIRLESS & XOLOITZCUINTLI
Female: normal, but misses are frequent
Male: normal
Litter Size: 3
Birth Weight: 4 oz.
Motherhood: free whelpers; good moms
Standard Deviations: drop ears; bad fronts; missing teeth; "coated" pups are culled
Reported Disorders: na

Breed: MINIATURE BULL TERRIER
Female: normal
Male: normal
Litter Size: 3–4
Birth Weight: 6 oz.
Motherhood: usually free whelpers; some eclampsia; good moms
Reported Disorders: see Standard, plus 139

Breed: MINIATURE PINSCHER
Female: normal; a few very dominant bitches
Male: normal; eager
Litter Size: 1–6
Birth Weight: 4–6 oz.
Motherhood: hardy, free whelpers if kept muscular & trim
Dewclaws: Remove all.
Tails: docked short (not quite to end of tan or to just cover anal triangle)

Ears: cropped to moderate length, narrow, curved & graceful
Standard Deviations: oversized; lack of eye or nose pigment; white spots; "thumb" marks; retained puppy teeth
Reported Disorders: 12, 27, 38, 130, 134, 173, 186, 208, 219

Breed: MINIATURE POODLE
Female: puberty often at 14 mo. or more; normal breeders
Male: normal; eager
Litter Size: 4–6
Birth Weight: 6–8 oz.
Motherhood: free whelpers; good moms
Dewclaws: Remove all.
Tails: docked; leave over ½ of tail (remove just over ⅓)
Standard Deviations: parti-colors; malocclusions; missing teeth, oversized
Reported Disorders: 3, 12, 13, 28, 32, 50, 53, 55, 63, 67, 69, 70, 71, 78, 82, 83, 100, 103, 104, 112, 115, 117, 118, 131, 134, 136, 151, 162, 173, 174, 175, 190, 191, 196, 197, 208, 219, 244, 262

Breed: MINIATURE SCHNAUZER
Female: variations in ovulation (esp. late); many "spoiled brats"
Male: Outside ties can be a problem.
Litter Size: 3–5
Birth Weight: 4–9 oz.
Motherhood: "lazy" bitches; 15% C-secs.
Dewclaws: Remove all.
Tails: docked, just short of tan (silver) mark
Ears: cropped moderately short, with no bell
Standard Deviations: white spots; pure white; soft, wispy coats; late tooth eruption; malocclusions; improper size
Reported Disorders: 1, 12, 13, 26, 28, 38, 42, 50, 69, 82, 89, 126, 134, 139, 151, 190, 191, 196, 197, 198, 208, 221, 256, 262

Breed: NEAPOLITAN MASTIFF

Female: normal but aggressive; introduce to male early in season
Male: normal
Litter Size: 12
Birth Weight: 16–24 oz.
Motherhood: free whelpers; good moms
Dewclaws: Remove rears.
Tails: docked; leave ⅔
Ears: cropped very short
Standard Deviations: na
Reported Disorders: 9, 35, 72, 115, 161, 203

Breed: NEWFOUNDLAND

Female: irregular ovulation; awkward & uncooperative
Male: awkward; need help; no tie & may have to hold male up
Litter Size: 6
Birth Weight: 20–24 oz.
Motherhood: long, slow whelpers; secondary inertia; last pups may be retained; not protective; good moms
Dewclaws: Remove rears if present.
Standard Deviations: malocclusions
Reported Disorders: 59, 78, 97, 101, 115, 126, 161, 175, 198, 232, 251, 252, 259, 262

Breed: NORWEGIAN ELKHOUND

Female: normal
Male: may not mature until 24–30 mo.
Litter Size: 5–7
Birth Weight: 8–10 oz.
Motherhood: free whelpers
Dewclaws: Remove rears.
Standard Deviations: malocclusions
Reported Disorders: 27, 36, 38, 61, 78, 103, 115, 168, 205, 206, 208

Breed: NORWICH-NORFOLK TERRIER

Female: normal if not spoiled
Male: normal if well trained; may need assistance bec. of short legs
Litter Size: 2–3
Birth Weight: 3–4 oz.
Motherhood: usually free whelpers; may

need help; some C-secs. in smaller bitches w. large pups
Dewclaws: Remove all.
Tails: docked just short of ½ (shorter than most terriers)
Standard Deviations: soft and/or long coats; malocclusions
Reported Disorders: 23, 130

Breed: NOVA SCOTIA DUCK-TOLLING RETRIEVER

Female: puberty 8–12 mo.; may cycle every 6 to 14 mo.
Male: normal, although some require assistance
Litter Size: 5–7
Birth Weight: 8–12 oz.
Motherhood: generally free whelpers, although some require help; good moms
Dewclaws: usually removed, esp. rears
Standard Deviations: malocclusions
Reported Disorders: 38, 50, 67, 115, 122, 126, 208, 251

Breed: OLD ENGLISH SHEEPDOG

Female: normal
Male: normal
Litter Size: 8
Birth Weight: 10–16 oz.
Motherhood: free whelpers; good moms
Dewclaws: Remove all.
Tails: docked as close to body as possible
Standard Deviations: malocclusions
Reported Disorders: 28, 34, 55, 63, 78, 87, 103, 115, 142, 208, 210, 261

Breed: OTTER HOUND

Female: irregular seasons & decreased fertility due to narrow genetic base
Male: may require AI, if rarely used
Litter Size: 7–8
Birth Weight: 20 oz.
Motherhood: free whelpers, unless older; very attentive moms for first 2 wk.
Dewclaws: removal optional
Standard Deviations: malocclusions
Reported Disorders: 50, 92, 115, 241

Breed: OWCZAREK NIZINNY
Female: normal
Male: normal
Litter Size: 5–7
Birth Weight: 10 oz.
Motherhood: free whelpers; good moms
Tails: docked short, like a Doberman Pinscher
Standard Deviations: faded nose and/or eye pigment; malocclusions
Reported Disorders: 78, 115, 175

Breed: OWCZAREK PODHALANSKI
Female: normal; late puberty
Male: normal
Litter Size: 6–9
Birth Weight: 14 oz.
Motherhood: free whelpers; good moms
Dewclaws: removal optional
Reported Disorders: 115

Breed: PAPILLON
Female: normal
Male: eager, but may need help if a lot smaller than female
Litter Size: 2–4
Birth Weight: 4–5 oz.
Motherhood: most lines free whelpers, but occasional primary inertia (in single-pup litters) or eclampsia
Dewclaws: remove rears; front optional
Standard Deviations: mismarks; retained puppy teeth; drooping ears; oversized; malocclusions; open fontanels
Reported Disorders: 27, 38, 50, 55, 78, 82, 117, 126, 130, 174, 208, 246, 262

Breed: PEKINGESE
Female: short estrus
Male: require help bec. of body shape & long coat
Litter Size: 3–5
Birth Weight: 4–6 oz.
Motherhood: delivery difficult; often need C-sec.; need help to sever cords & clean pups; good moms
Reported Disorders: 12, 28, 38, 67, 75, 117, 130, 131, 136, 151, 162, 173, 174, 208, 246, 251, 256

Breed: PEMBROKE WELSH CORGI
Female: normal
Male: normal
Litter Size: 6–7
Birth Weight: 10 oz.
Motherhood: most free whelpers; some dystocias; may be slow to start tending to pups
Dewclaws: Remove all.
Tails: If not born tailless, dock as close to the body as possible.
Ears: Tape if not up by 12 wk.
Standard Deviations: all white; "bluies"; "fluffies"; malocclusions
Reported Disorders: 27, 51, 53, 59, 82, 115, 131, 139, 182, 208, 210, 234, 262

Breed: PERUVIAN INCA ORCHID
Female: normal; late puberty
Male: normal
Litter Size: 6
Birth Weight: 10–12 oz.
Motherhood: free whelpers; good moms
Dewclaws: removal optional
Standard Deviations: missing teeth (associated with dominant hairless gene—cross with coated dogs to retain teeth)
Reported Disorders: 251

Breed: PETIT BASSET GRIFFON VENDÉEN
Female: normal
Male: normal; train young
Litter Size: 9–10
Birth Weight: 14–16 oz.
Motherhood: free whelpers; good moms; continue training their young as they grow
Ears: Ear injuries are common in hunting packs.
Reported Disorders: na

Breed: PHARAOH HOUND
Female: normal; late puberty & ovulation
Male: normal
Litter Size: 2–12

Birth Weight: depends on litter size
Motherhood: free whelpers; great moms
Dewclaws: Remove all.
Standard Deviations: too large or small; too much white
Reported Disorders: 165

Breed: POINTER
Female: normal
Male: normal but slow to mature
Litter Size: 6–14
Birth Weight: 10–18 oz.
Motherhood: easy whelpers; sometimes whelp early; good moms
Dewclaws: Remove all.
Standard Deviations: malocclusions
Reported Disorders: 17, 22, 27, 45, 55, 77, 78, 115, 160, 173, 207, 208, 251, 252

Breed: POMERANIAN
Female: normal; some dry heats
Male: normal
Litter Size: 2
Birth Weight: 3–4 oz.
Motherhood: slow whelpers; live pups can follow 2 hr. of mild but continuous contractions; although some free whelpers, inertias common & many C-secs.; good moms
Dewclaws: Remove rears.
Standard Deviations: retained baby teeth; open fontanels
Reported Disorders: 27, 50, 67, 78, 117, 123, 136, 162, 174, 175, 208, 219, 244

Breed: PORTUGUESE WATER DOG
Female: normal
Male: normal
Litter Size: 8
Birth Weight: 12–14 oz.
Motherhood: free whelpers, though may be slow between pups; good moms
Standard Deviations: open coats
Reported Disorders: 100, 115, 151, 208

Breed: PUG
Female: late puberty for Toy; may be 9–12 mo.

Male: early puberty; may be exhausted before consummation if fat or hot
Litter Size: 4–6
Birth Weight: 4–9 oz.
Motherhood: some free whelper strains; others have a lot of inertia & C-secs.; problems if overweight; always need help with cord & sacs; pups slow to thrive; pups get upper respiratory disease
Dewclaws: Remove all.
Reported Disorders: 12, 27, 46, 67, 75, 78, 173, 196, 197, 208, 230, 246

Breed: PULI
Female: normal
Male: normal
Litter Size: 5–7
Birth Weight: 7–9 oz.
Motherhood: free whelpers; good moms
Dewclaws: Remove all.
Standard Deviations: parti-colors; malocclusions; missing teeth
Reported Disorders: 27, 115, 208

Breed: RAT TERRIER
Female: normal
Male: normal
Litter Size: 5–7
Birth Weight: 6 oz.
Motherhood: free whelpers; good moms
Tails: docked short
Reported Disorders: 139, 174

Breed: RHODESIAN RIDGEBACK
Female: normal
Male: normal
Litter Size: 8–12
Birth Weight: 16 oz.
Motherhood: free whelpers; good moms
Dewclaws: Remove all.
Standard Deviations: lack of proper ridge
Reported Disorders: 1, 27, 34, 55, 60, 78, 115, 126, 259

Breed: ROTTWEILER
Female: often uninterested or aggressive; may have to muzzle

Male: low libido
Litter Size: 7
Birth Weight: 12–18 oz.
Motherhood: may whelp late; can be slow, but free whelpers in some lines; lack of maternal instincts a problem
Dewclaws: Remove all.
Tails: dock short, not flush w. body but shorter than a Doberman Pinscher; leave just one joint
Reported Disorders: 27, 38, 55, 63, 72, 78, 97, 115, 140, 158, 166, 208, 209, 210, 261, 262

Breed: SAINT BERNARD
Female: normal, but need help; can't support wt. of male
Male: assisted breedings common; wt., lack of muscling & overweight results in many AIs
Litter Size: 8–10
Birth Weight: 16 oz.
Motherhood: free whelpers
Dewclaws: Remove rears.
Reported Disorders: 10, 27, 34, 35, 51, 55, 59, 62, 67, 69, 72, 78, 82, 88, 87, 85, 101, 103, 115, 161, 162, 166, 169, 172, 203, 250, 252, 256

Breed: SALUKI
Female: puberty at 24 mo. or more; irregular ovulation; stress can take them out of heat
Male: hold bitches; low libido may be due to hypothyroidism
Litter Size: 5–8
Birth Weight: 16 oz.
Motherhood: free whelpers, but they like "their" people around
Dewclaws: all usually removed
Standard Deviations: malocclusions; sensitivity to barbiturates
Reported Disorders: 33, 50, 59, 103, 115, 126, 145, 208, 251

Breed: SAMOYED
Female: puberty at 24 mo. or more; then normal & regular
Male: outside ties frequent

Litter Size: 6–7
Birth Weight: 12 oz.
Motherhood: slow but free whelpers; good moms
Dewclaws: Remove rears.
Ears: Shave or tape ears if not up by 12 wk.
Standard Deviations: blue eyes; lack of pigment on eye rims & nose
Reported Disorders: 14, 27, 29, 36, 38, 50, 62, 67, 78, 85, 103, 115, 131, 134, 190, 191, 198, 208, 210, 223

Breed: SCHIPPERKE
Female: puberty at 12 mo. or even 2 yr.; some silent seasons
Male: normal
Litter Size: 4 (1–8)
Birth Weight: 4–5 oz.
Motherhood: usually free whelpers
Dewclaws: Remove all.
Tails: docked short; indentation so no tail is visible or can be lifted
Standard Deviations: malocclusions
Reported Disorders: 12, 27, 78, 208, 212

Breed: SCOTTISH DEERHOUND
Female: puberty late; may cycle 8–10 mo.; otherwise normal
Male: normal; eager
Litter Size: 8–9
Birth Weight: 12–24 oz.
Motherhood: some primary inertias, but generally free whelpers; good moms
Dewclaws: usually removed
Standard Deviations: "woolies"; "ring" tails
Reported Disorders: 50, 101, 166, 172, 186

Breed: SCOTTISH TERRIER
Female: generally normal; some irregularities
Male: normal; some elevations or AIs needed for short-legged males
Litter Size: 4–5
Birth Weight: 7–9 oz.

Motherhood: some primary inertias; pups have large heads, so some C-secs.
Dewclaws: removal optional
Tails: DO NOT DOCK.
Reported Disorders: 3, 13, 27, 32, 47, 53, 55, 87, 116, 126, 139, 147, 200, 202, 208, 241, 262

Breed: SEALYHAM TERRIER
Female: longer cycles than average
Male: frequent AIs due to heavy bodies & short legs
Litter Size: 4–5
Birth Weight: 6–8 oz.
Motherhood: some easy; others "lazy" & need assistance; good moms, independent & sensible
Dewclaws: removal optional
Tails: docked; leave ½
Standard Deviations: ears too small
Reported Disorders: 13, 27, 55, 103, 136, 139, 151, 208, 210, 239

Breed: SHETLAND SHEEPDOG
Female: variable estrus & ovulation; immature tracts; often not willing, esp. when sent away
Male: normal
Litter Size: 4–6
Birth Weight: 6–10 oz.
Motherhood: easy whelpers; a few C-secs.; good moms
Dewclaws: Remove all.
Tails: Glue or weight if not properly tipped by 8–10 wk.
Standard Deviations: oversized; undersized; brindle color; more than 50% white; walleye
Reported Disorders: 12, 27, 36, 37, 45, 50, 54, 58, 67, 69, 82, 85, 87, 115, 126, 151, 157, 174, 175, 207, 208, 246, 260, 262

Breed: SHIBA INU
Female: normal
Male: normal; eager breeders
Litter Size: 4
Birth Weight: 8–10 oz.

Motherhood: normal; free whelpers, although may go early; good moms
Standard Deviations: missing teeth
Reported Disorders: 115, 126, 174, 218

Breed: SHIH TZU
Female: irregular cycles; may not stand the first time
Male: sometimes "rough up" bitches; may be shorter than females
Litter Size: 3–6
Birth Weight: 4–6 oz.
Motherhood: free whelpers, but long (may be 6 hr. until live pup)
Dewclaws: Remove all.
Standard Deviations: unpigmented nose &/or eye rims; blue eyes
Reported Disorders: 27, 38, 60, 78, 131, 173, 205, 208, 209

Breed: SIBERIAN HUSKY
Female: often difficult; muzzle & assistant should be available
Male: normal; eager
Litter Size: 3–7
Birth Weight: 12–16 oz.
Motherhood: free whelpers, but slow (10–12 hr. for 6 pups common); may deteriorate in condition while nursing
Dewclaws: Remove all.
Reported Disorders: 28, 40, 45, 50, 69, 71, 78, 85, 103, 115, 138, 139, 151, 173, 208, 258

Breed: SILKY TERRIER
Female: silent heats common; false pregnancies common
Male: normal
Litter Size: 3–4
Birth Weight: 5–6 oz.
Motherhood: eclampsia may be problem during pregnancy; C-secs. sometimes necessary
Dewclaws: Remove all.
Tails: docked; leave ⅓ (⅛ in. past the tan mark)
Reported Disorders: 12, 27, 38, 50, 62, 82, 106, 117, 162, 174, 244

Breed: SKYE TERRIER

Female: normal
Male: normal
Litter Size: 6
Birth Weight: 8–10 oz.
Motherhood: free whelpers, although may be slow; good moms
Standard Deviations: kinked tail end; missing teeth; malocclusions
Reported Disorders: 96, 126, 137, 139, 255

Breed: SOFT-COATED WHEATEN TERRIER

Female: normal
Male: normal
Litter Size: 4–7
Birth Weight: 4–11 oz.
Motherhood: free whelpers, but make sure they're done
Dewclaws: Remove all.
Tails: docked; leave ⅔ (if short back & thick tail) or ½ (if long back & thin tail)—in general, leave ½ of tail plus ¼ in.
Ears: Glue ears into proper position if they are "flying" at 12 wk.
Standard Deviations: light eyes; lack of proper wheaten color; malocclusions; missing teeth; oversized
Reported Disorders: 27, 115, 205, 208, 262

Breed: SPINONE ITALIANO

Female: normal
Male: normal
Litter Size: 8–10
Birth Weight: 16 oz.
Motherhood: free whelpers; good moms
Dewclaws: Remove all.
Tails: docked; leave a generous ⅓ of tail
Reported Disorders: 72, 78, 115

Breed: STAFFORDSHIRE BULL TERRIER

Female: normal
Male: normal
Litter Size: 7

Birth Weight: 8 oz.
Motherhood: free whelpers; good moms
Standard Deviations: malocclusions
Reported Disorders: 28, 38, 78, 208

Breed: STANDARD POODLE

Female: late puberty (14–18 mo.); otherwise normal
Male: normal; eager early
Litter Size: 6–12
Birth Weight: 16 oz.
Motherhood: free whelpers; good moms
Dewclaws: Remove all.
Tails: docked; leave about ½ of tail (almost to top of head)
Standard Deviations: malocclusions; parti-colored
Reported Disorders: 28, 55, 67, 78, 82, 101, 115, 118, 122, 131, 133, 151, 168, 175, 205, 208, 213, 251, 262

Breed: STANDARD SCHNAUZER

Female: normal
Male: normal
Litter Size: 6–8
Birth Weight: 7–12 oz.
Motherhood: normal
Dewclaws: Remove all.
Tails: docked just at end of tan (lighter color) mark
Ears: cropped at 6–8 wk., slightly longer than for Miniature Pinschers; graceful, w. no bell
Standard Deviations: late eruption of teeth; malocclusions
Reported Disorders: 27, 28, 42, 115, 198

Breed: SUSSEX SPANIEL

Female: skipped seasons or one estrus/ yr.; variable ovulation
Male: frequent low libido; at kennel w. bitch, check for hypothyroidism &/or give testosterone shot 2–4 da. prior to breeding date
Litter Size: 2–8
Birth Weight: 9–14 oz.
Motherhood: never leave them alone; may not cut cord, etc.; good moms;

many losses in first 2 wk. due to genetic problems; slow-developing pups; late eye opening, etc.
Dewclaws: Remove all.
Tails: docked; leave nearly ½
Standard Deviations: malocclusions
Reported Disorders: 27, 115, 126, 131, 234

Breed: TIBETAN MASTIFF
Female: normal; cycle once/yr. in fall
Male: normal
Litter Size: 7–8 (more males than females)
Birth Weight: less than 12 oz., but grow VERY rapidly
Motherhood: free whelpers; rough & protective; dam may cull & wean pups herself
Dewclaws: Remove rears only.
Reported Disorders: 115, 121

Breed: TIBETAN SPANIEL
Female: normal; once per year
Male: normal
Litter Size: 3–4
Birth Weight: 4–5 oz.
Motherhood: free whelpers, but NEED owners
Standard Deviations: Underbites are normal.
Reported Disorders: 151, 208, 251

Breed: TIBETAN TERRIER
Female: slow to mature; some silent heats
Male: normal; eager early
Litter Size: 5 (more males than females)
Birth Weight: 7–8 oz.
Motherhood: normal; free whelpers (55–65 da.); good moms
Dewclaws: Usually remove all.
Standard Deviations: slow teeth eruption; missing teeth; malocclusions; poor pigment
Reported Disorders: 13, 27, 115, 126, 139, 203, 208, 262

Breed: TOY POODLE
Female: sometimes canal too short & small for normal tie
Male: good; may have to be elevated if smaller than female
Litter Size: 2–3
Birth Weight: 3–6 oz.
Motherhood: generally free whelpers, unless pups very tiny or a single-pup litter; good moms unless nervous
Dewclaws: Remove all.
Tails: docked; leave nearly ⅔ (wait until 5–7 da. if very tiny)
Standard Deviations: oversized; gay tails; malocclusions; parti-colored
Reported Disorders: 12, 13, 28, 38, 55, 67, 69, 117, 118, 134, 174, 175, 187, 208, 210, 244

Breed: VIZSLA
Female: normal
Male: normal; may be reluctant w. owners around
Litter Size: 6–8
Birth Weight: 10–14 oz.
Motherhood: free whelpers; good moms; protective
Dewclaws: Remove all.
Tails: docked; leave a generous ⅔
Standard Deviations: very light eyes; black nose; too much white on body; malocclusions
Reported Disorders: 28, 47, 50, 72, 78, 82, 85, 88, 115, 169, 172, 208, 262

Breed: WEIMARANER
Female: normal
Male: eager breeders; males don't tolerate one another
Litter Size: 6–9
Birth Weight: 10–16 oz.
Motherhood: free whelpers; good moms; pups often born with dark stripe down back that will go away
Dewclaws: Remove all.
Tails: docked; leave about ½ (1½ in., at taper or to cover genitals)

Standard Deviations: long coats; pink eye &/or nose pigment; white markings; malocclusions
Reported Disorders: 50, 59, 67, 78, 85, 86, 101, 115, 121, 124, 146, 161, 183, 186, 208, 235, 242, 247, 251, 252

Breed: WELSH SPRINGER SPANIEL
Female: normal
Male: normal
Litter Size: 4–6
Birth Weight: 8–12 oz.
Motherhood: free whelpers; good moms
Dewclaws: Remove all.
Tails: docked; leave ⅓
Standard Deviations: malocclusions
Reported Disorders: 16, 27, 82, 103, 115, 208

Breed: WELSH TERRIER
Female: normal
Male: normal
Litter Size: 5–6
Birth Weight: 4–9 oz.
Motherhood: normal; good moms
Dewclaws: Remove all.
Tails: docked; leave ¾ (even w. top of head—for thick tail, a bit longer; for thin tail, a bit shorter)
Reported Disorders: 27, 67, 103, 139, 174

Breed: WEST HIGHLAND WHITE TERRIER
Female: normal
Male: lazy; not always eager
Litter Size: 3–4
Birth Weight: 6 oz.
Motherhood: slow, lazy whelpers; some C-secs. due to prolonged time or small pelvis of dam; a few indifferent moms
Dewclaws: Remove all.
Tails: DO NOT DOCK.
Ears: Clip hair at 12 wk. & tape at 20 wk. if ears not up.
Standard Deviations: mismarks; lack of nose pigment; retained baby teeth; malocclusions

Reported Disorders: 12, 13, 27, 28, 38, 44, 47, 50, 104, 115, 117, 126, 130, 134, 139, 151, 155, 174, 201, 214

Breed: WHIPPET
Female: normal; late puberty
Male: normal
Litter Size: 4–8
Birth Weight: 8–12 oz.
Motherhood: very few problems
Dewclaws: Remove all.
Standard Deviations: light eyes; malocclusions; hypersensitivity to barbiturates & insecticides
Reported Disorders: 27, 39, 41, 50, 70, 139, 208

Breed: WIREHAIRED POINTING GRIFFON
Female: normal; puberty usu. over 1 yr.
Male: mature sexually very early; territorial
Litter Size: 8
Birth Weight: 13–16 oz.
Motherhood: easy whelpers; excellent moms
Dewclaws: Remove all.
Tails: docked; leave ½ to ⅔
Standard Deviations: oversized; coat too short & harsh; coat too long & soft
Reported Disorders: 72, 78, 115

Breed: YORKSHIRE TERRIER
Female: normal
Male: normal; eager
Litter Size: 1–4
Birth Weight: 4–6 oz.
Motherhood: want owners to help; inertia & eclampsia frequent; 20% C-secs.
Dewclaws: Remove all.
Tails: docked; leave ½ in. (or just beyond tan mark)
Ears: Clip hair if not up by 12 wk.
Standard Deviations: no fading (failure of black hair to turn steel-gray by 1 yr.); malocclusions; retained baby teeth
Reported Disorders: 8, 12, 27, 39, 50, 67, 76, 117, 123, 130, 134, 162, 174, 190, 191, 208, 210, 212, 244

APPENDIX II

Disorders

1. Achalasia
Other Names: idiopathic (or primary) megaesophagus; dilated esophagus
Description: esophagus dilated down to stomach from lack of proper nerves; begin vomiting food at weaning
Inheritance: autosomal recessive

2. Achlorhydria
Description: lack of adequate hydrochloric acid in stomach for digestion; chronic vomiting
Inheritance: unknown

3. Achondroplasia
Other Names: dwarfism
Description: abnormally shortened & bent long bones; "normal" in many breeds (e.g., Basset Hounds)
Inheritance: autosomal recessive

4. Acrodermatitis
Other Names: congenital zinc deficiency
Description: crusty, oozing skin; due to inherent inability to use zinc
Inheritance: autosomal recessive

5. Afghan Myelomalacia
Other Names: necrotizing myelopathy
Description: beginning by 1 yr., rapid onset of severe ataxia & paralysis
Inheritance: autosomal recessive

6. Amyloidosis
Other Names: swollen dock syndrome; familial Shar Pei fever
Description: early fever & swollen joints; leads to amyloid deposits in kidneys & other organs; often leads to renal failure by 4–6 yr.
Inheritance: autosomal recessive

7. Amyotrophic Lateral Sclerosis
Other Names: Lou Gehrig's disease; canine spinal muscular atrophy
Description: ataxia & abnormal gait at 1–8 mo.; may progress to complete paralysis
Inheritance: dominant w. variable expression

8. Anasarca
Other Names: walrus puppy; rubber puppy; water puppy

Description: usually lethal lymphedema of newborns; huge size (often 3 lb.) requires C-sec.
Inheritance: autosomal recessive

9. Anury
Description: lack of tail at birth (called brachury when just a stub)
Inheritance: autosomal recessive

10. Aphakia
Description: absence of the lens in the eye, often associated w. other eye abnormalities
Inheritance: autosomal recessive

11. Aplasia Cutis
Other Names: epitheliogenesis imperfecta
Description: skin defects present at birth; various body areas not covered by normal skin
Inheritance: unknown

12. Aseptic Necrosis of the Femoral Head
Other Names: Legg-Calvé-Perthes disease
Description: improper blood supply to femoral head leads to degeneration of hip joint, limping & pain; most common in smaller breeds & Terriers
Inheritance: autosomal recessive

13. Atopic Dermatitis
Other Names: contact or inhalent skin allergies
Description: itching & self-mutilation after antibody response in skin; immune-mediated
Inheritance: unknown

14. Atrial Septal Defect
Description: born w. hole between 2 upper heart chambers; heart murmur; weakness; severe lack of oxygen
Inheritance: polygenic

15. Autoimmune Hemolytic Anemia
Other Names: AHA
Description: severe & potentially fatal destruction of red blood cells by the body's own defenses; immune-mediated
Inheritance: unknown

16. Azospermia
Description: spermatogenic arrest; sudden sterility; may be immune-mediated
Inheritance: unknown

17. Bithoracic Ectromelia
Description: lack of front legs (scapula is the only foreleg bone present)
Inheritance: autosomal recessive

18. Black Hair Follicular Dysplasia
Description: black-haired areas are scaly, w. hair that is thin, dull & broken off; white/brown areas are normal
Inheritance: unknown

19. Borzoi Retinopathy
Description: retinal degeneration by 1–5 yr.; may lead to blindness
Inheritance: familial (more males than females) but still unknown

20. Brachygnathia
Other Names: overbite; overshot jaw; parrot mouth; shark jaw
Description: upper jaw is longer than lower jaw, which creates a malocclusion
Inheritance: unknown

21. Briard Retinopathy
Other Names: progressive retinal degeneration; stationary night blindness
Description: night blindness by 9 wk.; nystagmus; may not progress
Inheritance: familial (autosomal recessive suspected)

22. Calcinosis Circumscripta
Other Names: calcium gout
Description: lumps in skin caused by calcium deposits
Inheritance: unknown

23. Cardiomyopathy
Description: damaged heart muscle leads to lung edema, cough & weakness; often lethal
Inheritance: polygenic; threshold

24. Carpal Subluxation
Description: wrists congenitally out of joint; first appears at 3 wk.; this gene is allelic to (in the same place on a chromosome as) the gene for hemophilia A
Inheritance: recessive; sex-linked

25. Cataract, Unilateral
Description: lens opacity, occurring in only 1 eye
Inheritance: unknown

26. Cataract, with Microphthalmia
Description: cataract associated w. abnormally small eyes, often present at birth
Inheritance: unknown

27. Cataracts, Bilateral
Other Names: triangular subcapsular cataracts
Description: opaque lenses develop in both eyes, usually after 2 yr.
Inheritance: autosomal dominant (incomplete penetrance)

28. Cataracts, Juvenile
Description: bilateral lens opacities by age of 6 yr.; may lead to blindness
Inheritance: autosomal recessive

29. Cerebellar Abiotrophy
Other Names: neuronal abiotrophy; cerebellar degeneration
Description: starts at 8 wk.; progressive weakness leading to total paralysis
Inheritance: autosomal recessive

30. Cerebellar Degeneration
Description: cerebellum degenerates; may be static or progressive
Inheritance: unknown

31. Cerebellar Hypoplasia
Description: abnormal gait & lack of body control; present at birth & nonprogressive
Inheritance: unknown

32. Cerebrospinal Demyelinization
Other Names: ataxia
Description: progressive loss of spinal cord nerve covering; exhibit inability to coordinate voluntary muscular movements, leading to paralysis, at 2 to 4 mo.
Inheritance: unknown

33. Ceroid Lipofuscinosis
Other Names: juvenile amaurotic idiocy; Batten disease; neuronal ceroid lipofuscinosis
Description: begins by 2 yr. of age; symptoms include visual impairment, ataxia, personality changes, seizures and/or paresis; due to lack of brain enzyme
Inheritance: autosomal recessive

34. Cervical Vertebral Instability
Other Names: CVI; wobbler syndrome; spondylomyelopathy
Description: unstable vertebrae in lower neck; weakness and ataxia; may lead to paralysis; usually at C3–C7 (in Basset, Hounds, at C2–C3)
Inheritance: unknown

35. Cherry Eye
Other Names: hypertrophy and prolapse of the nictitating membrane gland
Description: red, swollen gland at inner corner of eye in puppy; irritating; usually requires surgery
Inheritance: unknown

36. Chondrodysplasia
Other Names: dwarfism
Description: shortened, deformed front legs, w. downhill stance
Inheritance: autosomal recessive

37. Choroidal Hypoplasia
Description: mild abnormality of central retina; may be symptomless
Inheritance: unknown

38. Cleft Lip/Cleft Palate
Other Names: harelip
Description: nonclosure of bones & soft tissue of upper jaw &/or roof of mouth; present at birth
Inheritance: autosomal recessive

39. Coliform Enteritis
Other Names: immunoproliferative small intestinal disease
Description: persistent, nervous diarrhea; may be immune-mediated
Inheritance: unknown

40. Colobomas
Description: pitted areas of retina near optic disk; asymptomatic
Inheritance: may not be hereditary

41. Color-Mutant Alopecia
Other Names: blue-dog dermatitis
Description: hyperkeratinization & alopecia associated w. the *dd* (dilute) color gene seen in both blues (dilute of black) and fawns (light gray dilute of red)
Inheritance: autosomal recessive

42. Comedo Syndrome
Other Names: Schnauzer bumps
Description: crusts on back due to plugged hair follicles; itching
Inheritance: complex

43. Congenital Nystagmus
Description: eyes flick back and forth uncontrollably
Inheritance: unknown

44. Copper-Associated Hepatopathy
Other Names: chronic active hepatitis; copper toxicosis; Wilson's disease
Description: selective accumulation of copper in liver; leads to inevitable liver failure
Inheritance: autosomal recessive

45. Corneal Dystrophy
Other Names: corneal leukoma
Description: white patches on eye surface
Inheritance: autosomal recessive

46. Corneal Ulcer
Other Names: indolent ulcer; recurrent corneal erosion; ulcerative keratitis
Description: superficial erosion of cornea; resistant to treatment & often recurs; may be more common in spayed females
Inheritance: unknown

47. Craniomandibular Osteopathy
Other Names: CMO; lion jaw; hog jaw
Description: thickened lower jaw; victims have fever & pain & can't move jaw; usually outgrow it, but if not, they starve
Inheritance: autosomal recessive

48. Cranioschisis
Other Names: cranial dysraphism
Description: congenital fissures in skull bones, brain & membranes herniate through
Inheritance: autosomal recessive (lethal)

49. Cricopharyngeal Achalasia
Description: spasm of muscles in pharynx; can't swallow solid food; mostly seen in Toys
Inheritance: autosomal dominant

50. Cryptorchidism
Other Names: undescended testicle(s)
Description: bilaterals sterile; unilaterals fertile but barred from showing; widespread in many breeds
Inheritance: threshold; recessive (?)

51. Cutaneous Asthenia
Other Names: Ehlers-Danlos syndrome,

dominant collagen dysplasia, dermatosparaxis
Description: loose, stretchy, & fragile skin that is easily torn
Inheritance: autosomal dominant

52. Cyclic Hematopoiesis
Other Names: cyclic neutropenia, gray Collie syndrome
Description: lethal; cycles of low white blood cell counts lead to overwhelming infections; associated w. the silver/gray gene in Collies; can also occur in other breeds
Inheritance: autosomal recessive

53. Cystinuria
Description: high cystine excreted in urine; prone to stone formation; symptoms seen only in males
Inheritance: recessive; sex-linked

54. Deafness, Dominant
Description: born without ability to hear in either one or both ears; does not occur in heterozygote
Inheritance: autosomal dominant (in homozygous merles)

55. Deafness, Recessive
Description: born unable to hear in either one or both ears; often associated w. white color, especially white heads & ears
Inheritance: autosomal recessive

56. Degenerative Myelopathy
Other Names: chronic degenerative radiculomyelopathy
Description: muscle wasting & progressive ataxia of rear; pain-free
Inheritance: genetic predisposition

57. Demodectic Mange, Generalized
Other Names: red mange; puppy mange
Description: generalized mange unresponsive to therapy; secondary infections; may be immune-mediated
Inheritance: unknown

58. Dermatomyositis
Other Names: epidermolysis bullosa (if in skin only)
Description: inflammation of skin (leading to hair loss, scaling & scarring) & muscle (leading to weakness & atrophy)
Inheritance: autosomal dominant w. variable expression

59. Dermoid
Other Names: corneal dermoid cyst
Description: congenital cyst on cornea; contains skin, glands & hair
Inheritance: unclear

60. Dermoid Sinus
Description: tubelike cyst into back; may communicate w. spinal cord
Inheritance: autosomal recessive

61. Diabetes Insipidus
Other Names: water diabetes
Description: extreme polydipsia/polyuria (abnormal thirst & urination); origin from either kidneys or pituitary gland
Inheritance: unknown

62. Diabetes Mellitus, Adult Onset
Other Names: sugar diabetes
Description: lowered insulin production; predisposed in some breeds
Inheritance: unknown

63. Diabetes Mellitus, Juvenile Onset
Other Names: sugar diabetes
Description: onset of insulin deficiency at 2 to 6 mo.
Inheritance: autosomal recessive

64. Diaphragmatic Hernia
Description: Abdominal contents are continuous w. either chest cavity or heart sac.
Inheritance: unknown

65. Digital Hyperkeratosis
Description: early onset of pad

overgrowth, pad splitting & pain; pads
become infected
Inheritance: unknown

66. Dislocated Hips
Description: born w. hips out of sockets
Inheritance: complex

67. Distichiasis
Other Names: double eyelashes
Description: extra row of eyelashes,
usually on lower lid but also on upper;
irritates cornea; causes tearing
Inheritance: unknown

68. Dysmyelination
Description: abnormal brain/spine
covering; various nervous signs; may
not be progressive
Inheritance: unknown

69. Ectasia Syndrome
Other Names: Collie eye anomaly
Description: symptoms range from
choroidal hypoplasia to optic nerve
coloboma to retinal detachment; occurs
in several breeds
Inheritance: autosomal recessive

70. Ectodermal Defect
Other Names: hypotrichosis
Description: appearance of symmetrical
areas of thin hairless or partially haired
skin; covers up to 2/3 of body
Inheritance: unknown

71. Ectopic Ureter
Description: unilateral or bilateral,
usually female; urine dribbling since
birth or weaning
Inheritance: unclear; familial

72. Ectropion
Other Names: loose eyelids
Description: hanging lower lids
accumulate irritants & create red,
inflamed eyes; common in many breeds
Inheritance: unclear

73. Elbow Hygroma
Other Names: elbow bursitis
Description: fluid-filled, saclike
enlargement on side of elbows
Inheritance: unknown

74. Elbow Joint Deformity
Description: deformed articular surface of
the elbow joint
Inheritance: unknown

75. Elongated Soft Palate/Stenotic Nares
Description: pinched nostrils &
obstructed airway; snoring; gagging;
exercise intolerance; common in
brachycephalic breeds but not exclusive
Inheritance: unknown

76. Enchondromatosis
Description: multiple cartilage bumps on
bones near joints; if severe, can cause
lameness
Inheritance: unknown

77. Enostosis
Other Names: juvenile osteomyelitis,
panostitis, "pano"
Description: acute, shifting lameness of
large, growing dogs; deep bone pain;
self-limiting
Inheritance: unclear

78. Entropion
Other Names: diamond eye
Description: eyelids roll in; hair rubs on
cornea; effects are irritation, tearing &
visual losses from scarring; occurs in
many breeds
Inheritance: polygenic

79. Eosinophilic Colitis
Other Names: ulcerative colitis
Description: bouts of chronic colitis
associated w. eosinophilia
Inheritance: unknown

80. Eosinophilic Myositis
Other Names: masticatory myositis
Description: degeneration of upper jaw

muscles; can't open mouth; immune-mediated; treatable w. early recognition
Inheritance: unknown

81. Epidermal Dysplasia
Description: keratin defect; starts w. red skin & itching; later skin darkens & becomes seborrheic
Inheritance: unknown

82. Epilepsy
Description: recurrent seizures, w. onset at 1 to 3 yr.; some epilepsy is not hereditary
Inheritance: complex; recessive (in some breeds)

83. Epiphyseal Dysplasia
Description: bone growth disorder; causes sagging, swaying rear legs
Inheritance: autosomal recessive

84. Esophageal Diverticula
Description: pouches in esophagus; causes vomiting or gagging; considered "normal" in Bulldog pups
Inheritance: unknown

85. Factor VIII Deficiency
Other Names: hemophilia A; AHF
Description: slowed clotting time; prolonged bleeding at tail docking, hematomas, etc.
Inheritance: recessive; sex-linked

86. Factor XI Deficiency
Description: minor bleeding disorder; potentially severe after trauma or surgery
Inheritance: autosomal dominant; incomplete penetrance

87. Factor IX Deficiency
Other Names: hemophilia B; PTT deficiency; Christmas disease
Description: prolonged bleeding time; heterozygotes bleed more than in hemophilia A
Inheritance: recessive; sex-linked

88. Factor I Deficiency
Other Names: fibrinogen deficiency; hypofibrinogenemia
Description: lamenesses; nose bleeds; surgery or trauma may result in fatal hemorrhage
Inheritance: autosomal dominant (incomplete penetrance?)

89. Factor VII Deficiency
Description: no detectable bleeding, but may be bruising or prolonged postsurgical bleeding
Inheritance: autosomal recessive (also reported as an incomplete dominant [?])

90. Factor X Deficiency
Other Names: Stuart-Prower syndrome
Description: severe bleeding in newborns & young adults; homozygotes are usually stillborn or die within weeks; heterozygotes have mild to severe bleeding but may live
Inheritance: autosomal dominant; incomplete penetrance

91. Factor XII Deficiency
Description: no bleeding; prone to infections &/or thrombosis (clot formation)
Inheritance: unknown

92. Factor II Deficiency
Other Names: hypoprothrombinemia
Description: clotting disorder, usually associated w. nosebleeds & gum bleeding
Inheritance: unknown

93. Fanconi's syndrome
Description: renal tubules degenerate, leak sugar then proteins & salts in urine; leads to complete renal failure
Inheritance: autosomal recessive

94. Flank Sucking
Description: bizarre, repetitive behavior of sucking on a flank
Inheritance: unknown

95. Fly-Biting Syndrome

Description: dogs jump up & snap at imaginary flies; may be associated w. low-grade epilepsy
Inheritance: unknown

96. Foramen Magnum Dysplasia

Description: malformed occipital bone next to skull creates pressure on brain stem; can include hydrocephalus
Inheritance: unknown

97. Fragmented Choronoid Process

Other Names: FCP
Description: bony processes of upper radius fragment; causes front lameness; usually requires surgery
Inheritance: polygenic

98. Friedreich's Ataxia

Description: sclerosis of lower spinal cord; ataxia
Inheritance: unknown

99. Fucosidosis

Description: begins at 1 to 3 yr.; symptoms include change in temperament, seizures, visual deficits, tremors, imbalance, deafness, circling, head pressing, jaw champing & other bizarre behavior
Inheritance: autosomal recessive

100. Gangliosidosis

Other Names: amaurotic idiocy, Tay-Sachs disease, Norman-landing disease, Derry's disease, Sandhoff's disease
Description: born normal; retarded & blind by 1 yr.; symptoms range from staggering to seizures; caused by congenital lack of necessary brain enzymes
Inheritance: autosomal recessive

101. Gastric Torsion

Other Names: GDV, bloat/torsion, twisted stomach
Description: stomach rotates on long axis; causes shock & death; usu. in deep chested, narrow &/or tucked-up breeds
Inheritance: unknown

102. Gingival Hyperplasia

Description: gums respond to chronic periodontal disease by thickening & overgrowing teeth
Inheritance: unknown

103. Glaucoma, Primary

Other Names: congenital glaucoma
Description: increased fluid pressure in globe leads to pain, eye destruction & blindness
Inheritance: autosomal recessive

104. Globoid Cell Leukodystrophy

Other Names: Krabbe's disease
Description: progressive stiffness & ataxia due to lack of brain enzyme
Inheritance: autosomal recessive

105. Glossopharyngeal Defect

Other Names: bird tongue
Description: abnormally shaped tongue creates inability to swallow
Inheritance: autosomal recessive (lethal)

106. Glucocerebrosidosis

Other Names: Gaucher's disease
Description: begins by 6 mo.; symptoms include severe incoordination, stiff gait, tremors & hypermetria (exaggerated movements beyond their grain)
Inheritance: unknown

107. Glycogenosis

Other Names: glycogen storage disease; Cori's disease
Description: low blood sugar due to inherent liver enzyme deficiency; causes weakness & liver enlargement & destruction
Inheritance: autosomal recessive

108. Goiter
Description: enlarged thyroid gland
Inheritance: autosomal dominant

109. Granulocytopathy
Description: abnormal neutrophils can't
fight bacteria; stunted growth &
constant infections
Inheritance: unknown

110. Hairlessness, Dominant
Description: occurs only in heterozygote;
homozygote combination lethal;
associated w. abnormal mouth & teeth,
e.g., Mexican Hairless, Peruvian Inca
Orchid & Chinese Crested breeds
Inheritance: autosomal dominant

111. Hairlessness, Recessive
Other Names: alopecia universalis
Description: congenital lack of hair
follicles, i.e., American Hairless
Terrier; not associated w. other
abnormalities
Inheritance: autosomal recessive

112. Hemeralopia
Other Names: day blindness
Description: reduced ability to see in
bright light
Inheritance: autosomal recessive

113. Hermaphrodite, True
Other Names: chimera
Description: both ovaries & testes;
usually appears as a female externally,
w. enlarged clitoris
Inheritance: XX/XY or *XX/XXY*

114. Hiatal Hernia
Description: poor ligament attachment
allows part of stomach to bulge into
chest cavity; tendency in
brachycephalic breeds
Inheritance: unknown

115. Hip Dysplasia
Other Names: CHD
Description: progressive developmental

deformity of hip joints; mild to
crippling
Inheritance: polygenic; threshold (?)

116. Histiocytosis
Description: reticuloendothelial
dysfunction leads to histiocytic
accumulation in various organs;
probably immune-mediated
Inheritance: unclear

117. Hydrocephalus
Other Names: water on the brain
Description: increased fluid pressure
within skull damages & destroys brain
tissue; sometimes associated w. open
fontanels
Inheritance: polygenic; complex

118. Hyperadrenocorticism
Other Names: Cushing's syndrome
Description: excess cortisone; symptoms
include potbelly, hair loss, weakness &
increased thirst; from functional tumor
of either adrenal or pituitary gland
Inheritance: unknown

119. Hyperchylomicronemia
Description: lack of digestive enzyme;
high triglycerides; abdominal distress;
polyneuropathies
Inheritance: unknown

120. Hypertrophic Neuropathy
Description: nerve degeneration begins at
8 wk.; progresses to tetraplegia (total
paralysis)
Inheritance: unknown

121. Hypertrophic Osteodystrophy
Other Names: HOD
Description: painful, swollen joints &
bones; fever; may outgrow it but often
left w. bone deformities; most
prevalent in giant breeds; may be
associated w. oversupplementation
Inheritance: unknown

122. Hypoadrenocorticism

Other Names: Addison's disease
Description: weakness; salt & fluid imbalances; congenital form probably lethal
Inheritance: autosomal recessive (in some breeds)

123. Hypoglycemia, Neonatal

Other Names: juvenile hypoglycemia
Description: sudden low blood sugar due to stress; ataxia & convulsions; outgrow it; most common in tiny Toy puppies
Inheritance: unknown

124. Hypomyelinogenesis

Description: born w. improper nerve covering; tremors & incoordination; may improve & even be normal by 1 yr.
Inheritance: recessive; sex-linked

125. Hypospadia

Description: abnormally developed penis & sheath; may be associated w. other abnormalities
Inheritance: unknown

126. Hypothyroidism, Acquired

Description: thin, poor hair coat; reproductive problems; obesity; may be immune-mediated
Inheritance: unknown

127. Hypothyroidism, Congenital

Description: congenital TSH (thyroid stimulating hormone) & iodine deficiency; usually lethal
Inheritance: unclear

128. Ichthyosis

Other Names: fishskin disease
Description: scalelike thickening of skin; present at birth & progresses
Inheritance: unknown

129. Immune Deficiencies

Description: ineffective immune response; variety of problems
Inheritance: probably more than one disease

130. Inguinal Hernia

Other Names: rupture
Description: abdominal contents bulge out under skin in groin; most common in females, but does occur in males occasionally
Inheritance: threshold

131. Intervertebral Disk Disease

Other Names: slipped disk; herniated disk
Description: disks herniate & press on nerves & cord; causes pain, weakness or paralysis, mostly in neck or lower back
Inheritance: complex

132. Intestinal Lymphangiectasia

Description: Malformed lymph channels in intestine lead to protein-losing enteropathy & death from starvation.
Inheritance: unknown

133. Iris Atrophy

Description: Iris in eye deteriorates.
Inheritance: unknown

134. Keratitis Sicca

Other Names: keratoconjunctivitis sicca; KCS; dry eye; xerophthalmia
Description: lack of or loss of ability to produce tears; leads to eye damage & potential blindness
Inheritance: unknown

135. Kidney Aplasia

Other Names: renal agenesis
Description: born w. only 1 or neither kidney; usually fatal; one of the recognized causes of fading puppy syndrome
Inheritance: unknown

136. Lacrimal Duct Atresia

Other Names: nasolacrimal duct atresia
Description: improper ducts drain eye; tears spill down face
Inheritance: unknown

137. Laryngeal Hypoplasia
Other Names: collapsed larynx
Description: voice box improperly developed; may collapse & cause a variety of breathing difficulties
Inheritance: Autosomal recessive

138. Laryngeal Paralysis
Description: larynx can't open properly; have muted bark, cough & later roaring inspiration
Inheritance: autosomal dominant

139. Lens Luxation
Description: lens slips out of position; leads to secondary glaucoma
Inheritance: autosomal recessive

140. Leukoencephalomyelopathy
Description: beginning at 1–3 yr., demyelinization of brain & cord, incoordination & possibly total paralysis
Inheritance: familial but unknown

141. Lissencephaly
Description: born w. few if any convolutions in brain; severe retardation
Inheritance: unknown

142. Lymphoedema
Description: pitting edema of hind legs in pups; usually outgrow it, but occasionally can be fatal
Inheritance: autosomal dominant

143. Macrocytic Anemia
Description: associated w. chondroplastic dwarfs; pleiotropic effect of dwarf gene
Inheritance: autosomal recessive

144. Malabsorption Syndrome
Description: congenital or acquired inability to absorb digested food; leads to inevitable starvation
Inheritance: unknown

145. Marfan's Syndrome
Description: displaced eye lens; thin, elongated toes (spider toes); heart problems
Inheritance: autosomal dominant

146. Mastocytoma
Other Names: mast cell tumor
Description: malignant & often rapidly spreading nodular skin tumors
Inheritance: unknown

147. Melanoma
Description: malignant tumor of pigment cells, often dark in color, in mouth or on skin; invades rapidly
Inheritance: unknown

148. Methemoglobinemia
Description: blood enzyme deficiency; brown mucous membranes; blood doesn't turn red in air; weakness
Inheritance: unknown

149. Microcheilia
Description: abnormally small mouth opening
Inheritance: unknown

150. Microcytosis
Other Names: familial microcytosis
Description: blood cells too small; can't fight infection
Inheritance: unknown

151. Microphthalmia
Other Names: microphthalmos
Description: very small globe; usually associated w. 1 or more other eye abnormalities
Inheritance: unknown

152. Microphthalmia w. Colobomas
Description: born w. small, nonfunctional eyes; does not occur in the heterozygote
Inheritance: autosomal dominant (homozygous merles)

153. Mitral Valve Malformation
Other Names: mitral valve defect
Description: defect in valve between

upper & lower heart chambers; heart murmur & weakness
Inheritance: complex

154. Myasthenia Gravis (Congenital)
Description: muscle disease; premature fatigue helped w. rest; megaesophagus; drooping eyelids; collapse
Inheritance: autosomal recessive

155. Myotonia
Other Names: dystrophic myopathy
Description: by 8 wk., stiff gait, muscle atrophy & swollen tongue; may not progress
Inheritance: unclear

156. Narcolepsy/Cataplexy
Description: excessive daytime sleep; periods of severe muscle weakness
Inheritance: unclear

157. Nasal Solar Dermatitis
Other Names: Collie nose
Description: sunlight hypersensitivity; blistering & erosion of nose; occurs in several breeds
Inheritance: unknown

158. Neuroaxonal Dystrophy
Other Names: NAD
Description: abnormal development of cells in brain; signs vary as to area of brain affected
Inheritance: autosomal recessive

159. Neuronal Degeneration
Description: born normal; show ataxia, tremors, abnormal behavior & seizures by 3 to 6 mo.
Inheritance: unknown

160. Neurotropic Osteopathy
Other Names: sensory neuronopathy
Description: brain disease associated w. ataxia, urinary incontinence, gastrointestinal dysfunction & self-mutilation of extremities
Inheritance: autosomal recessive

161. Nictitating Membrane Eversion
Description: haw has poor attachments; cartilage is rolled; everts, showing red swelling & curved cartilage
Inheritance: autosomal recessive (uncertain)

162. Odontoid Process Dysplasia
Other Names: atlantoaxial subluxation; hypoplasia of dens
Description: lack of firm fusion between first & second neck vertebrae; cord pressure; mild pain to paralysis; occurs mostly in Toys
Inheritance: unknown

163. Oligodendroglioma
Description: slow-growing, benign brain tumor
Inheritance: unknown

164. Oligodontia
Description: congenital lack of many or most teeth
Inheritance: autosomal recessive

165. Optic Nerve Hypoplasia
Description: lack of development of optic nerve; blindness only if bilateral
Inheritance: unknown

166. Osteochondritis Dessicans
Other Names: OCD
Description: growth disorder of joints; cartilage death, pain & lameness; may occur in many joints
Inheritance: polygenic, plus nutritional factors

167. Osteochondrosis, Spinal
Other Names: runners
Description: bone & cartilage degeneration in back; arched back; stilted gait; hips higher than shoulders
Inheritance: unknown

168. Osteogenesis Imperfecta
Other Names: snowshoe feet
Description: abnormal bone development;

flat feet; elbows out; knockknee; loose ligaments
Inheritance: unclear

169. Osteogenic Sarcoma
Other Names: osteosarcoma
Description: malignant bone tumor; more frequent in giant breeds
Inheritance: unclear

170. Osteopetrosis
Description: bones too solid; lack marrow space; leads to fewer blood cells
Inheritance: unknown

171. Otocephalic Syndrome
Other Names: otocephaly
Description: low-grade form has no jaw & hydrocephalus; high-grade form has no structures anterior to brain stem; very rare
Inheritance: autosomal recessive

172. Pancreatic Hypoplasia
Other Names: pancreatic atrophy; chronic pancreatitis
Description: lack of digestive enzymes; gray, greasy feces; chronic wt. loss despite huge appetite; insulin-producing cells usually remain normal
Inheritance: autosomal recessive

173. Pannus
Description: blood vessels & pigment migrate over cornea; can lead to blindness; usual form starts laterally & moves inward; "atypical" form begins on inside & moves outward
Inheritance: unknown

174. Patellar Luxation
Other Names: slipping kneecaps; slipped stifles
Description: poor structures that hold kneecap in place, one or both; starts at 4–6 mo.; can be medial (inward, in Toys) or lateral (outward, in Giants)
Inheritance: polygenic

175. Patent Ductus Arteriosus
Description: failure of fetal arteriovenous shunt to close soon after birth; loud heart murmur; exercise intolerance; may be lethal
Inheritance: polygenic threshold

176. Pectus Excavatum
Other Names: cobbler's chest
Description: flattened chest & curved-in breastbone
Inheritance: unknown

177. Pelger-Huët Anomaly
Other Names: Pelger-Huët Nuclear Anomaly
Description: abnormal white blood cells; homozygote has infections, bone deformities or fetal death; heterozygote may be benign
Inheritance: autosomal dominant

178. Pelvic Bladder
Description: bladder back in pelvic canal; may be asymptomatic or may cause incontinence; can be associated w. other abnormalities
Inheritance: unknown

179. Perianal Fistula
Description: open, draining tracts around anal orifice; surgical correction required
Inheritance: familial

180. Persistent Atrial Standstill
Description: slowed heart rate; dogs with symptoms of weakness will need pacemaker
Inheritance: unknown

181. Persistent Frenulum
Description: band of tissue attached to tip of penis makes it come out bowed; easy to correct surgically
Inheritance: unknown

182. Persistent Pupillary Membrane
Description: strands of tissue across

pupil; may be symptomless or may lead to opacities
Inheritance: autosomal dominant (with a range of expression)

183. Persistent Right Aortic Arch
Description: abnormal artery constricts esophagus halfway to stomach; vomiting; must be corrected surgically
Inheritance: polygenic; threshold

184. Phosphofructokinase Deficiency
Description: periodic destruction of red blood cells; mild to moderate signs
Inheritance: unknown

185. Pituitary Cysts
Description: can lead to obesity, genital atrophy & water diabetes; most common in brachycephalic breeds
Inheritance: unknown

186. Pituitary Dwarfism
Description: normally proportioned dwarf, immature & retarded; may be fatal
Inheritance: autosomal recessive

187. Plantaris Muscle Fibrosis
Other Names: hoppers
Description: certain leg muscles degenerate; dog can move only by hopping
Inheritance: unknown

188. Polycystic Kidneys
Description: fluid-filled cysts in kidneys; may be without symptoms or may lead to renal failure
Inheritance: unknown

189. Polyostotic Fibrous Dysplasia
Description: Bone cysts form in wrist area.
Inheritance: unknown

190. Portosystemic Shunt, Extrahepatic
Description: born with abnormal vessels around liver; leads to liver disease
Inheritance: unknown

191. Portosystemic Shunt, Intrahepatic
Description: born with abnormal circulation within liver; leads to liver disease
Inheritance: unknown

192. Primary Ciliary Dyskinesia
Description: bronchi lining lacks cilia; can't rid lungs of particles & microbes; many infections
Inheritance: autosomal recessive

193. Primary Uterine Inertia
Description: At term, cervix dilates, but uterine contractions never begin.
Inheritance: unknown

194. Prognathism
Other Names: underbite; undershot; Bulldog mouth
Description: lower jaw longer than upper jaw; malocclusion; desired norm in some breeds
Inheritance: unknown

195. Progressive Axonopathy
Description: rear ataxia by 8 wk.; progresses to paralysis
Inheritance: autosomal recessive

196. Pseudohermaphrodite, Female
Description: has ovaries, but internal or external genitalia appear masculine; chromosomal anomaly
Inheritance: XX

197. Pseudohermaphrodite, Male
Description: has testes, but internal & external genitalia appear like those of a female; chromosomal anomaly
Inheritance: XY

198. Pulmonic Stenosis
Description: artery from heart to lungs is narrow at its origin; right heart enlargement; heart murmur
Inheritance: polygenic; threshold

199. Pyloric Stenosis
Description: excess gastrin; spasm of stomach exit valve; projectile vomiting
Inheritance: unknown

200. Pyometra
Description: malodorous vaginal discharge; excess thirst; toxic; may be fatal
Inheritance: unknown

201. Pyruvate Kinase Deficiency
Other Names: PKD; hemolytic anemia
Description: anemia (regenerative) due to premature red blood cell destruction
Inheritance: autosomal recessive

202. Quadriplegia with Amblyopia
Description: progressive paralysis with blindness
Inheritance: autosomal recessive (lethal)

203. Radius, Premature Closure (or Radius Agenesis)
Other Names: radius curvus; bowed front
Description: early closure (or improper growth) of radius; ulna then overgrows, creating bowed front leg
Inheritance: unknown

204. Recurrent Tetany
Other Names: Scottie cramp
Description: when excited, dog has stiff gait; not progressive; occurs in several breeds
Inheritance: Autosomal recessive

205. Renal Cortical Hypoplasia
Other Names: familial renal disease
Description: degeneration of both kidneys, beginning at about 1 yr.
Inheritance: autosomal recessive

206. Renal Glucosuria
Description: defect allows leakage of glucose in urine; nonprogressive; tend to urinary infections
Inheritance: unknown

207. Retinal Atrophy, Central Progressive
Other Names: central PRA; CPRA
Description: retina degenerates; near or total blindness by age of 3–5 yr.
Inheritance: autosomal dominant; incomplete penetrance

208. Retinal Atrophy, Generalized Progressive
Other Names: general PRA
Description: retina degenerates; first, night blindness; then total blindness before middle age
Inheritance: autosomal recessive

209. Retinal Detachment
Description: retina detaches in 1 or both eyes; may lead to blindness by 3–4 yr.
Inheritance: familial, but unknown

210. Retinal Dysplasia
Description: abnormally formed retina; not progressive; may or may not affect vision
Inheritance: autosomal recessive

211. Reverse Rear Legs
Description: born w. abnormal joints in rear legs
Inheritance: unknown

212. Schistosoma Reflexus
Description: open belly at birth; abdominal organs on outside; usually fatal
Inheritance: unknown

213. Sebaceous Adenitis
Description: hair follicles & oil glands begin degenerating at 1–3 yr.; hair loss & scaly, abnormal skin develop
Inheritance: autosomal recessive

214. Seborrhea
Other Names: hyperkeratinization; greasy skin disease
Description: increased production of

upper skin layers & glands; skin scaly,
oily, itchy & malodorous; hard to treat
Inheritance: unknown

215. Seborrhea, Congenital
Description: like other seborrhea but
present at birth
Inheritance: unknown

216. Selective Cobalamin Malabsorption
Description: moderate anemia with
abnormal blood cells; can lead to
cachexia & dementia
Inheritance: unknown

217. Selective IgA Deficiency
Description: lack of antibody proteins
yields constant infections, esp. of skin,
lungs, ears, etc.
Inheritance: unknown

218. Short Spine
Other Names: baboon dogs
Description: all vertebrae very short;
creates very short back; have scoliosis;
spine slopes to hip
Inheritance: autosomal recessive

219. Shoulder Luxation
Other Names: slipped shoulder; shoulder
dislocation
Description: starts at 3–4 mo.; looseness
may lead to medial luxation of
shoulder
Inheritance: unknown

220. Silica Urinary Stones
Description: Star-shaped stones form in
urinary bladder.
Inheritance: unknown; may be dietary
factor

221. Sinoatrial Syncope
Other Names: sinoatrial arrest, prolonged
sinus pause
Description: slowed heart rate; may cause
fainting
Inheritance: autosomal recessive

222. Sphingomyelinosis
Other Names: Niemann-Pick disease
Description: ataxia; hypermetria; head
tremors; loss of equilibrium; may
proceed to blindness & death
Inheritance: unknown

223. Spina Bifida
Other Names: open spine
Description: vertebrae don't cover nerves
in lower back; incontinence & gait
abnormalities; more common in tailless
breeds
Inheritance: autosomal dominant
(uncertain)

224. Spinal Abiotrophy
Other Names: motor neuronopathy
Description: uncoordinated movement
(ataxia)
Inheritance: autosomal recessive

225. Spondylolisthesis
Description: narrowed channel for spinal
cord in midneck; pain & ataxia
Inheritance: unknown

226. Spondylosis Deformans
Description: bridging spinal arthritis;
ankylosis; may be asymptomatic or
may lead to paraplegia
Inheritance: unclear

227. Spongioform Encephalopathies
Description: abnormal fluid-filled cavities
in various areas of brain; variety of
brain signs, depending on area
involved
Inheritance: unknown

228. Squamous Cell Carcinoma
Description: malignant, erosive skin
tumor; occurs on unpigmented areas
Inheritance: unknown

229. Stationary Night Blindness
Description: starts by 6 wk.; may or may
not be associated with PRA
Inheritance: unknown

230. Stenosis of Atrioventricular Bundle
Other Names: atrioventricular bundle stenosis
Description: fainting spells beginning in the first few months of life
Inheritance: unknown

231. Stockard's Paralysis
Description: degeneration of lumbar spine, partial paralysis by 12 wk.
Inheritance: 3 dominants

232. Subaortic Stenosis
Other Names: SAS; aortic valve stenosis
Description: aorta narrowed below its valve at birth; heart murmur; enlarged left heart; may have signs, depending on degree
Inheritance: polygenic; threshold

233. Supernumerary Incisors
Description: seven incisors in upper jaw
Inheritance: unknown

234. Swimmer Puppy
Description: flattened chest in newborns; can progress unless assisted; then usu. recover
Inheritance: unknown; other factors involved

235. Syringomyelia
Other Names: spinal dysraphism; hopper's disease
Description: dog stands in a crouch & hops to move; nonprogressive; associated with myelin dysplasias
Inheritance: unknown

236. Systemic Lupus Erythematosus
Other Names: SLE, lupus
Description: multisystem immune-mediated; shifting lameness; polyarthritis; polymyositis; skin lesions; great mimicker
Inheritance: unknown

237. Tarsal Subluxation
Other Names: intertarsal subluxation
Description: overangulated hock with partial luxation, unstable joint & associated lameness
Inheritance: unknown

238. Testicular Hypoplasia
Description: lack of proper development of testes; low or no sperm counts, starting at puberty
Inheritance: unknown

239. Tetralogy of Fallot
Description: severe heart disorder with 4 major defects present; murmur & other signs of heart failure; sometimes fatal
Inheritance: polygenic; threshold

240. Thrombasthenic Thrombopathia
Description: inherently abnormal platelets; minor clotting problems
Inheritance: unknown

241. Thrombopathia
Other Names: giant platelet disease
Description: minor bleeding disorder; platelets are abnormally large & low in numbers
Inheritance: autosomal dominant; incomplete expression

242. Thymic Atrophy
Description: by 1–3 mo. stunted growth, wasting & suppurative pneumonia
Inheritance: unknown

243. Toxic Gut Syndrome
Description: acute onset of diarrhea, shock & death
Inheritance: unknown

244. Tracheal Collapse
Description: incomplete cartilage rings allow trachea to collapse; dry, honking cough; turn blue on exercise; in brachycephalic & miniature breeds
Inheritance: unknown

245. Tracheal Hypoplasia
Other Names: tracheobroncheal hypoplasia
Description: cartilage rings of windpipe too small; severe lack of air; chronic pulmonary infections; not surgically correctible
Inheritance: unknown

246. Trichiasis
Description: ingrown eyelashes, esp. on upper lid; irritate cornea
Inheritance: autosomal dominant; incomplete penetrance

247. Tricuspid Valve Dysplasia
Description: bad valve between heart chambers causes many other heart problems to develop
Inheritance: unknown

248. Type 2 Myofiber Deficiency
Other Names: Labrador Retriever myopathy
Description: by 3–6 mo., stiff, awkward gait; bunny hopping; muscle atrophy; usu. not progressive after 6 mo.
Inheritance: autosomal recessive

249. Tyrosinemia
Other Names: Harada's disease; tyrosinase deficiency
Description: early onset of eye & skin lesions; lack of blood enzyme
Inheritance: unclear (is autosomal recessive in cats)

250. Ulna, Premature Closure
Other Names: fiddle front
Description: ulna stops growing while radius continues; results in wrists-in/front-feet-out posture
Inheritance: autosomal recessive

251. Umbilical Hernia
Other Names: rupture; "outie"
Description: bulging of abdominal contents in sac at umbilicus; common; usu. harmless unless very large
Inheritance: threshold

252. Ununited Anconeal Process
Other Names: elbow dysplasia
Description: growth plate in elbow doesn't fuse; secondary degenerative joint disease; pain & limp; surgical correction required
Inheritance: polygenic

253. Urea Cycle Enzyme Deficiency
Description: can't metabolize urea; liver disease w. brain signs
Inheritance: unknown

254. Uric Acid Excretion
Other Names: urate defect
Description: tendency to form urate stones in bladder
Inheritance: autosomal recessive

255. Urine-Dribbling Puppies
Other Names: leakers; tiddlers
Description: may be associated with many defects of bladder, urethra &/or urachus
Inheritance: unknown

256. Uroliths
Other Names: bladder &/or kidney stones; urogenital urolithiasis
Description: tendency for stones to form in urinary system, esp. bladder; frequent painful bloody urination; may need surgery
Inheritance: complex; tendency may be hereditary

257. Vaginal Hyperplasia/Prolapse
Description: protrusion of swollen vaginal tissues at vulva; may be hormonal in origin; mostly in very large &/or brachycephalic breeds
Inheritance: unknown

258. Ventricular Septal Defect
Description: hole between two lower heart chambers; pumping defect; weakness; turn blue
Inheritance: polygenic

259. Vertebral Anomalies

Other Names: hemivertebrae; butterfly
vertebrae; block &/or fused vertebrae

Description: some vertebrae are
compressed or abnormally shaped; may
be symptomless or may exhibit pain,
incoordination & spinal curvature; most
common in brachycephalic and/or
"screw-tail" breeds

Inheritance: complex

260. Vestibular Disorder

Other Names: peripheral vestibular
disorder

Description: incoordination and loss of
balance

Inheritance: autosomal recessive

261. Vitiligo

Description: loss of skin color, esp.
around nose, lips & face; may also
include hair, pads & nails

Inheritance: unknown

262. Von Willebrand's Disease

Other Names: pseudohemophilia

Description: bleeding syndrome w.
several abnormal factors

Inheritance: autosomal dominant;
variable expression

263. *XX* Sex Reversal

Description: chromosomal configuration
& gonadal sex don't agree; *XX* but
with testes & masculine appearance

Inheritance: unknown

Index

All breeds are listed alphabetically in Appendix I, Breed Specifics and Predispositions.

Pages shown in **boldface** contain detailed coverage of the item.

flattened chest, 163
fluids, replacing, 142, **156–157,** 158
food, *see* feeding
formula, 97, 147, 148–149, **150**
foster mothers, 140, **149–150**

gag, 130
gangrene, 122, 145
gas, 155
genes, 21–22
    additive, 24–25
    dominant/recessive, 22–23
    homozygous/heterozygous, 23–24
    mode of inheritance, 25–26
    phenotype/genotype, 31–32
    sex-linked, 33–34
    test breeding, 32–33
genitals, small, 73
genotype, 31–32, 35, 36
gestation, 46, 88, 91, 93, 95, 97, 106,
        110, 121, 127; *see also* pregnancy
glans penis, 67, 81, 83
glucose solution, 132, 138, 147
gums, 119, 127, 133

hand-feeding, 141, 142, 147, 149,
        150–153, 156, 158
head-first position, whelping, 120, 123
heart defects, congenital, **165**
heat cycle, 5, 7, 17, 45, 46, **47–49,**
        51–52, 54, 56, 58–59, 62, 72, 80,
        86
    abnormal, 80
    delayed/early heats, 49
    extended heat, 52
    silent heat, 51, **52,** 58
    split heat, 52
heat source, whelping, 104, 114, 133,
        134
hernia, umbilical, 159–160
herpesvirus, 158
heterozygous/homozygous genes, 23–
        24
hormonal problems, 52–54, 77, 80, 98,
        124, 142
hormonal treatment to induce cycle, 51,
        75
hormones, 4, 7, 33, 49, 51, 54–55, 62,
        74, 88, 94, 115, 128
    lack of, 52–54, 77, 80
hostility toward young, 138, **139–140,**
        150
hydrocephalus, **163–164**
hydrops amnii, **124**
hyperactivity, puppy, 146

immunity, 45, 148, 158
inbreeding, 35–36, 38–39
incubator, **133–134**
inertia, 121, 126, 127
    primary, **124**
    secondary, **125**
infanticide, **139–140**
infection, 5, 6, 46, 54, 55–56, 75, 80,
        83, 93, 98, 109, 119, 123, 127,
        135, 138, 140–142, 145, 153,
        155–158
injury, 49, 56, 64, 80, 83, 98
inoculations, 9, **45,** 148
International Canine Genetics, Inc., 94,
        96
interval between puppies, 114, 119

juvenile vagina, 46, 83

kit
    stud, **66**
    whelping, **103**

labor, 97, 98–99, **103–116,** 120, 121,
        124, 125, 126
lactation, 46, 97; *see also* milk
Lactinex/lactobacillus, 142, 156
libido, low, 54, 55, 56, 77, 83
linebreeding, **35–39**
listlessness
    during pregnancy, 108–109
    puppy, 146–147
losses, whelping, **138–139, 148–149**
luteinizing hormone, pituitary, 62

malpresentation, **123–124,** 125
mastitis, 94, 139, **141,** 142, 143
maternal instincts, 149, 150
    lack of, 128, **137–138**
meconium, 111
medication for puppies; *see* individual
        diseases
merle-colored lines, 165
metestrus, 48–49, 60, 61
metritis, acute, 141–142
milk, 45, 46, 92, 94, 115, 129, 138,
        139, 140, 142, 147, 148, 149,
        150–153, 155, 156, 161, 166
    mastitis, **141**
    substitutes, **150**
milk fever, **140–141**
mismating, 88–89
misses, 18, 43, 46, **52–55,** 59
mouth-to-mouth resuscitation, 130
mucous membrane, 119, 127, 133